HMAS CANBERRA

KATHRYN SPURLING

HMAS CANBERRA

CASUALTY OF CIRCUMSTANCE

To those who served on HMAS *Canberra I* in war and peace, those who followed on HMAS *Canberra II* and those who serve on HMAS *Canberra III*. The RAN continues to do the name 'Canberra' proud.

And to my son, Bryden Scott Spurling.

Published in 2022 by New Holland Publishers
First published in Australia in 2017 by New Holland Publishers
Sydney • Auckland

Level 1, 178 Fox Valley Road, Wahroonga, NSW 2076, Australia
5/39 Woodside Ave, Northcote, Auckland 0627, New Zealand

newhollandpublishers.com

A record of this book is held at the National Library of Australia.

ISBN 9781760794750

Group Managing Director: Fiona Schultz
Project Editor: Diane Jardine
Designer: Andrew Davies
Production Director: Arlene Gippert
Printed in Australia by SOS Print + Media Group

10 9 8 7 6 5 4 3 2 1

Keep up with New Holland Publishers:

 NewHollandPublishers
 @newhollandpublishers

CONTENTS

PREFACE

I consider it an honour and privilege to write this foreword for *HMAS Canberra: Casualty of Circumstance.*

Many books have been written about the Battle of Savo Island and the loss of HMAS *Canberra.* The battle was short, dramatic and memorable. As a survivor I can vouch for the authenticity of the events depicted in Kathryn Spurling's history.

Kathryn's service with, and knowledge of, the RAN has given her a deep understanding. She tells the story of a young ship's company facing adversity with courage, doing their duty in surreal situations, and caring for each other. It is a good read.

But more than that *HMAS Canberra: Casualty of Circumstance* is the account of a young Australian Navy attempting to establish its own identity and to escape the influence and attitudes of RN officers and senior RN non-commissioned officers.

I joined the RAN in the late 1930s at the tender age of 16, unaware of the class system that existed within the service – the distinction between officers and the lower deck.

The British Admiralty and the RN component of the RAN did not understand the tendencies of Australians; and in maintaining the British way of doing things, they sowed the seeds for this tragic moment in naval history.

Lieutenant Commander Henry Longdon Hall, MBE, OAM, RAN (rtd)

FOREWORD

It was with great pleasure I accepted the invitation to provide a foreword to the latest book by naval historian Dr Kathryn Spurling, *HMAS Canberra: Casualty of Circumstance*.

It gives me great pride to be the Chief Minister of the city associated with this ship – a ship with such a fascinating history, and a crew who served our country with distinction in peacetime and in war.

Dr Spurling has brought this history to life with a gripping account of the last terrifying minutes in which HMAS Canberra's fate was sealed. She pays tribute to the 93 men whose lives were cut short by telling their stories, sharing their motivations for joining the Royal Australian Navy and providing insights into life onboard the ship. Dr Spurling gives the reader a real sense of the men whose lives were so indelibly marked by this tragedy.

The City of Canberra's relationship with its namesake continues today. The officers and crew of HMAS Canberra II visited this city often, exercising its granted right to Freedom of the City until it's decommissioning in 2005. More recently our city has struck up a new relationship with the ship's company of the HMAS Canberra III which will continue a strong tradition and give our landlocked city its connections to the men and women of the RAN who sacrifice much in the service of Australia and its people.

I would like to congratulate Dr Spurling on the meticulous research which so obviously underpins this book and on having the courage to probe and question the decisions of the past. It is only with careful scrutiny of the mistakes of the past that we learn for the future.

I commend this book to the reader and hope you gain a renewed respect for the crew of HMAS *Canberra I*.

Andrew Barr MLA
Chief Minister of the Australian Capital Territory

INTRODUCTION

My God this is bloody awful.

Sub Lieutenant MacKenzie Gregory, RAN[1]

Sub Lieutenant MacKenzie 'Mac' Jesse Gregory, Royal Australian Navy (RAN), stood peering into the blackness of a night shrouded in heavy clouds. He was Officer of the Watch (OOW), having only recently qualified for such responsibility. And responsibility it was, to be charged with the safety of the His Majesty's Australian Ship (HMAS) *Canberra* and its crew of 819 in a war-ravaged Pacific Ocean. The warship moved gracefully at 12 knots through the slight chop in what was known as The Slot — the space within the Solomon Islands between Savo Island to the north east and Guadalcanal to the south west. It was part of a fleet defending amphibious landings in what was the commencement of the Guadalcanal campaign.

During the first half of 1942, Japanese forces appeared unstoppable, their rapid advance and precision of naval and military execution nothing less than extraordinary. With the sea lines of communication between the United States (US) and Australia in jeopardy, on 2 July 1942, the US Joint Chiefs of Staff ordered Allied forces to attempt to halt the Japanese advance. Operation Watchtower was launched. Success would depend on the re-occupation of the Solomon Islands.

Troops landed by the Imperial Japanese Navy (IJN) had captured

Tulagi on 3 and 4 May 1942. This was part of the Empire of Japan's strategy to cover the flank of, and provide reconnaissance support for, their advancing military forces on Port Moresby, New Guinea, as well as to further protect their major base at Rabaul, New Britain. A Japanese seaplane reconnaissance base was established and work commenced to build an airfield at Lunga Point on the larger island of Guadalcanal. Watchtower was not only the first US combined amphibious operation since 1898, but also the first combined Allied naval and military operation in the Pacific. If it were to be successful, the ensuing days and months would mark the transition of Allied operations from defensive to strategic offensive.

The crew of HMAS *Canberra* was confident in the Allied force of which their cruiser was an integral part. Vice Admiral Frank Jack Fletcher, United States Navy (USN), on the aircraft carrier USS *Saratoga*, commanded the Allied force. In charge of the amphibious forces was Rear Admiral Richmond Kelly Turner, USN. Major General Alexander Archer Vandegrift, United States Marine Corps (USMC), was in command of the 16,000 Allied (primarily marine) infantry. In command of the three Australian and five American cruisers, 15 destroyers and assorted minesweepers – known as Task Force 62.2 – was the Royal Navy's Rear Admiral Victor Alexander Charles Crutchley. Crutchley had been awarded the Distinguished Service Cross (DSC) and the Victoria Cross (VC) during World War I and had assumed command of the RAN Fleet on 13 June 1942.

Crutchley believed the threat would be from the air so to protect the transports delivering troops to shore, he divided the Allied warships into three groups. The southern group – HMAS *Australia* and HMAS *Canberra*, USS *Chicago*, and destroyers USS *Patterson* and USS *Bagley* – patrolled between Lunga Point and Savo Island. The northern group – the cruisers USS *Vincennes*, USS *Astoria* and USS *Quincy*, and destroyers USS *Helm* and USS *Wilson* – were conducting a box-shaped patrol between the Tulagi anchorage and Savo Island. The eastern group – the cruisers USS *San Juan* and HMAS *Hobart* and two US destroyers – guarded the eastern entrance between Florida and Guadalcanal Islands. The destroyers USS *Blue* and USS *Ralph Talbot*, radar guard ships, seaward of Savo Island, patrolled the southern and northern passages to warn against the approach of any enemy shipping. The remaining seven destroyers provided close-in protection of transport anchorages.

Bad weather enabled the Allies to launch surprise attacks on the night of 6 August and morning of 7 August but resistance thereafter was fierce and bloody. The landing of marines slowed and there was congestion on the beaches; the operation dragged into another night and day. Allied crews had undertaken days of action, bombardment of shore positions and anti-aircraft warfare in the oppressive tropical heat. With a heavy sky diminishing the threat of air attack and his belief that the Japanese would not have the audacity to attack by sea at night, Crutchley permitted crews to go to Condition II on the night of 8 August meaning that approximately half were at action stations and the remainder either below in their bunks or asleep next to their action stations.

In the earliest hours of the morning of 9 August, US military personnel, weighed down with guns and equipment, their guts constricted with emotion and their senses on high alert, continued to wade through waters onto white tropical sands. By comparison Sub Lieutenant 'Mac' Gregory, standing on the bridge of HMAS *Canberra*, had it easy. His feet were dry, he was comfortably attired, a steward arrived with a hot drink – there was just that heavy sense of responsibility and the familiar fear of the unknown. His training did not completely negate the foreboding and the middle watch midnight to 0400 was the hardest, when the body and mind were at their most vulnerable.

It didn't help that the flagship, HMAS *Australia*, had vanished from the front of the column with the flag officer (the admiral). Admiral Turner had called Crutchley and Vandegrift to his command ship, the transport *McCawley*, off Guadalcanal, to discuss the implications on the operation of the decision of Vice Admiral Fletcher to withdraw his carriers the next day. Crutchley left Captain Howard D. Bode, USN, of *Chicago* in charge of the southern group. Crutchley did not inform the commanders of the other cruiser groups of his absence – the force had been divided into three groups, each led by a cruiser.

Bode decided not to place his ship in the lead of the southern group, as was customary for the senior ship, and went back to sleep. Turner, Crutchley, and Vandegrift discussed the sightings of a Japanese force of warships but decided this was likely a 'seaplane tender force' of little interest to the Allied fleet. Crutchley elected not to return *Australia* to the southern force, instead stationing his ship near the Guadalcanal transport anchorage. He did not inform other Allied ship commanders of this decision or of the heavy cruiser's location.

HMAS *Canberra* continued three cables ahead of USS *Chicago*, exposed, yet accountable for the safety of many, zig-zagging slowly back and forth parallel to and five miles from Guadalcanal. Occasionally lightning flashes penetrated the darkness before another rain squall reduced visibility again to as little as 100 yards. The destroyer USS *Patterson* was somewhere on the starboard side and the destroyer USS *Bagley* somewhere on port. Conversation on the bridge was sparse as each man diligently engaged in separate but interconnected duties, wondering how many air attacks they would face in the new day. The sound of aircraft overhead had been heard at 0100 and the Principal Control Officer, Lieutenant Commander Ewan James Byam Wight, RAN, reported it to the Commanding Officer Captain Frank Edmund Getting, RAN. A junior officer on USS *Quincy* asserted that these must be enemy aircraft but the consensus of his seniors was that his claims were 'mildly hysterically'[2] and they dismissed the aircraft as being 'friendly'.

Throughout the ship, crew slumbered fitfully and Captain Getting took the rare opportunity to leave the bridge and sleep. Sub Lieutenant 'Mac' Gregory checked his watch, 0143, almost time to waken Navigator Lieutenant Commander Jack Statton Mesley, RAN. Mesley had gone to sleep less than an hour earlier but *Canberra* was due to make a course change as the cruiser neared the north-westerly extremity of the patrol. In virtually the same instant, Wight saw an explosion about 6,000 yards (5486 metres) off the starboard bow. Could it possibly be a torpedo? USS *Patterson* had commenced signalling 'Warning, Warning. Strange ships entering harbour!'

The signal was by Talk Between Ships (TBS) but only the American ships were fitted with TBS. *Patterson* was observed to make an abrupt course change and Wight sounded the general alarm.

'Mac' Gregory was suddenly engulfed in chaos.

> Suddenly all hell broke loose and there was an explosion to the north which was probably a Jap torpedo. The port lookout reported a ship ahead – nobody on the bridge could see it.[3]

Canberra's crew rushed to action stations as torpedoes raced along the starboard side. Captain Getting entered the bridge and assumed command. The navigator entered the bridge announcing to 'Mac' 'I have the con'. Relieved of his responsibility, the 20-year-old Sub Lieutenant climbed up to the forward control above the bridge to take his regular duties as rate officer and to estimate the course and speed of enemy warships for the transmitting station. Flares lit up the sky and the Australian cruiser was silhouetted in stark illumination. 'Mac' looked through his binoculars only to have the lenses fill with six Japanese cruisers and one destroyer approaching rapidly in line ahead attacking formation. 'My God this is bloody awful' he said to himself.

'Mac' was enveloped by deafening, pervasive noise which crushed the mind and riveted the body. Shrapnel strafed the space and the young Able Seaman standing next to 'Mac' was felled by a large piece of shrapnel to the back of the head. A shell exploded into *Canberra*'s bridge with devastating effect. The gunnery officer was decapitated. Captain Getting fell to the deck mortally wounded. The Seagull aircraft burst into flames. Within minutes, 28 shells tore into the ship. Flames devoured decks, equipment and flesh. The cruiser groaned, stopped dead in the water and began to list starboard.

HMAS *Canberra*'s fight was over before it had begun. Not only was the cruiser and those within the victims of a surprise Japanese offensive but also the men onboard *Canberra* were victims of a litany of archaic, misguided policies, standards and beliefs promoted by the British Admiralty and successive puppet RAN Flag Officers. The errors would be exacerbated by an international cover-up concerning friendly fire.

A MOST IMPRESSIVE NEW SHIP

*On boarding our new ship we were much
impressed ... and not a little proud.*

Torpedoman John Bastock, RAN.[4]

For 'Mac' Gregory the journey had started in January 1936 when he was one of thirteen 13-year-olds from Victoria, New South Wales and South Australia entering the Royal Australian Naval College (RANC). Selection was very competitive and applicants had to be of the right social group. Connections with the RN or RAN were advantageous. First there was a written examination, then a thorough medical followed by the very important interview by a board of naval officers. A prestigious career would follow those who completed the four years and proved themselves to be suitable RAN officer material.

The RANC had been located on the picturesque coastline of Jervis Bay in New South Wales. By 1930 retaining the college in this remote area became an 'intolerable financial burden'[5] particularly in light of the federal government's decision that no cadet midshipmen would be entered the college during the following year due to the severe financial difficulties affecting Australia.[6] The RANC was moved to the RAN's main naval training depot, HMAS *Cerberus* at Westernport, a large tidal bay in southern Victoria opening onto Bass Strait. The physical separation of the RANC from sailor training was accentuated not least of all by 'a large green cypress hedge which delineated college boundaries'.[7] The Naval Board 'stressed the importance' of the college being 'a separate entity and its own traditions and esprit de corps'.[8]

For Mac Gregory the division between officers and sailors was particularly significant. His father was serving in the RAN, not as an officer but as a sailor. Jesse Herbert Gregory, born 30 July 1890, was an Englishman who as a soldier had survived the muddy, bloody fields of the Somme.

'Dad didn't talk much about the war. He was a very proud person' Mac recalled.[9] He enlisted in the RN and came to Australia on loan to the RAN. It took little time before he decided to forfeit his right to a government-funded return passage to England in favour of bringing his wife and extended family to Australia.

Officer Steward Jesse Gregory was a man of the old world who accepted his place on the social ladder. He proudly served officers and 'really did look after the admirals he had'.[10] Jesse Gregory rose in rank to Chief Petty Officer Steward. He was in charge of the School for Stewards at the Flinders Naval Depot, was Personal Steward to First Naval Member Sir Ragnar Colvin, and remained in the RAN until 1945 when he left to take up a position as a High Court assistant. But Chief Gregory wanted more for his son. He aspired for his son to become a naval officer, a member of the upper deck, not the lower deck. His dedicated service proved instrumental.

> I always thought that it probably helped. I never really knew how I'd got into the navy. I thought maybe I was the token lower deck person's son to get into the naval college. I was the only one of a serving sailor.[11]

Cadet Midshipman MacKenzie Gregory started at the RANC on 1 January 1936. Chief Jesse Gregory was delighted; at the time he was serving his second draft in the cruiser HMAS *Canberra*.

For Cadet Midshipman Gregory and his class, the ensuing years at *Cerberus* went by in a harried blur, every hour seemingly crowded with academics, naval studies, sport and drill, punctuated with 'glorious leave'.[12] Hierarchically, the RANC was most difficult for the first year cadet midshipmen. Mac described first year as 'being absolute dog's bodies for ... all senior to us in 1936'. [13]

Punishment of cadet midshipmen by senior cadets could be harsh. One of the more innocuous punishments is described by Mac.

One's behind would feel the wrath of a size ten gym shoe application with vigour to it, for at least six wallops.[14]

At the end of each year, a very elaborate passing out parade was performed by all cadets, 'all done without orders, but on a specific beat of the drums in the naval band'.[15] The final manoeuvre saw cadets in line abreast advance towards the saluting dais and halting in front. A great deal of training was undertaken to ensure a perfect straight line and 'woe betide any cadet stupid enough to muck up a rehearsal, let alone on the actual day'.[16]

In 1937 parade drill was demanding for most, regardless of rank, as Norman Charles King discovered. The King family had migrated from England to find a better life. The environment was warmer, drier and healthier but when Great Britain suffered financial upheaval, the Commonwealth fell into depression. Norm was born on 21 March 1920 and had to leave school at the age of 13 to help support his family. He applied for a fitter and turner apprenticeship with the railways but the more exciting prospect was the application he submitted to the RAN. Norm tried not to get too excited because the RAN had been hit with restrictions and only 10 per cent of recruit applications were successful – his 'chance of getting the call seemed remote'.[17] Recruits up to age 18 were designated as Junior Entry, over 18 as Adult Entry. Norm was overjoyed to be accepted two days before his seventeenth birthday and rated 'Stoker III'. Some believed his was the lowest rank and rating in the permanent RAN but Norm didn't care; the opportunities seemed limitless and his salary of 36 shillings a fortnight a fortune and the 10 shillings he sent home to his mother would really help.

When the RANC moved to HMAS *Cerberus* at Westernport, the new entry recruit school was given over to the cadet midshipmen as an

Jervis Year 1936. Top Row, left to right: Rupert Treloar, John Lorimer, Laurie Merson, David Nicholls, Max Reed. Middle Row: Mackenzie Gregory, John Shearing, Lieutenant Commander H.C. Wright RAN Term Officer, Bob Scrivenor, Jack Lester. Front: Neil McDonald, Norm White, Hugh McDonald.

academic block. Another block was built in 1936 in time for Norm King's recruit class. 'Sixteen lads aged between sixteen and eighteen ... were escorted by train to Flinders [*Cerberus*] '[18] For the newest volunteers who straggled around the sweeping road to their accommodation for the first time, five months training lay ahead: 'five months of total discipline and authority'.[19] They were rapidly subjected to the attention of navy barbers and loud-voiced petty officers (POs) who were found to have a remarkably limited and expletive-filled vocabulary. An elementary lesson – how to sling a hammock between steel bars six feet from the floor – proved more straightforward than actually getting into the hammock, 'for most of us it was a comedy of errors, in one side and straight out the other' recalled Stoker III Norm King.[20] A bugle call at 0600 commenced each new day. Instructors were rigorous in their encouragement of those slow to lash and stow their hammocks. The first uniform issue provided some mirth, the short recruits seemed to get the long uniforms and the tall recruits the short uniforms – but it was probably a case of one size fits all.

In the first three months recruits concentrated on squad and rifle drill, marching around and around the parade ground – 'hard slogging'. 'We were told that whether we liked it or not, by the time we had finished the course we would be and look, "a fine body of men"'. King's class almost made it.

> We marched with fifteen arms swinging as one. Fifteen rifles
> sloped at the correct angle and fifteen feet in perfect step.
> Number sixteen in the squad, Billy Ridd, was the odd man out.
> His arms and legs were not synchronised. If he concentrated on
> his arms, his feet let him down and vice versa.[21]

Stoker III Wilfred Alwyn 'Billy' Ridd (21481) was given more 'jankers' (punishment) than most, ordered to 'double' (double march) around the parade ground for two hours wearing a full pack and rifle at the slope. But 'it didn't help poor Billy Ridd'. Ridd barely survived recruit school but went on to have a distinguished RAN career, retiring as a Petty Officer Stoker Mechanic in 1949.

Added incentive to become fitter and faster came at 'scran' (meal) time. Once dismissed, famished recruits ran to the mess. First ones in the queue grabbed whatever was on offer. According to Norm King, the choice diminished towards the end of the food line and one 'had to be satisfied with the carrots, pumpkin or turnips'.[22] The ensuing months were filled with lectures and practical instruction in specialised subjects. For stokers, this meant steam boilers, turbines and other forms of ship propulsion. Every recruit had lectures on world affairs.

> We were told that our purpose in life was to serve the British
> cause. That the British navy was the most powerful force for
> good in the world. Our task was to protect those areas shaded
> red on the map of the world. It was imperative to the wellbeing

Divisions, HMAS Cerberus, *c. 1930s.*

of all races, that British warships kept the sea lanes open and, British gunboats, by patrolling the rivers of Asia kept the heathens under control.[23]

Following graduation from HMAS *Cerberus*, the majority of the new ordinary seamen and stokers were sent to Australia's largest warships, HMAS *Canberra* and HMAS *Australia* for sea training.[24] Norm King's official number was 21476 and he was delighted to be drafted to *Canberra* with mates and fellow South Australian Stoker IIs, Alan Albert Dare (21475) and Reginald Alfred Johnson (21477). It was September 1937 when the newest crew members, bursting with enthusiasm and false confidence, looked out at the white hull of HMAS *Canberra* for the first time. It was impossible not to be impressed – the cruiser was breathtaking.

One of two Kent Class Design of County Class heavy cruisers built by John Brown & Co. as part of a naval redevelopment programme, *Canberra* was laid down on 9 September 1925 and launched by Her Royal Highness Princess Mary, Princess Royal and Countess of Harewood, on 31 May 1927. *Canberra* and sister ship, *Australia*, had a displacement of 9,850 tons standard and 13,600 tons full load. The cruisers were 630 feet in length with a beam of 68 feet 4 inches and a draught of 22 feet 4 inches. A top speed of 31½ knots and 80,000 horsepower came from Brown-Curtis geared turbines, 4 screws and 8 three-drum type boilers. Armament consisted of 8x8 inch guns, 4x4

HMAS Canberra, *c. 1930s.*

inch anti-aircraft guns, four 2 pounder pom-poms, four 3 pounders and eight 21 inch torpedo tubes.

Princess Mary returned on 9 July 1928 to commission the warship. The event was filled with pomp and ceremony and, for the ship's officers, the occasion was filled with fine wine and food. Luncheon was planned to run from 1345 to 1530 but Princess Mary objected. She decided that one and three quarters of an hour was far too long as the trip 'would be tiring'.[25] Australia's London naval representative answered that although they would attempt to 'carry out her wishes' to reduce the time to one and a quarter hours, the luncheon was the proposed length because 'certain speeches are unavoidable'.[26] It is unclear if Princess Mary left when she wished or suffered all the long-winded speeches by politicians, diplomats and senior naval dignitaries. It was just another glitch in the far from smooth process of securing RAN ships.

The 1921 Washington Naval Treaty was designed to limit naval construction in an effort to reduce the risk of an arms race (as had led to World War I). The treaty, signed by the governments of the United

Kingdom, the United States, Japan, France, and Italy, particularly targeted the manufacture of battleships. Capital ships were now limited to cruisers not exceeding 10,000 tons standard displacement and 8 inch guns. The British Empire was restricted to 15x8 inch cruisers (146,800 tons) and 6 inch cruisers not exceeding a total of 192,000 tons. The treaty was not welcomed by all nations and ultimately non-compliance created an imbalance, in particular the development of the Imperial Japanese Navy (IJN). As part of the British Empire, Australia had to abide by decisions made by the British Government and the Admiralty when it came to commissioning Australian warships.

A casualty of the treaty was the Indefatigable Class Cruiser, the first HMAS *Australia*, a flagship that had evoked nationalistic euphoria when it led the new RAN fleet up Sydney Harbour for the first time on 4 October 1913. The cruiser, manufactured at the behest of the British Government, had cost the new Commonwealth of Australia the princely sum of £2,000,000. On 12 December 1921 the 17,055-ton ship was decommissioned and on 12 April 1924 was towed to sea by tugs and sunk off Sydney. The British Government then cancelled expenditure for the new Singapore naval base, a project to which Australia had been generously contributing in the belief that it would not only alleviate its own fleet expenditure but also assure a powerful base with a strong resident RN fleet on its doorstep. The Australian Government had no alternative but to institute a five-year naval expansion programme and tenders were invited for the construction of two cruisers.

In what would prove a recurring theme of poor judgement and mismanagement of the nation's large-scale defence purchases, the Australian Cabinet approved the construction of both cruisers offshore, in Britain. Though the cruisers offered much, particularly good handling and an ability to steam long distances at high speed, there was criticism. 'Some experts considered them needlessly large for cruiser work [and] lacking in armour'.[27] There were sensational headlines and condemnation in the Australian media with headlines such as: 'British Blunder Cost Us Dear – *Canberra* and *Australia* Not Only Useless, But a Menace'.[28]

Adverse assessment concerned both ships' vulnerability to attack

Members of the commissioning crew travelling on SS Beltana *to England, c. 1928.*

due to their lack of effective armament and the thickness of the hull. 'If war did occur, they would be smashed and riddled with shells ... "death traps" to the men aboard'.[29]

One of the first Australians to experience the cruiser was Torpedoman John Bastock (1405). Bastock had entered the RAN in 1923 at age 15. After surviving the severe boy seaman training in the hulk HMAS *Tingira* moored in Sydney's Rose Bay, he served in the aging cruisers, *Melbourne*, *Brisbane* and *Sydney*. Bastock was a member of the commissioning crew of *Canberra* all of whom travelled to Britain onboard SS *Beltana*. The RAN men were hoping for something a lot more glamorous than the *Beltana*, a former World War I troopship with very basic accommodation.

Nonetheless, the sailors realised that this was a trip around the world at government expense; something beyond the reach of working and middle class men in May 1928. Exotic ports of call and great camaraderie added pleasure to the journey, until Able Seaman Douglas Sutherland Brett (11857) was accidently killed on 24 June. Like Bastock, Brett joined as a Boy Seaman, in 1919. He had only ever wished to join the navy having followed the exploits of the RAN during World War I; disappointed he was just too young to serve. His father James agreed to

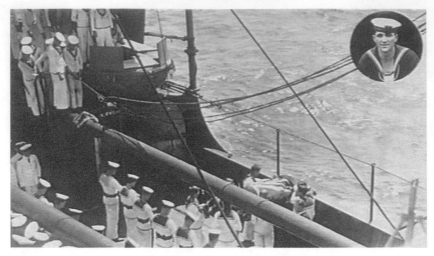

Burial service onboard Beltana *for Able Seaman Doug Brett* (INSET), *c. 1928.*

Chief Petty Officers Mess, HMAS Canberra, *c. 1935.*

sign the papers in 1919 when Douglas was just 14. Life at sea came with inherent dangers but Brett could not have imagined he would die at sea on a dilapidated transport. His body was committed to the depths with full naval honours. As with most naval burials, there was no grave at which the family could mourn.

Having rattled and rolled its way across the world, *Beltana* finally anchored off Greenock in Scotland in 19xx. From there, the crew were taken to Clyde to Australia's newest warship. RAN personnel were impressed with the stately appearance of the cruiser and according to Torpedoman Bastock, 'not a little proud'.[30] They revelled in the pristine cleanliness and newness of the ship and 'the smell of fresh paint'. The media photographs tended to show the less-crowded quarters such as the Chief Petty Officers' Mess.

After the cramped quarters of Australia's first cruisers, this was luxurious and Bastock and other sailors delighted in the 'roomy mess deck, with their punkah louvre ventilation'.[31] The ventilation was a little too drafty for the Australians in the cold, dank, Scottish air, but offered welcome relief when the ship was in home waters and during tropical summers of the Southern Hemisphere. This was an easy ship to admire, with its spacious upper deck, 'the sleek 8-inch gun mountings with their twin guns high enough for them to walk under'.[32]

Months of work-up trials followed after the commissioning and another exciting royal visitation. *Canberra* arrived in the historical naval town of Portsmouth, England on 14 July and three days of around-the-clock activity commenced to make both *Canberra* and sister cruiser, *Australia*, spotless for King George V. In 1928, even for the most hardened cynic, there was no greater thrill than to line the rails and cheer, be inspected by, and march past in close proximity with the King. It would be a day boasted about in correspondence and conversations for a lifetime.

Over the next three months the crew familiarised themselves with the workings of their ship in sea trials with the RN Atlantic Fleet. Torpedo and gunnery exercises were conducted and unfortunately both *Canberra* and *Australia* showed some serious flaws. *Australia* retired from an RN gunnery exercise due to electrical malfunction to gun turrets and ammunition hoists. *Canberra* opened fire and chaos reigned when recoil and concussion injured several, including the Commanding Officer (CO) Captain George Lawrence Massey, RN.[33] Able Seaman Ralph Ward Pound (14507), who was a boy seaman on *Tingira* with John Bastock, was injured but could not help but be amused when his distinguished captain 'and his stool took off ... without a word of farewell [from the bridge] down the ladder to the signal deck among the scattered flags and halyards and signalmen sprawling on the deck'.[34]

Fortunately, injuries were not serious however, when the CO regained his composure on the bridge, he discovered the ship's telephones no longer functioning and communications restricted to voice pipe. John Bastock and his electrical party 'were fully occupied all next day replacing broken light fittings'.[35] Humour and broken light fittings aside one erudite analysis stated:

> there was clearly a lot to be repaired and rectified – one of the troubles was that considerable quantities of aluminium had been used for fittings, and most of it was not strong enough to take the shock of gunfire.[36]

Canberra returned to Portsmouth dockyard for repairs giving weight to the concern about the strength of the ship's superstructure. The shipbuilder admitted to the excessive use of the lighter aluminium rather than steel in order to reduce the weight of the ship in keeping with the Washington Treaty's agreement to a limit of 10,000-ton for cruisers. Some of the aluminium was replaced by brass but it was not enough to quell concerns. At least there was an enjoyable short reprieve for *Canberra* sailors and officers with a farewell dance given by the Lord Mayor of Portsmouth on 30 November. Five days later, new and old romances were disrupted as the crew lined the guard rails to watch England disappear in the mist, and thoughts turned to Australia.

On 7 December 1928 *Canberra* moored at Gibraltar and off-duty personnel enjoyed the mysteries of the ancient citadel for two days. The ship's company changed their blue caps for white and on 12 December, the cruiser arrived in the ethnically diverse Canary Islands to take on fuel and replenish supplies. Tropical rig was now worn by the sailors which included wearing sun helmets.

The sun helmets seemed to be uniform issue from a bygone age, having been part of the officer military uniform as far back as the Indian Mutiny of 1857, the Anglo-Zulu wars of 1879 and the second Boer War, 1899 to 1902. The 'Wolseley' variety of helmet was used by the Royal Naval Division during the Gallipoli Campaign. Navy ratings

HMAS Canberra *crew cheering King George V, c. 1928*

King George V boarding HMAS Australia, *c. 1928.*

The forward guns of HMAS Canberra, *c. 1930.*

were given helmets similar to the Wolseley with a round brim angled down and with the tally band identifying the ship. Someone totally comfortable in the sun helmet was Petty Officer Claude Choules, a man respected by all men aboard *Canberra*.

Born in Pershore, England on 3 March 1901, Claude Stanley Choules was caught up in the excitement and sense of duty as World War I raged. He joined the RN as a Boy Seaman in 1916 just one month after he turned 14 and began his service in HMS *Impregnable*, a naval training ship at Devonport dockyard. In 1917, he joined the battleship HMS *Revenge*. In 1918, from the decks of *Revenge*, he watched the surrender of the German Battle Fleet at Firth of Forth and then the scuttling of the German fleet off Scapa Flow.

Claude had a preference for big ships and served in the battleship *Valiant* with the Mediterranean Fleet between 1920 and 1923. Another draft saw him involved in the construction of HMS *Eagle*, the RN's first purpose-built aircraft carrier, and he then spent two years with *Eagle* and the RN Mediterranean Fleet as a petty officer. In 1926 Claude Choules was one of 26 senior sailors loaned to the RAN by the RN and became an instructor at Flinders Naval Depot. Deciding he favoured the exciting prospects on offer in this youthful navy and nation, Claude transferred permanently to the RAN only to be returned to England to undergo Chief Torpedo and Anti-submarine Instructor courses. He became a member of the supervising party for the construction of HMA Ships *Australia* and *Canberra*.

> We had plenty to do. One of our duties was to weigh every piece of equipment coming into the ship in order to conform to the Washington Treaty, which demanded a 10,000-ton limit for cruisers.[37]

Every piece of equipment had to be properly installed and tested. Choules was pleased to then be drafted as a member of the *Canberra* commissioning crew. Old-time navy through and through, Choules could never have realised what lay ahead. In 1928 he was just intent on ensuring that the young sailors in his charge were well trained and responsible as the cruiser sailed home with stops at Freetown, Lagos, Cape Town, Simonstown and Durban. Choules gained permission from Captain Massey to take ship cutters, their crews and fishing nets into a deserted beach off Sekondi, Gold Coast (Ghana). The nets were hauled

HMAS Canberra *Petty Officers, c. 1928.*

PO Choules onboard Canberra *dressed in summer dress, c. 1928.*

Choules as a young sailor, date unknown.

ashore bearing 'enough fish to feed the ship's company of over 700 men'.[38] No junior sailor was brave enough to refer to Choules, popular as he was, by the nickname by which his direct peers knew him, 'Chuckles'. Torpedoman John Bastock responded positively to PO Choules's tutelage and qualified as Leading Torpedoman then as Leading Seaman by 16 February 1929 when *Canberra* pushed through choppy seas off Sydney Heads, steamed up the harbour and, to the delight of all onboard, docked at its home mooring.

Surprisingly, Choules took an RAN discharge in 1931and moved to Western Australia. He was uncomfortable in civilian life and rejoined the RAN in 1932 as Chief Petty Officer (CPO) Torpedo and Anti-submarine Instructor. During World War II, he was Chief Demolition Officer and Acting Torpedo Officer at Fremantle. At Esperance in Western Australia, he disposed of the first mine to wash up on Australian soil. Choules was also charged with the responsibility of destroying Fremantle facilities and oil

Chief Petty Officer Claude Choules became Australia's last surviving WWI veteran when he died at the age of 110 in 2011.

storage tanks should the enemy invade. After World War II, he transferred to the Naval Dockyard Police (NDP) until retirement. Still unable to stay away from the ocean, Claude Choules spent 10 years on his own boat cray fishing off the Western Australian coast. He died on 5 May 2011 aged 110, believed to be the world's last surviving World War I combat veteran. The RAN named a Bay Class Landing Ship Dock, HMAS *Choules*, commissioned on 13 December 2011, only the second RAN vessel named in honour of a sailor.

Unfortunately, such longevity was not in the future for HMAS *Canberra*, the cruiser that Chief Choules had been proud to be an integral part of, nor for the career of Torpedoman John Bastock which ended just as it was about to flourish.

*The majority were in their middle thirties and to us
raw recruits they seemed like old men.*

Stoker II Norman King, RAN[39]

Stoker II Norm King and classmates, Alan Dare and Reg Johnson, joined HMAS *Canberra* straight from HMAS *Cerberus* training in September 1937. They were surprised by the age of the *Canberra* crew who looked like old men to their young eyes.

The old-timers told stories – true, exaggerated and false – to the naïve new crew members of the *Canberra*. By comparison the 1930s seemed bland to the young sailors, not reflective of the fighting navy of previous decades that the old-timers romanticised.

Listening to veterans who had been onboard the cruiser for years – some on their second draft – it seemed the RAN's primary purpose was showing the flag. Financial stringencies had reduced extended sea time, exercises and gunnery training. There were grand photographs of the warship in various Australian harbours. There was *Canberra* sailing beneath the incomplete Sydney Harbour Bridge in 1930 and taking part in activities when the bridge opened on 19 March 1932. This was a rare cause for celebration during a crippling depression and Australians took great pride in the 'extraordinarily skilful'[40] workmanship of the bridge. In typically Australian style, this world-breaking structure was

Poster for the celebrations of the opening of the Sydney Harbour Bridge, March 1932.

nicknamed The Coathanger.

The ceremony had its own drama. Following official speeches, the Premier of NSW, Labor politician Jack Lang, prepared to open the bridge by cutting a ribbon at the southern end. As he was about to do so, Francis de Groot, a member of the New Guard – a 1930s right-wing paramilitary group opposed to Lang's policies – moved forward on horseback and slashed the ribbon with a sword. He was promptly arrested and later convicted of offensive behaviour. The ribbon was hurriedly retied and Lang cut it with flourish. This show of defiance appealed to some sailors whose 'dressed'[41] ship looked resplendent at its mooring in sight of the bridge which now linked both shores of Sydney Harbour. A 21-gun salute and a Royal Australian Air Force (RAAF) fly-past concluded the official ceremony. For non-duty *Canberra* crew, this marked the opportunity to go ashore to enjoy the festivities with characteristic navy gusto.

After arriving in Australia, *Canberra* operated primarily in Australian waters. The longest voyage was in September 1931 when

HMAS Canberra *sailing under the Sydney Harbour Bridge, October, 1930.*

Canberra moored in Sydney Harbour for the Sydney Harbour Bridge celebrations, 1932.

the cruiser visited New Caledonia and Fiji. The ship's peaceful routine became monotonous for the crew. Midshipman Richard Innes Peek, who was born on 30 July 1914 at West Tamworth in New South Wales and entered the RANC in 1928, passed out with high grades before joining *Canberra*. Like his peers, he had been eager to commence his sea training but found life on the cruiser unexciting and struggled to fill his midshipman journal with enthusiasm. All the excitement was on the other side of the world. There was a search for the RN submarine *M2* that had been suspended; the 60-man crew lost.

The brevity of Peek's 31 January entry drew the displeasure of the inspecting officer. 'Divisions, church and captain's inspection as usual. Social pictures in the evening', he had written[42] Peek endeavoured to sound more enthusiastic but barely disguised his boredom.

1st February. Regatta practice continues with increased activity as the day approaches. His Excellency Sir Isaac Isaacs arrived in Hobart and the Commodore went ashore to meet his train.
2nd February. A march past is being rehearsed both for Hobart and the Sydney Bridge celebrations.[43]

HMAS Canberra *band was kept busy with official events and wardroom receptions, c. 1930s.*

Finally Midshipman Peek found something more exciting to write about and sailors such as Torpedoeman Bastock were delighted to be tested when on 10 February a torpedo was fired. Unfortunately, it took 'a bad turn' and *Canberra* chased 'at all available speed'[44].

An attempted recovery failed and the torpedo sank in 28 fathoms. Over the next four days, divers and sweeping failed to locate the torpedo and the cruiser departed. On 16 February the crew was informed that the 'Naval Board had decided that we should return and search for the torpedo immediately after the Regatta'.[45] According to CPO Claude Choules, the torpedo tubes in this class of ship:

> were much higher above the waterline than in previous cruisers
> and our torpedoes were sometimes damaged due to the height
> they had to fall before reaching the water. We eventually
> obviated this with several modifications.[46]

Canberra was triumphant in the Hobart Regatta over other RAN ships, including arch rival, *Australia*. After leaving Hobart, a 'full calibre shoot' was conducted with mixed success. The following day,

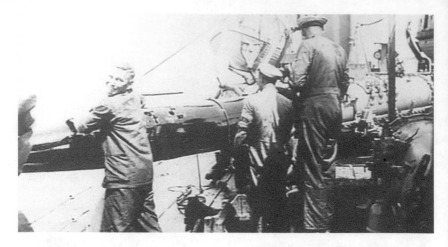

Canberra *personnel engaged in torpedo firing, c. 1935.*

24 February, 'a serious accident almost occurred' when there was a problem with 'men manning the tackle' and the same day a 'searchlight control was exercised after dinner' which failed because a 'small bulb was found to be missing'. On 25 February there was to be a 'sub-calibre bombardment' with aircraft from HMAS *Albatross* spotting. Owing to the conditions the 'results were not very satisfactory'.[47] *Canberra* weighed anchor and proceeded to Hobart where a strong wind made mooring alongside difficult and 'we grazed the pier denting several plates'. It was back to parades, divisions, open days and social activities – and so it continued.

Peek was again reprimanded for his brevity, lack of sketches and untidy writing. His writing improved but not his assessment of *Canberra*'s war gaming abilities. On 3 March, gunnery practice was only 'moderately good'. On 7 March the night exercise against HMAS *Tattoo* did not go well because 'P2 4 inch jammed after the first round'. Much of Midshipman Peek's journal entries for the month concerned the painting of the ship: '150 gallons of ship's side grey was used alone' to which his senior officer added 'More detail'. Much activity in preparation for the Admiral's inspection consumed the ship's company time and energy during the last fortnight of March and gave Peek little to write about but 'paint ship'.

In August the only excitement was of Midshipman Peek's making and did not enhance his self-esteem: 'Court of enquiry assembled on board this morning to enquire into the cause of my mishap in the cutter'.[48] In September 'children's party attended by 30 children was held at 1500 and the midshipmen found 10 children somewhat too many' – more painting of ship.

Officers' children's Christmas party, complete with slippery dip and crane basket rides, c. 1930s.

HMAS Canberra *officers with midshipmen, 1931.*

In November Able Seaman Eric Thompson died from a burst appendix when the navy was unable to evacuate him to hospital soon enough. A ship's company dance was postponed and his shipmates turned out in force for his funeral at Rookwood Cemetery, Sydney. In Peek's journal 1 December was simply marked 'yet another children's party'.[49]

The following year seemed no more exciting. Captain Charles Farquhar-Smith, RAN, was relieved by Captain Frederick Cyril Bradley, RN on 29 May 1933. [50] July was time for the 'winter cruise' and the ship steamed north to Queensland for visits to Brisbane and Lord Howe Island as well as some exercises in Hervey Bay.

On 15 July, Peek's journal provides a sailor's insight into what became known as the White Australia Policy, what was in fact the *Immigration Restriction Act*, 1901.

> The Dean of Canterbury has made a speech declaring that it would be a 'great gesture' to allow Japan to populate those areas of Australia which the 'white races are not able to populate'. Truly a great gesture! But the speaker does not take into account the abhorrence on reasonable grounds of anything but a 'white Australia'. It is a known fact that the Japanese breed much more

rapidly than the English and the great fear is that once allowed to start, the Japanese will be uncheckable in somewhat the same way as the humble rabbit is at present. It is wondered why this speaker did not suggest Canada or another 'great gesture' but perhaps he found that owing to its proximity the uproar caused would eventually come back to him. Finally the speaker does not know his facts when he says 'areas which the white peoples are not able to populate' there are no such areas as he would realise if he took the trouble to read or merely glance through the Commonwealth publication 'Australia Unlimited'. [51]

For this uncharacteristic eloquence and perhaps nationalistic sentiment, Midshipman Peek received a congratulatory comment from his superior. Following his year in *Canberra*, Midshipman Richard Peek, as customary for every Australian midshipman, travelled to England to be attached to the RN for further training. His RAN career would be a very distinguished one rising eventually to the rank of Vice Admirable.[52]

The lackadaisical tempo continued and *Canberra* visited Brisbane for exhibition week, the annual agricultural show of Queensland. Payne wrote:

where the ships were seen by a large number of country people staying in the city. From Brisbane, H.E., the Governor of New South Wales and Lady Game were taken to Lord Howe Island.[53]

August 1933 marked a change in scenery with *Canberra* sailing to New Zealand. A five-day 'mock battle' was conducted off Russell on the North Island – with an Australian attack by *Canberra* and *Australia* and staunch resistance from ships *Dunedin* and *Diomede*. Victory went to the Australians but the invasion and occupation of New Zealand was deemed superfluous though the arrival of both cruiser crews in Auckland probably seemed like an invasion. The *New Zealand Herald* was polite in its description.

RUSSELLO.
A Naval Occasion.

AFTER we had sunk the convoy
   And wished its crew a bon voy-
    Age to down below
                 low-low-low,
    Then we had to hustle—
    Hustle off to Russell-o.
Though "Australia" was a B.F.
   To have let us get a D/F
    On her wavelength low
                 low-low-low,
    Then we had to hustle—
    Hustle off to Russell-o.
Though we are tired of action stations
  And war at morning, noon and night ;
And though the Seagull, without flying,
  The Fairy Queen has put to flight.
Though the starshell flew around us
  And the rain-squall nearly drown'd us,
    We'd a good Vignot
             oh-oh-oh.
    Then we cut a caper,
    Won the war, on paper,
    On the way to Russell-o.

Pages from Sea Noises, *book by G.C. Ingeton and H.L. Boyd, c. 1930s.*

Silently, punctually and unobtrusively in the custom of the
Navy … the Australian and New Zealand Squadron … arrived
in Auckland. People who watched the ships from the vantage
points were witness to an impressive spectacle as the steel grey
warships rounded North Head and steamed majestically up to
the doors of the city.[54]

There was time in 1933 for Lieutenant Geoffrey Chapman Ingleton
and Chief Henry Boyd onboard *Canberra* to create a book entitled *Sea
Noises*. The 240 copies sold quickly. New Zealand ports were featured
and mention made of the many thousands of visitors who clambered
onboard to regard 'the clean appearance and the efficiency of the ships'.
Showcased were ten songs written and sung 'many times in the mess'

during the cruise, preferably with 'a glass of beer in one hand and at least two inside'.[55] For each port of call there were a number of 'lagers' or 'tots'. Songs, illustrated with artistic flourish, included 'Back Again to Rotorua', 'A Rotten Song' and 'Taranaki'. The song 'Russell-O' is the only song which referred to operational duties. The last song was 'Sydney'.

> Back to Sydney shore! Back to Sydney shore! What a glorious sight to see: Sweethearts waiting on the Quay. Pretty girls galore congregate at four, waiting for their sailor boys on the Sydney shore.[56]

References to alcohol, sweethearts and girls simply accentuated the dominant interests of navy men. The song 'Wellington' could be interpreted as comment on the continuous requirement for navy personnel to entertain the public.

What most irked members of the lower deck was that, whereas officers were permitted to drink alcohol and, indeed, were encouraged to entertain onboard, non-commissioned personnel were commonly not.[57]

> There were Colonels and Majors and Captains by the ton,
> Waiting to welcome us at Wellington.
> Governors and Generals and pressmen out for fun
> Waiting to welcome us at Wellington.
> They all stood along the wharf
> As we came steaming in,
> And when the bar was opened – well,
> You should have heard the din.
> Some came for luncheon and stayed till after tea.[58]

Dignitaries were feted by officers. Cocktail parties were held on the upper deck and official guests in the Captain's or Admiral's cabins or in the wardroom. *Canberra* was dubbed 'the glamour ship' because of its assigned duties. Invariably it assumed the role of flagship with the Admiral onboard.

Admiral Dalglish and Captain Walker gave a cocktail party on board HMAS *Canberra* to which about 150 naval officers and their wives and friends were invited.[59]

In whatever port the cruiser was moored, the routine remained the same.

HMAS *Canberra* and HMAS *Hobart* will be the fete this week before leaving for the summer cruise to Tasmania. This Friday Admiral Custance will entertain at cocktails onboard HMAS *Canberra* ... Most of the officers' wives make this an annual date for a trip to Hobart.[60]

RAN produced postcards carried the word 'cruise' in keeping more with a pleasure trip than a navy truly preparing to safeguard a nation against any contingency. The 'cruising' continued. In 1935, *Canberra* escorted the HMS *Sussex* with the Duke of Gloucester onboard during the Duke's visit to Australia. In August 1936, *Canberra* brought Admiral Sir Murray Anderson to Sydney for his investiture as Governor of New South Wales.

Such assignments were prestigious for some but less so for others. For crew, 'the glamour ship' meant constant ship cosmetic work. The sailors were known to say: 'If it moves, salute it; if it doesn't, paint it'.

The continuous need for *Canberra* to be 'shipshape' for official and public visits meant that for seamen and engineering staff presentation was more fundamental than operations.

The increased number of officer dinners and receptions resulted in longer, physical and monotonous duty for sailors who were required for preparation, and duties during and after the special occasions. Traditionally, two of the least favoured duties were painting and 'holystoning' performed at the whim of the Commodore. Generations of ratings regarded this as their hardest duty and few were sad to see wooden decked ships replaced by steel.

The experience of holystoning was vivid for *Canberra* Ordinary Seaman Lloyd 'Saltie' Saltmarsh.

We used to get up in the morning and scrub the decks, up at 6 o'clock and worked until 7 and we would be scrubbing the decks and then about once a fortnight or it might be once a month, we used to have to holystone the decks and there were two stones about half the size of a brick and they had a round hole in the top, and that's why they are called holystones, which you were supposed or you could fit a handle to use, scrub the woodwork up and down. But we never quite got to the stick in the hole business, it used to be down on your hands and knees and you'd have a holey stone in each hand and you would scrub up and down ... until you cleaned the deck.[61]

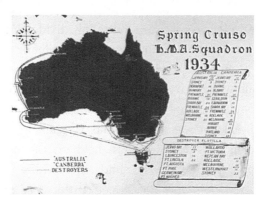

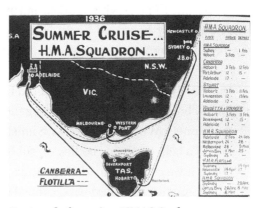

Postcards featuring HMAS Canberra, *c. 1930s.*

Canberra crew were commonly divided into three watches. For stokers, that meant four hours on in the boiler or engine rooms and eight hours off around the clock. With a third of the crew on watch, there was no allowance given to those who had been on night watch. At 0600 the bugle sounded 'Wakey, Wakey'. Hammocks were lashed up and stowed. Breakfast was at 0700 and 'Captain's rounds' were at 1000. At 1100 divisions (parade) were held on the upper deck. Frenzied activity preceded Captain's rounds. Everything was scrubbed, wooden tables and stools were holystoned, cutlery and plates were polished and food trays burnished.

'We scrubbed with soft soap and hot water the deck ... we even polished the spittoon inside and out'.[62]

As the officers – the captain, executive officer (XO), divisional officer and chief PO – approached 'we stood stiffly to attention alongside our table'[63] as everything was closely inspected. Sailors held their breath and prayed they would not be the ones who received the wrath of their seniors.

It was impressed upon young stokers that they were extremely fortunate not to be serving on coal-burning ships, on which the work was notoriously hard and dirty. Nonetheless, working conditions on *Canberra* for young stokers were 'deplorable'.

Our time was spent cleaning and red leading smelly and filthy bilges, boiler cleaning and scraping the soot from the inside of the funnels. Whatever the job we finished up covered in soot or filth. To help clean our bodies we rubbed ourselves down with oil, or if we could get hold of it butter. Despite these precautions and no matter how hard we scrubbed ourselves the grime stayed in the pores of the skin. Clean clothes and especially our white summer uniforms would be grubby within minutes.[64]

As modern as *Canberra* was, ablutions (bathrooms) had no showers, only rows of small stainless steel bowls. Sailors rubbed themselves

HMAS Canberra *decorated for the arrival of Admiral Sir Murray Anderson.*

Removing layers of paint that were a fire risk, c. 1930s.

Holystoning, c. 1930.

down with sweat rags and soapy water. New sailors quickly learnt that if their idea of hygiene was below standard, older members of the crew would take to them with a stiff brush until they 'voluntarily' raised their standard.

The class divide within the RAN was further magnified by an Australian media preoccupied with officers and their wives. Articles in popular magazines were commonplace. For example, the *Australian Women's Weekly* reported on 6 October 1934 that:

> Lieutenant T. F. Percival, RAN ... married Miss Joy Taylor, daughter of Mr J Taylor, of St Kilda Rd.[65]

On 20 October 1937, the *Sydney Morning Herald* featured a photograph of sailors suspended over *Canberra*'s hull painting in preparation for 'the southern cruise, which takes place each year about Melbourne Cup time'.[66] Headlines centred on the heavy rains in Australia, the resulting flooding and the possible impact this would have on the spring racing carnival, as well as the approaching Australian elections and Prime Minister Joseph Lyons' declaration that:

Australia is at the cross-roads. She must choose between Empire unity or Australia aloof and pursuing a policy of national independence.[67]

However, such significant matters of national interest were diminished by the large advertisement declaring it was 'Time to Order Your Xmas Suit' for the special price of £4/4/– and an even larger advertisement for the 'New Austin fifteen-nine' for £389, which 'revolutionises motor car value with this full 5-seater 112-inch wheelbase Austin'. The stability and security of the world had been deteriorating throughout the decade but the media, the Australian Government and the people they represented preferred to dwell on less serious issues. They believed in the superiority of the British race and that the Empire would protect them.

Back in May 1927 on the chilly docks of Clydebank in Scotland when Princess Mary had broken a bottle of Australian red wine across the bows of the cruiser (which she would later commission as HMAS *Canberra*), the Australian High Commissioner, Sir Joseph Cook, declared:

Sailors painting the hull of Canberra, 1939.

we in Australia are hoping that man for man, ship for ship, discipline for discipline, the Australian will fit into the Imperial navy like a section of a bookcase fits into the whole. That is Australia's hope, because we are proud to be a section of the Imperial family.[68]

Almost a decade later the *Sydney Morning Herald* stated:

The Governor-General Lord Gowrie stated 'the peace of the world and the future of civilisation were hanging in the balance, and the extent of the British Empire's ability to make her influence felt would be the deciding factor'.[69]

Despite this confidence in the British Empire's ability to influence world affairs, turbulence in Europe was rapidly escalating that would herald the demise of the British Empire. The ascendancy and aggression of nations not loyal to the British Empire had been remarkable. Adolf Hitler was on the move. Having forced the passage of the *Enabling Act 1933* in Germany, granting himself the right to enact laws without parliamentary consent and constitutional limitations, Hitler went on to become Fuhrer of Germany on 19 August 1934. On 16 March 1935, Hitler violated the Treaty of Versailles by introducing military conscription. In March the following year, German troops occupied the strategically important Rhineland. During the first two weeks of March 1938, Hitler's Germany announced the 'Anschluss' (union) with Austria and in August the German military mobilised. On 12 September 1938 at a Nuremberg Nazi Party rally, Hitler denounced Czechoslovakia as being a fraudulent state.

British Prime Minister Neville Chamberlain (far left) with Adolf Hitler (centre) in Munich, 30 September, 1938 to sign what would become the Munich Agreement.

On his return to England, PM Chamberlain declared 'peace in our time' was assured.

At a conference held in Munich, Germany and major European powers, excluding the Soviet Union and Czechoslovakia, agreed that Nazi Germany could annexe portions of Czechoslovakia, to be designated 'Sudetenland'. British Prime Minister Neville Chamberlain flew back to England flourishing the Munich Agreement and declaring 'peace for our time'.

In October 1935, Benito Mussolini's Fascist Italy invaded Abyssinia (Ethiopia) and eight months later annexed that nation. On 25 October 1936, Nazi Germany and Fascist Italy signed a treaty of cooperation and the Rome-Berlin Axis was announced on 1 November 1936. On the other side of the world, Japan invaded Manchuria, signed the Anti-Comintern Pact with Nazi Germany on 25 November 1936 and invaded China on 7 July 1937.

The world was teetering on world-wide conflict but during 1937 when Stoker Norm King joined *Canberra*, the tempo within Australia and the nation's navy was bewilderingly blithe. He may have struggled to separate fact from fiction in the 'dits' (stories) told by the 'old men' who made up the bulk of the crew but, as a very junior sailor, King soon understood the priorities of those in RAN authority.

He wrote in his journal: 'A typical Sunday routine at sea. The ship steaming up the East Coast of Australia to show the flag.'[70]

Canberra steamed to the Whitsunday Passage visiting Townsville and Cairns.

> We cruised the calm and beautiful waters inside the Barrier Reef anchoring off different islands every day. The crew given recreational leave, we rowed ashore in the cutters and whalers, explored the islands and skylarked on the beaches.[71]

The warship continued pushing through Australian waters to the northern tip of the country where the youthful stoker was impressed by the indigenous peoples' welcome but declined the cooked kangaroo, preferring to partake in the feast hauled onboard.

It was on to the Dutch East Indies for more cruiser diplomacy. King was becoming more settled; it was feeling like 'home [away] from home'. It was fascinating to relax on the upper deck and watch the ocean roll past, the sea unusually calm. When it rained 'it came down in buckets', but as the rain cleared, the sky and sea 'were blue and it was beautiful'. Dolphins surfed the warship's wake and whales were seen spouting plums of spray. It seemed idyllic. Then they continued on to Indonesia.

For Australian country and city boys alike, Bali was definitely an eye-opener.

> Lovely girls carrying things on their heads and nothing from the waist up. They seemed quite pleased to be photographed and we were happy to oblige, so much for the landscape views. All I remember of Batavia (Jakarta) is big fat Dutch men and women being pulled around in rickshaws by skinny little native men.[72]

Back to Australia they prepared to embark on the yearly southern cruise for the Hobart regatta. The strapping 18-year-old King was delighted to be selected for the first cutter crew, not just for the recognition and the glory, but also because the legendary competitiveness between *Australia* and *Canberra* resulted in the cutter crew being given a 'special diet of steak' leading up to the regatta. If his team beat the team from the sister cruiser, he was confident he would face lighter duties on the return trip to Sydney.

There were all sorts of fun and games for the crews during the regatta. One keenly contested between the two cruisers, was a bizarre version of the board game Ludo, better known to sailors as 'Ukkers'.

> We had a big canvas board, Ludo board and it was about nine feet square and painted in appropriate colours. And the dice was about 6 inches square, the shipwright used to make the dice and we used to have it in a bucket, shake it in a bucket and throw it out you know, roll the dice out. And that used to be a bit of onboard fun.[73]

Following a most successful 1938 regatta, *Canberra* sailed to Jervis Bay and then onto the Sydney home port on 23 March 1938. On 1 April 1938, command of the cruiser was relinquished by Captain Alexander Guy Berners Wilson, DSO, RN, and assumed by Captain Wilfred Rupert Patterson, RN. It was then time to undertake the annual winter cruise,

Canberra *crew with catch of the day, c. 1930s.*

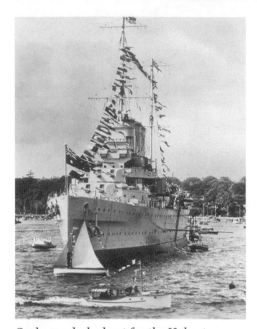

north to Queensland and in time for the fun activities of the Brisbane Exhibition week.

But beneath the gloss and veneer not all was stable within the RAN. In many ways Australia's navy was a reflection of the past rather than the present and was totally unprepared for the future.

During the 1930s, the fickleness of government budgets and defence policy caused disruption within the RAN and austerity cuts severely impeded

Canberra *decked out for the Hobart Regatta, 1930s.*

operational effectiveness. Simultaneously, few of those in RAN positions of highest authority understood or respected those who served in the

Keen competition between Canberra *and* Australia *boat crews, c. 1930s.*

Ukkers, a popular game played on deck, c. 1930s.

HMAS Canberra *approaching Dalgety's Wharf, Brisbane, c. 1930s.*

Captain W.R. Patterson, RN on HMAS Canberra *bridge, c. 1939.*

lower deck. During the decade, the permanent force aged and the opportunity to enlist willing volunteers was lost as a myopic personnel policy was pursued. Should the nation be committed to war, not only would there be a severe manpower shortage, but the imbued attitudes and beliefs of those in authority would make them less practised in, and less inclined towards, embracing the most modern equipment and strategies.

We did not attract officers of a high calibre and later I realised that my training had suffered because of this.

Vice Admiral Henry Burrell, RAN[74]

Rear Admiral George Francis Hyde, RAN, c. 1930s.

On 20 October 1931, Rear Admiral George Francis Hyde, RAN, took command of the Royal Australian Navy on his appointment as First Naval Member, Australian Commonwealth Naval Board (ACNB). Hyde was born in Portsmouth, England in 1877. With his family unable to afford RN College fees, he commenced his seafaring career at 17 as a merchant navy apprentice. Hyde was then able to join the Royal Naval Reserve (RNR) as a midshipman and, at the turn of the century, was undergoing RN Gunnery School training. By July 1912, he had transferred to the RAN and during World War I served as Executive Officer of the Australian flagship, HMAS *Australia*. Promotion to Vice Admiral came in November 1932. On 12 July 1936, he was promoted to full Admiral and created Knight Commander of the Bath (KCB) in the 1937 New Year Honours list, the first seagoing member of the RAN to hold this rank, and the only one awarded a KCB.

Hyde commanded the RAN between 1931 and 1937, a period marked by disrupted RAN personnel policy and lower deck unrest. Depression-era economic problems facing successive Australian governments caused difficult decisions to be made, particularly with regards to personnel, but it was the RN socialisation of the First Naval Member and other ACNB members, and their hard-line loyalty to the British Admiralty and British Empire, which exacerbated the situation and impacted on RAN operational effectiveness.

In 1931 and 1932, there were 'malicious' attempts to damage the engines of HMAS *Albatross*.[75] In 1932, a mutiny occurred on the permanent depot ship HMAS *Penguin* based in Sydney. The CO passed on the men's complaints to the ACNB. The Board reacted angrily believing the requests were 'so subversive of discipline' they should not be considered and criticised *Penguin*'s CO for accepting the requests and failing to recommend sailors concerned be discharged SNLR (Services No Longer Required). The Board was determined 'to dispense with the services of the men who refuse duty'.[76] Shortly afterwards a large number of sailors assembled in the HMAS *Cerberus* drill hall and only the conciliatory efforts of a naval chaplain averted mutiny and the men agreed to disperse.

HMA Ships Australia *and* Canberra *(foreground) in Sydney Harbour, c 1930s.*

In November 1932, HMAS *Canberra*, in the company of *Australia,* the seaplane carrier *Albatross* and destroyer *Tattoo*, had travelled south to undertake a training exercise in Bass Strait. The squadron docked in Melbourne and it was reported that 200 men 'had walked off the ships' and after 'refusing duty had carried a resolution to leave their case in the hands of the Naval Board'.[77] The Minister for Defence, Sir George Pearce, stood in the Federal Parliament to admit that sailors 'had issued an ultimatum to the government' but it remained a 'gross reflection on the men of the Navy to suggest that insubordination existed'.[78] It was subsequently reported that the 'gathering' in Melbourne had indeed occurred and there was:

> evident discontent ... due to the delay in dealing with properly
> presented complaints and to a suspicion that both sympathy

Canberra *and* Australia *leading naval exercise, c. 1940.*

and understanding were lacking at headquarters (because naval) administration ... [was] woodenly unresponsive and exasperatingly slow.[79]

Discontent had been simmering on *Australia* for some time. The twin cruisers commonly interchanged personnel, often drafts from one to the other ensued, and the cruisers steamed on exercises together, one behind the other depending on which was the flagship. Problems on one were easily the concern of sailors on the other.

Petty Officer Edward Walter James Dickerson (10615) was highly regarded by the men. A career navy man, he had enlisted in the RN in 1918 aged 16 and decided to call Australia home and transfer to the RAN in 1924. As a petty officer (PO), he was sent back to England as a member of the commissioning crew of *Australia*. Following a year as an instructor at HMAS *Cerberus*, he drafted to *Australia* as a gunnery instructor. In July 1932, this popular PO, of whom his Divisional Officer wrote 'Petty Officer Dickerson is highly recommended by me for any position of trust'[80] was charged with 'behaviour with contempt to a superior officer' to Midshipman Rendall Hay Collins. The 17-year-old Collins had admonished PO Dickerson in front of his gun crew for what Collins believed was incorrect gunnery drill. Dickerson retorted: 'I think I know how to teach 4-inch gun drill' or words to that effect. Whilst his comment was a chargeable offence, tactful consultation between the parties –*Australia*'s Executive Officer and *Australia*'s CO, Captain F.C. Bradley, RN – could have quickly defused the situation. But Dickerson was ordered to face a court martial. Though it was known that Midshipman Collins had been involved in an earlier enquiry at *Cerberus* for 'failing to tell the truth', no leniency for Dickerson was granted. Collins, the court believed, was an 'officer and a gentleman' and therefore would not make a false statement in a deliberate endeavour to injure the accused.[81] Dickerson was reduced to Leading Seaman, deprived of two good conduct badges (stripes) and drafted to *Canberra*.[82] The reaction of the cruiser ships' companies was immediate and brought to a head the simmering discontent on issues, particularly 'the excessive application of discipline'.[83]

A smoke screen onboard Canberra, *reflective of 1930s RAN smoke and mirrors administration.*

In 1936, Sub Lieutenant Collins was discharged on the medical grounds of short sight.[84] He was transferred to the retired list but appointed to the emergency list in 1939, re-entering the RAN and promoted to Lieutenant. He served as a training school gunnery instructor, a land depot gunnery officer and then as a staff officer during the war. Collins was demobilised in 1946 and remained on the Navy list until 1956. Dickerson regained his PO rank in 1935 and was promoted to Chief Petty Officer (CPO) in 1938. During World War II, he served on many warships and was discharged in 1945. Though he had served for 27 years, mostly in gunnery at sea, his claim for a war pension was rejected.

The Naval Board continued to refute media allegations concerning unrest within the lower deck. For example, the Board demanded legal action be taken against *Smith's Weekly* following the publication of articles 'calculated to have a bad effect on the naval service'.[85] This did not occur. In November 1932, the Board did instigate legal action under

Canberra *steaming up the Brisbane River, c. 1933.*

the *Crimes Act* against the publisher of *Truth* when the newspaper also published an article citing widespread sailor dissension.[86] The ACNB believed the newspaper was attempting to incite mutiny. The case went to trial and the jury retired for just 17 minutes before bringing in a verdict of 'not guilty'.[87]

In 1934 sailors refused to obey the command for hands to fall in onboard HMAS *Moresby*. Seven sailors were discharged SNLR for being 'the probable ringleaders'.[88] Melbourne-born Engine Room Artificer (ERA) Frederick William Reville (19878) served in *Canberra* between 1934 and 1935. He wrote home about the unrest.

> They are still having trouble on *Australia*. I believe. Things
> thrown overboard and small electric wires cut, so that the old
> bloke's [Hyde] denial of discontent in the paper falls a bit flat ...
> I wonder how it will finish up.[89]

In August 1935 *Canberra* left Sydney for the spring cruise. As the cruiser steamed north, it was discovered that someone had taken the breech blocks from the four 4-inch anti-aircraft guns and thrown them overboard.[90] It was alleged that on arrival in Brisbane all members of

Photographs of happy sailors onboard HMAS Canberra *did little to assuage rumours that the cruiser was anything but a happy ship, c. 1939.*

the 4-inch gun crews had their fingerprints taken by police and 'the man responsible was discovered and discharged'.[91]

By December 1934 the Australian Government asked Hyde to explain the causes of the lower deck unhappiness. The Admiral stated that in his opinion disciplinary troubles in the RAN could be traced to:

1. unsatisfactory pay conditions
2. unsatisfactory food
3. bad officers
4. subversive influence of persons whose direct objective is the causing of disaffection.[92]

This official assessment by the highest RAN authority was both accurate and superficial.

Pay rates for sailors had been set in accordance with those of Commonwealth public servants following World War I, causing much resentment because there was little similarity between the two occupations. A sailor had a binding enlistment of 12 years. Mandatory retirement age for a sailor was between 40 and 50 whereas for public servants, it was 60 to 65. The average working week for a member of the Commonwealth Public Service was 37 hours, overtime was paid and time off in lieu granted – weekend work was unusual. Sailors had a minimum working week of 50 hours and additional hours when leave was cancelled. No overtime was paid. Serving on a ship deployed at sea for weeks or months, free time was a rare commodity and confined to the ship. Any comparison with civilian employment was nonsensical.

In 1925 an able seaman's salary was £127/8/– per annum, a male public servant's salary £162 per annum. Under the *Financial Emergency Act 1929*, the Australian Government implemented a 22½ per cent pay cut to the salaries of all government employees. An able seaman's basic salary was reduced from 7/– (70 cents) a day to 5/8d (58 cents) a day or £103/12/8d per annum. By 1932, a sailor-formed Lower Deck Welfare Committee stated that the disparity was unacceptable and that public service salary gains between 1919 and 1929 had not been handed on to sailors yet sailors had been subjected to the same pay cut. Sailors received additional allowances, included as gross wages, but sailors were required to use them, for example, to ensure their uniforms (kit) passed the careful scrutiny of superiors. Able Seaman James McBain (15117) applied for a naval discharge on the grounds that his pay was 'inadequate to support wife and mother' and he could earn more in civilian employment.[93] The Lower Deck Welfare Committee stated that:

> the Naval Board refuses to understand or accept the
> humanitarian side of lower deck wages. The Naval Board is
> unsympathetic to the lower deck.[94]

The ACNB needed to juggle capital, maintenance and personnel costs but the Board and Admiral Hyde believed 'the [RAN] rating is substantially better off than his opposite number in the Royal Navy'.[95] When lower deck pay rises were introduced in the RN in 1936, the RAN did not adopt them. Whilst Hyde had transferred to the RAN from the RN, the bulk of his service time had been spent serving in RN ships. His opinion of sailors was based on his service primarily within the RN, with RN lower deck and in the Northern Hemisphere. His lack of appreciation of the differences between RN and RAN, British and

Australian-born lower deck, aggravated the personnel conundrum.

Rear Admirable Henry Feakes, RAN, believed Hyde was an 'unshakeable' supporter of a policy of the closest association with the RN, which blinded him to the differences. Feakes believed the highest RAN authority was:

> strong in character, an excellent seaman, a sound organiser,
> his one handicap was one not unusual in the individualist long
> accustomed to use of autocratic power. He was totally unable
> to tolerate any difference of opinion from that strongly held by
> himself.[96]

A long-held view within a navy born of the RN was that Australian midshipmen needed to serve extensively with the RN in European waters. This offered training and seafaring experience but it was also seen as a way in which young Australians could absorb the beliefs and standards of the RN – standards deemed necessary to become a naval officer and gentleman. At the same time, there was a preference for RN sailors on loan or exchange to serve as the basis of the RAN lower deck, rather than the recruitment of Australians.

After the RAN was established in 1911, there was a necessity for experienced and fully trained sailors to man the Australian fleet and to instruct Australian recruits. It was advocated in 1920 that the RAN required 576 officers and 6,052 sailors.[97] In 1920, 33 per cent of the RAN were RN personnel. In March 1920, ACNB agreed that the shortage of junior sailors had been caused by 'poor personnel planning and policy implementation', yet the recruitment of Australian volunteers was suspended on 10 June 1920.[98] In September 1920, ACNB admitted that 'nearly all the ratings now serving in destroyers are Royal Naval ratings'.[99] By 1921 the percentage of RN personnel within the RAN had doubled from that in 1917.[100] By 1923 the RAN permanent naval force had dwindled to 3,854.[101]

A valuable RAN rating foundation was achieved through Australians being recruited via the Boy Training Scheme. This was discontinued in 1926 and though it was indicated that this was a 'temporary' measure, it was nearly 40 years before an RAN junior recruit scheme was reintroduced. The ACNB also closed naval reserve units in many cities. Of a naval budget in 1925–26 of £2,071,512 (exclusive of capital ship building), just £3,700 was spent on recruiting Australians.[102] It had become clear as early as 1911 to the Australian Minister for Defence, George Foster Pearce that there was a breakdown in the training schedule of Australian recruits. He laid the blame with the Admiralty for failing to provide instructors whilst also diminishing opportunities for the advanced training, which would eventually allow Australians to take on instructor duties.[103] For the Admiralty and the ACNB, the recruitment and promotion of Australians was viewed as less desirable. RN sailors were seen as being more compliant, more class-conscious, more likely to defer blindly to discipline from a higher order rather than from a respect earned from proven professionalism and man management.

The Admiralty had long 'paid too little attention to personnel'.[104] The result was that RN lower deck conditions of service lagged 'a generation behind the standards of civilian society'.[105].This less caring attitude towards sailors now extended into every aspect of RAN life. 'Scran' (rations) clearly affected the quality of life onboard warships and again Australians were used to better and greater quantity than their RN counterparts. Under the *Financial Emergency Act*, ration allowances were reduced. It was also alleged that in 1932 Chief Petty Officers and Petty Officers (most likely British born) were given superior rations to lower ranks who were more likely Australian-born, so as 'create a rift within the ranks'.[106] Certainly dry tea was no longer issued to messes containing men lower than the rank of Petty Officer. Instead the tea was brewed in a general gallery – three quarters of a pound per 300 men – and soda ash used to improve its colour.[107]

Service on the cruiser was inherently dangerous. Whilst this was understood by sailors they believed that if an accident occurred, RAN assistance and compensation should be forthcoming, but compensation for death and injury was contested by the ACNB and resulted in less than adequate relief.

AB Harry Wimbles (15244) served in *Canberra* as a member of a gun crew for two years before being drafted to *Australia* in mid-

1930. Within six months he was discharged due to 'deafness caused by gunfire'. The Naval Board chose to award him only a fifth of the lump sum he could have been awarded.[108] In 1930, the Naval Board judged that Tasmanian-born HMAS *Canberra* cook, Eric Sims (18323), was severely injured 'through irregularly placing his hand in the dough mixer when the machinery was in motion'. The Board did concede that 'this man's culpability was not of such a degree as to warrant the withholding of compensation under the regulations', awarded the 21-year-old 30 per cent of the compensation permitted, and discharged him. In 1935 during a *Canberra* night shoot exercise off Jervis Bay, a PO steward developed appendicitis and the surgeon commander recommended that the patient be put ashore for immediate surgery at Berry Hospital. It was alleged that the captain was persuaded by the gunnery officer to wait until the conclusion of the shoot. When the sailor was hospitalised the following morning, his appendix was found to have burst and he died. Able Seaman Phillip Jay (14349) serving on *Canberra* wrote about the consequences of this incident.

> It was hushed up but for the next couple of years you only had
> to say you had a pain in the guts and you were in Randwick
> Hospital in nothing flat.[109]

Tuberculosis was a common cause of lower deck discharge between 1920 and 1935. The living conditions of sailors proved a fertile ground for the disease. The Admiralty had advised the ACNB that the 'causative factors' arose from:

> service afloat from crowded accommodation, absence of
> sunlight in the spaces, insufficient ventilation, and heat and
> humidity between decks.[110]

The Department of Repatriation believed that beyond doubt chronic disease developed faster amongst servicemen than within the civilian population.[111] Nonetheless ACNB continued to contest compensation on the grounds that the disease was not attributable to naval service.

Arthur William Amos (13855) was born in Sydney on 14 October 1905. Having left school early to help support his family, he worked as a labourer whenever and wherever he could and was pleased to gain RAN entry. According to naval medical authorities, Amos contracted tuberculosis as a 'direct result of an attack of catarrhal influenza during an epidemic of that disease in HMAS *Canberra*'.[112] The ACNB dissented on the grounds that:

> sub-clause (iii) of para 3 of ACD602 implies a condition where a part of a ship's company by an act of duty is exposed to some particularly unhealthy influence and not to a case of disease prevailing in the ship whether epidemic or otherwise, to which the whole of the ship's company is exposed in the ordinary course of duty.[113]

It is very unlikely that Amos understood the verbose nature of the regulation or appreciated that he was ineligible for compensation for tuberculosis because he had contracted the disease when his resistance had been lowered by influenza, which had also quickly accelerated to epidemic proportions in the fertile grounds of the cramped mess decks of HMAS *Canberra*.

Tuberculosis was seldom evident within the upper deck as fewer officers shared sleeping quarters, there was a separate area for meals, and their rations were better. If an officer did contract tuberculosis, his compensation was far more generous. Lieutenant Lloyd Falconer Gilling was born in Goulburn, New South Wales. He served in HMAS *Canberra* and contracted the disease. Gilling was awarded 100 per cent compensation.[114] Sick Bay Attendant George Henry Jennings (18431) was highly regarded by his superior officers, persistently receiving 'superior' on his yearly reports for ability and 'very good' for character. Jennings contracted the disease whilst nursing tuberculosis patients in the naval wing at the Prince of Wales Hospital, Sydney. He was discharged from the service and paid only 50 per cent of the compensation applicable.[115]

Between 1927 and 1937, whilst the RAN lower deck averaged

3,626 sailors, 73 were discharged SNLR, 51 sailors were discharged 'unsuitable', there were 296 desertions and 394 sailors chose not to re-engage.[116] In *Canberra* between 31 March 1932 and 30 September 1933, 703 sailors faced 22 warrants and 712 punishments, making it a particularly unhappy ship.[117] Charges included 'Did Sleep in Improper Place, namely a Mess Table' perhaps actually indicative of the congested living quarters.[118] Harshness was exemplified in the case of Officer Steward Samuel Lewis Solomons (10336) who was charged with 'did not immediately obey the order ... to serve drinks in an officer's cabin'.[119] The officer concerned was the RN Instructor Commander, a schoolmaster. Solomons received seven days stoppage of leave, for the first time in his 12-year navy career lost his 'very good' classification, which affected future promotion, and was drafted to another ship.

Captain Bradley, RN, had commanded *Australia* during years of particular unrest, which included the Dickerson court martial. The message to the ACNB that 'Admiralty approve of loan service being extended' meant Bradley assumed command of HMAS *Canberra* on 1 June 1933. Captain Charles Farquhar-Smith had proven a hard taskmaster but Bradley intensified the unrelenting, by-the-letter discipline.

On 25 August 1933, *Canberra* entered Jervis Bay and prepared to anchor. Officers were normally served their evening meal in the wardroom at 1740 but on this occasion five leading stewards simply 'walked off the job', refusing to serve. The five were charged with being absent from their place of duty and each received five days' stoppage of leave.[120] The following day, 17 able seamen refused to stow their hammocks at 0530 and only complied when so ordered by their petty officers. Each received two days stoppage of leave. At 0930, two leading seamen, three able seamen and an ordinary seaman did not report to their divisions and gathered in the lower conning tower. The master-at-arms hastily convinced them to return to their place of duty and hence their charges were reduced – they received five days stoppage of leave.

RAN documentation on sailor punishment (Punishment Returns) attests to anomalies in the awarding of and severity of punishment. Comparison with RN Punishment Returns for the same period shows the RAN awarded considerably more punishments. When compared with the RAN, 'the Royal Navy was a very cohesive force with no serious disciplinary problems'.[121] Members of the lower deck understood the necessity for discipline and the requirement for their superiors to maintain discipline in accordance with the *Naval Discipline Act*. But adherence to the strict disciplinary code of the RN as set in an act of 1866, left little room for interpretation and cultural dissimilarities. Whilst Admiral Hyde cited 'bad officers' as a contributory factor to unrest within the RAN, he believed this could be cured by harsher adherence to RN discipline so that there would be 'immediate and implicit obedience of commands'.[122] His interpretation was not universally shared by Australian-born officers.

Henry MacKay Burrell, born on 13 August 1904 in the picturesque Blue Mountains township of Wentworth Falls, entered the RANC in January 1918. Travelling to England in May 1928 on SS *Beltana*, he was a member of the commissioning crew of HMAS *Canberra*. Burrell excelled and was duly promoted while he served in HMA Ships *Tattoo*, *Stuart* and *Brisbane* between 1932 and 1935. He was unimpressed by many of the RN officers who administered the RAN.

Jervis Bay was a frequent anchorage for Canberra *and other naval vessels,* c.1936

We did not attract officers of a high calibre and later I realised that my training had suffered because of this. It was patently clear to me that the social life of many of my seniors took precedence over the service.[123]

The following three years were spent in the Northern Hemisphere with the RN, and Lieutenant Commander Burrell, RAN, received an adverse report from the Commanding Officer of HMS *Devonshire* for being 'too familiar with the sailors'. Burrell did not agree: 'In my view the ship would have been more effective if officers and ratings had been in closer touch'.[124] Burrell later rose to the rank of Vice Admiral and assumed the position of RAN Chief of Naval Staff on 24 February 1959.

One HMAS *Canberra* sailor wrote of the inaptitude of his torpedo officers

> [they did not demonstrate] a great deal of goodwill ... One thing we did realise, if the petty officers and the men under them didn't know their jobs, the officers were fairly useless.[125]

This comment may have been exaggerated but nonetheless conveyed the impression that sailors did not assume officers were their betters; respect was not an automatic right; respect needed to be earned.

Chief Stoker John Douglas Key Radley (13592) agreed. Having joined the RAN as a Stoker II in November 1922, Radley served in *Canberra* between 1932 and 1935, during the high punishment period. He offered an astute insight.

> As a general rule the seaman is treated like one of the lowest creatures ... discipline is necessary and must be enforced ... but there are different ways of giving orders and enforcing

Vice Admiral Henry Burrell, CB, RAN, c. 1959.

discipline. One way results in a rebellious discontented feeling. The other results in work being done conscientiously and willingly. Unfortunately the latter way is too often forgotten.[126]

In 1935, Chief Stoker Radley was a rare breed, an Australian-born, RAN-trained, senior non-commissioned officer. The majority of his peers did not commonly share his view of Australian sailors. During *Canberra's* maiden voyage to Australia, the heavy-handed and unpopular Chief Petty Officer Darby Allen was washed overboard. In heavy seas, the Captain manoeuvred the ship so that a lifeline could be thrown and the chief rescued. Sailors watched from guard rails and set up the cry 'let the bastard drown'.[127]

Much has been made of how different Australians were, particularly Australian servicemen during World War I, where the Australian Imperial Force (AIF) 'depended on the personal qualities of its leaders'.[128] Australian uniqueness may have been exaggerated but there were differences resulting from the tyranny of distance (from Europe), climate and environment (wide-open spaces), good diet, lack of established class order and political proclivity (five Labor governments between 1901 and 1931). One senior RN sailor was introduced to RAN junior sailors in 1925. He did not approve of 'their manners, their airs and graces'.[129] He wrote of his disappointment upon finding Australian sailors were unlike English sailors, despite their common heritage. Other factors annoyed him such as their 'affluence' and 'their popularity with the ladies'. He found them blatantly disrespectful, questioning of discipline and too democratic. 'Not one of them has been at sea long enough to know the laws even, let alone criticise them'.[130] Furthermore, he did not approve of the solidarity amongst the Australian ratings, which he believed led to 'organised disloyalty'. In 1942, this senior sailor agreed to a draft to an Australian-manned destroyer. Again he

CPO Stoker Douglas Radley, c. 1929.

condemned the Australian sailors for being 'slack, slovenly, shambling' and 'New World democrats'. His attitude changed.

> I saw these diggers whom I was so wont to belittle, work with
> such keenness, such willingness, such spirit indomitable that
> I have yet to meet elsewhere.[131]

Admiral Hyde preferred to believe no specific 'Australian temperament' existed and certainly not one that 'makes Australians less amenable to discipline'.[132] He demanded the strictest RN discipline possible as a way of accomplishing the Admiralty's desire that the RN and RAN achieve absolute personnel interchangeability, that young RAN personnel had the 'closest associations with the Royal Navy'.[133] Hyde formally enunciated the programme whereby the majority of RAN officers 'spent as much or more time with the RN before their promotion to captain as they spent in Australia'.[134] Their training should be identical to that given RN officers, which encouraged 'conformity and obedience to orders, and discouraged originality and initiative'.[135] Hyde continued to be unwavering in his belief that 'bad officers' were officers who showed 'timidity', who demonstrated a desire to be popular and 'fail to award a fair but firm punishment to offenders'.[136]

The assimilation of RAN sailors had to be aligned to the RN as closely as possible to achieve 'unquestioning discipline and absolute subordination to authority'.[137] Within warships, compliance to orders developed to a level of outlandish interpretation. HMAS *Canberra's* Able Seaman Phillip Jay wrote of frequent 'hands to go to general drill'.[138] Commands such as 'raise the anchor by deck tackle' involved prolonged physical effort for sailors but had relevance for an emergency. Some were supposed to amuse the crew, such as the order 'to flagship with fried egg', requiring a sailor to fry an egg and row with it to the flagship.[139] Sailors saw little humour when officers' stewards were ordered to Garden Island 'to bring back ten cats'.[140] The cats were wild. The stewards returned with four cats, sporting severe scratches and torn uniforms.

It was a favourite item of the admirals we had at the time, as well as with many skippers all of them RN and with fiendish delight in thinking up the most grotesque things for the lads to do.[141]

On 29 September 1935, Engine Room Artificer (ERA) Fred Reville wrote home that he was losing patience with how *Canberra* sailors were being sent on 'mystery hikes', 'dumped' ashore 'in some desolate hole' and told to find their way over a rough course as quickly as possible. On this trip to North Queensland, he was also unimpressed with the lack of leave.

We laid about seven miles off Townsville the other day and only officers allowed ashore. It was very annoying and they wonder why the men are discontented – to be able to see the lights and know that all we had to do was to sit and look at them made me feel I would have given a quid to get ashore. Need a good feed. They pick the most impossible places to anchor.[142]

Carefully worded grievances could be submitted through a divisional officer, but grievances were not always passed further up the chain of command lest it reflect unfavourably on the officer's own career. Of the 300 recommendations submitted to ACNB by the Welfare Committee over five years, just six were adopted. In 1933, the ACNB shut down the Welfare Committee leaving the lower deck without an institutional voice.[143] The *Daily Telegraph* asserted that sailors were not the problem; rather the fault lay with the administrators who treated Australian ratings like delinquent children. 'If silly things are being done in the name of discipline, they should be stopped,' the newspaper declared.[144] 'The Australian is the most easily disciplined person provided that he sees the reason for the thing he is asked to do'.[145]

Smith's Weekly joined the chorus stating that sailors:

needed handling, but when they get what they summarise very succinctly as a 'fair go' there is not a body of men more amenable to discipline.[146]

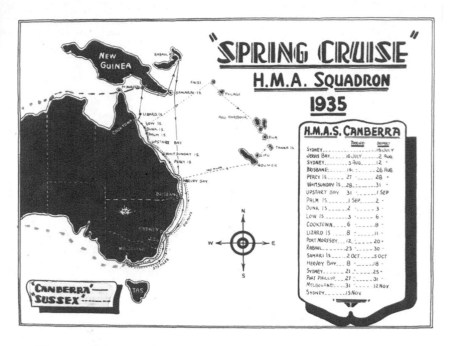

An illustration showing the extensive social calendar for HMAS Canberra *in 1935.*

This inflexible approach to sailors' rights and discipline worked to the advantage of the ACNB during a period when they believed they needed to reduce numbers by the premature discharge of 700 officers and sailors. It was sailors who faced the brunt of reduction policies. Between 1929 and 1932, officer numbers were reduced by 26 per cent, ratings by 40 per cent.[147] Sailors were offered free discharges. When this did not result in the desired drop in numbers, the slightest suspicion or infringement, injury or illness could be career ending. The use of the term, 'services no longer required' (SNLR) had traditionally been given to those discharged for criminal offences and venereal diseases; now SNLR was appearing on the records of ratings not guilty of such serious demeanours.

In a climate of retrenchment, any man who believed it was his democratic right to offer an opinion was very soon discharged. The label 'to the prejudice of good order and naval discipline' appeared increasingly on service certificates. Grounds for discharge now included

Anti-aircraft gunnery training onboard Canberra, *c. 1932.*

HMAS Canberra, *4-inch gunnery, c. 1939.*

any sailor who 'either on medical grounds or as regards character and/ or efficiency would be no particular loss to the service'. Another grounds for discharge was simple – 'this rating will be no loss to the service [because the sailor would] not likely to make good seaman'.[148] An internal ACNB memo cited 195 sailors as 'unsuitable'. Explaining that it would difficult to discharge under this term because it was difficult to prove deficient mental or physical state, or even 'incompetence', the recommended new term was to be 'on reduction'[149] which means exactly what it says, 'the reduction of numbers'. A further 83 Australian sailors were given 'compulsory discharges'.[150] Forced discharges also meant the RAN kept any deferred pay entitlements due to those discharged.

Leading Seaman John Bastock, the enthusiastic *Canberra* torpedoman whose service card had only been marked with 'very good' and 'superior', was discharged. Lieutenant Geoffrey Chapman Ingleton and Chief Henry Boyd the author, illustrator and printer of the joyful 1933 *Sea Noises* songbook were both dismissed. But herein lay another anomaly. Whereas sailors were readily discharged, every effort was made to retain officers and, if this was not possible, great effort was made to find them gainful employment. Ingleton was discharged on half pay in September 1935. Half pay was terminated six months later when he was appointed to a draughtsman's position with the Hydrographic Department.

The careers of officers and ratings (seamen) were viewed very differently – the former carefully nurtured, that latter, not at all. Administrators made much of the fact that it took eight years to train an officer but rarely admitted it took three or four years to train an able seaman, approximately seven years to train a leading hand and much longer for a sailor to qualify for Petty Officer (PO) or Chief Petty Officer (CPO). Sailors could be no less determined than officers to make the navy their lifetime career.

The modernisation of navies had increased particularly after World War I. Much had altered in the 60 years since Hyde's seafaring life commenced – change and advances in technology necessitated personnel reappraisal. Whereas in past eras sailors could be trained quickly, modern warships required better educated, technically competent men. Where once applicants scribbled occupations such as farm boy, labourer, hay binder or coal cart man on RAN enlistment forms, during the 1930s recruits were more liable to write 'clerk' or a trade.

The programme of personnel reduction that had been fiercely pursued would belatedly be seen as counterproductive. It would be admitted that within a cruiser complement of 600, approximately 200 specialist gunnery, torpedo and signal ratings were required. It took four years for a sailor to achieve a high degree of efficiency in these specialities. Whilst visual signalling may have changed little, the use of more sophisticated wireless, codes and cyphers became increasingly vital – fluency in all communication categories required time to achieve expertise.

David Mort had been RAN boy and man. Enlisting in January 1917 as a 14-year-old, Boy Seaman Mort, from his home town of Sydney, survived the taxing HMAS *Tingira* training, progressing from Boy II to Boy I to Signal Boy to Ordinary Signalman II before he could even commence his permanent RAN career on reaching the age of 18. As member of the *Canberra* commissioning crew, his career continued to flourish and favourable reports saw him promoted through Leading Signalman to Yeoman Signals to Chief Yeoman Signals. But during his return posting to HMAS *Canberra* in 1934, his career began a downward spiral. For the first time 'moderate' was written on his service card in 1934 and 1935.

Clearly something had changed in his attitude to his chosen career in the navy or the attitude of those in charge changed. Mort was demoted to Yeoman Signals and drafted off *Canberra*. The following year he left the RAN.[151]

Hyde blamed disciplinary problems on the 'subversive influence of persons whose direct objective is the causing of disaffection'. Sailors were not necessarily politically aware but they were by necessity a close-knit group sharing a bond among men who went down to the sea in ships. The 1930s were certainly an era

Signalman David Mort, c. 1918.

when democratic notions were in ascendancy. In this environment, the conservative establishment tended to attribute problems in the RAN to communist influences but there seems no proof of this. As early as 1927, the ACNB decided it needed to reduce numbers and so instituted a 'process of weeding out ratings'.[152] During the following decade, sailors who complained were placed on a list of those having 'communist tendencies' and their careers were further restricted. Hyde admitted that it was difficult to secure proof but that the RAN should adopt the practice of discharging 'as unsuitable any rating against whom there are sufficiently suspicious grounds'.[153] It was convenient for naval administrators to resort to the 'bolshie' communist label in assigning responsibility for the defiance of authority, for it absolved them of responsibility.

Hauling down a flag signal on HMAS Canberra *during training at sea, c. 1939.*

The file 'Recruits for the Navy' thickened as sailor selection and retention bordered on paranoia when it came to eliminating any individual who could be a possible troublemaker'.[154] Trained sailors who had accepted a free discharge and found civilian employment difficult to secure or not to their liking and who endeavoured to re-enlist were subjected to unreasonably intense scrutiny. The ACNB requested the Commonwealth Investigation Branch scrutinise sailors who wished to re-engage. Questions included:

Is he sane? Is he working? What is his reputation in the neighbourhood? Under what conditions is he living? Does he seem in comfortable circumstances? Has he a motor car?[155]

In 1933, RAN personnel had fallen to 2,783.[156] Between 1934 and 1937, defence expenditure in Australia doubled to about nine per cent of federal revenue yet sailor recruitment continued to rise only very slowly to 3,775. By 1936, serious rating shortages were becoming more obvious. In 1936, the full lower deck complement for destroyers *Vampire* and *Voyager* was 119 but by year's end, these ships had crews of 18 and 14 respectively. The decade had started with unrest and continued with sailors of sister cruiser *Australia* threatening 'serious trouble'. A newspaper article reported on 'crimes of various kinds were being frequently committed' under the headline 'Crew of "Australia" in Deep Discontent'.[157] As the cruiser had escorted the Duke of Gloucester onboard HMS *Sussex* back to England, the Admiralty recommended to the ACNB that *Australia* remain in the North Sea and then the Mediterranean. The ship's company was not informed of the ship's programme and the months turned into two years.

The Australian Government's Minister for Defence, Sir Robert Archdale Parkhill, became increasingly concerned. The Naval Board had continued to assure him dissent was simply 'isolated complaints of a few disgruntled individuals'.[158] The media declared that real grievances did exist and would find no 'breathing space in contented ships', but would 'flourish in an atmosphere in which official ears are deaf to genuine complaints'.[159] Another editorial argued that it was 'this blind-eye-to-the-telescope

A grainy cartoon of a sailor with communist emblem on his shirt astride HMAS Canberra *appeared in* Smith's Weekly, *c. 1932.*

attitude' that had aggravated the situation.[160] Parliamentarians had long joined the debate. Labor's David Watkins blamed the style of discipline enforced by 'officers who have been imported'.[161] He was not alone within the Australian Parliament to argue that Australian volunteers did not respond well to the 'harsh laws that governed the discipline of the ratings of the British Navy'.[162] One of the strongest statements had come in 1929 from Richard Crouch, the Labor Member of Corangamite in Victoria.

> We are at present running a navy. It is called the RAN. It is
> far more Royal than Australian. We pay for it, but have hardly
> any control over it, and it is mainly officered by men who have
> received their training in England ... They are against Australian
> methods ... After the Australian Navy has been in existence for
> eighteen years we now have in our forces men brought from
> England who are replacing Australians. It is absurd ... our
> Government should have the last word in matters pertaining to
> the Australian Navy.[163]

Between 1929 and 1937, the situation did not improve.

Admiral Hyde and his board resented the Australian Government's interference and refused to introduce structural changes. The need for a personnel policy that could resolved differences and misunderstandings, and which could nurtured loyalty within the lower deck, continued to go unacknowledged.[164] The relationship between minister and the head of the navy continued to deteriorate. So too did Hyde's health. In 1933, he was operated on for cancer of the mouth. Hyde's stamina was failing and he suffered several falls. Parkdale made it clear to the British Admiralty that he did not wish Admiral Hyde's appointment to be extended. Parkhill also wanted Rear Admiral Richard Lane-Poole, RN, Rear Admiral Commanding His Majesty's Australian Squadron, returned to Britain. The Admiralty agreed to recall Hyde but not Lane-Poole, conceding:

> such conflicts of personality were all too liable to arise when

Minister for Defence, Sir Robert Archdale Parkhill (in bowler hat) inspecting HMAS Canberra *crew, c. 1930s.*

> British officers were appointed to senior posts in Dominion
> navies ... and one has to admit that a certain type of Englishman
> would never go down well with the Australians.[165]

In a driving accident in June 1937, Hyde killed a pedestrian. The coronial enquiry absolved Hyde of blame but the accident took its toll and on 28 July 1937, Hyde died in Melbourne of pneumonia.

Admiral Hyde had faced the difficult task of resolving the issues afflicting the RAN, greatly exacerbated by an indecisive Australian Government defence policy and financial stringencies. What resulted was 'quite a remarkable number of misunderstandings' that 'caused mistakes in Australian naval administration'.[166] Nonetheless, like so many senior British officers whose careers had started well before the turn of the century, Hyde struggled with progress during his commission in Australia.[167] He and so many other senior officers came from another society, culture and time which placed tradition before reason and discouraged Australian nationalism. The RN personnel model imposed on the RAN was an ill-fitting one. There was a failure to accept the evolution of a more democratic navy, an RAN loyal to Britain but also one moulded by other loyalties, concerns and temperament. Similarly, those in charge were as ill at ease with the rapid technical advances of the modern navy as they were with the Australian sailors needed to crew. The RAN would struggle to recover from this neglect and misdirection.

I am going to like this ship very much.

Midshipman Kenneth James Hopper, RANR (S)[168]

Flight Officer John Bell felt the shuddering and the noise was all invasive. The imagination could run riot, the 'what ifs' gnawing at the conscious, momentarily bonding with the constricted feeling in the gut. It was against his sense of self-preservation that he gunned the throttle even more, so that the shaking and noise increased to the highest pitch. Bell had been told he was both brave and foolhardy; some shook their heads and said he was crazy but they didn't understand this was the ultimate thrill.

The activity outside was

Pilot Officer John Napier Bell, c. 1930s.

reaching a climax. Bell knew the routine completely and had the uttermost confidence in the HMAS *Canberra* seaplane launching party. The catapult officer watched his crew prepare the trolley. With safety pins removed, the trolley was moved to the firing position. Satisfied, the catapult officer informed the direction officer who notified the captain. *Canberra*'s Commanding Officer ordered a course change so that the cruiser was in the most conducive wind position. It seemed like an eternity, lost in a vacuum of noise and vibration, but it wasn't long before the order to launch was transmitted from the bridge below to the catapult room. The breech sailor loaded the cordite cartridge and reported 'loaded and ready' and the direction officer signalled Flight Officer John Napier Bell, RAAF (162). Bell's hand emerged from the small cockpit and the sailor manning the tow pushed the launch lever forward. The Seagull that Bell was flying hurtled off the cruiser. There was the slightest pause before the aircraft roared and began to climb under its own propulsion.

The bitter fight about who should control aircraft attached to RAN ships had been ongoing since 1923. In May 1923, following the lead of the RN, the RAN introduced a new aircrew category, the Australian Fleet Air Arm. The RAAF was very opposed. In 1925, with Australian Government sanction, the ACNB asked the Admiralty to design a seaplane carrier to be named HMAS *Albatross*. The design was poor and immediately following completion, the consensus was that *Albatross* was 'subject to many grave deficiencies chiefly in the matter of speed and lack of provision for flying on' and that the process had been too hasty 'partly as a result of political pressure'.[169] The RAN air wing had barely lifted off before it was grounded. *Albatross* had been designed to fly the Fairey IIID, but this aircraft was replaced by the Seagull III, an aircraft 'not stressed for catapulting' so a catapult was not installed.[170]

The between-the-wars period was characterised by huge technical advances but it was also a time stricken by financial limitations. The Australian Government decided to disband the separate navy air arm in January 1928 and the RAAF assumed the responsibility. Amphibious aircraft were henceforth flown by No. 101 Flight RAAF (and its successors, No. 5 Squadron, then No. 9 Squadron). Commissioned in

1929, *Albatross* had a brief initial career before the RAN was forced to lay up the seaplane carrier in 1933. The Seagull V arrived two months later which, considering the aircraft was found to be too tall for the *Albatross* hangar, was perhaps fortuitous. In 1938 *Albatross* was traded to the RN as part payment for HMAS *Hobart*. The RAN's first foray into a fleet air arm was suspended for a further decade.

On 19 March 1930 *Albatross* lost its first aircraft when a Seagull crashed into the sea off south east Tasmania, killing 21-year-old Leading Seaman Telegraphist Air Gunner Donald 'Tag' McGowan (13919).[171] Soon after, *Canberra* rescued a Seagull A9-7 crew in the same stretch of ocean. The aircraft was involved in a navigation exercise with *Albatross*. Better navigational skills were needed as the crew flew further out to sea than anticipated. Running low on fuel, they signalled *Albatross* and landed within sight of the coast. Their co-ordinates were incorrect, there was no way to contact the mother ship and currents were driving them ever more southward. Hours went by and their despair worsened as the drifting amphibian rocked ever closer to the treacherous Southern Ocean. Like some old Hollywood movie, HMAS *Canberra* came steaming over the horizon, ensign flying. Unable to winch the aircraft and anxious crew onboard, the cruiser's crew loaded the skiff with two-gallon cans of motorboat fuel, one hundred gallons in all, which they then transferred to the aircraft in many trips in heavy seas. The fuel was not a real alternative for the rich aviation fuel the Seagull needed and the aircraft was unable to complete an open-sea take-off. Under the protection of *Canberra*, the A9-7 taxied quite a distance until a calm water take-off could be attempted. Again the Seagull stubbornly failed to lift off and by now the lengthy submersion meant that the fabric on the wooden hull was falling away. The destroyer *Anzac* arrived and, with the Seagull crew bailing madly, the seaplane was towed to safety.[172]

A crane was installed on *Canberra* and a Seagull III was mounted on a platform amidships. Exercises off New Zealand in 1933 sparked huge public interest. 'Curiosity was chiefly centred on the warship's flying boat, snugly secured on deck and the substantially built crane'.[173]

It was a precarious and physically demanding method to launch and retrieve and the aircraft could only be lowered and returned to the

Manoeuvres with the Seagull III, *c. 1930s.*

During manoeuvres at sea with lifeboats and the Seagull III, *c. 1930s.*

Accidents during the loading stage were common, c. 1930s.

deck in less than 20-knot wind-affected seas.

Even then due to weight and other shortcomings, Seagull III episodes could be much more exciting than aircrew or cruiser crew desired.

The RAAF ordered 24 Seagull Vs with the first arriving in 1935. For their time, the Supermarine Seagull A2, designed specifically for use on Australia's cruisers *Canberra, Australia, Sydney, Hobart* and *Perth*, were revolutionary. Known in British service as the Walrus, this was a three-seat amphibian powered by one 775 hp Bristol Pegasus V19-cyclinder radial engine. Aircraft length was 37 ft 7 in (11.45 m) and wingspan was 45 ft 10 in (13.97 m). The firm that built the Seagull also built the Spitfire but that was the only commonality. One description of the former was 'speed – practically negligible; endurance – just enough'. Manufacturers gave the maximum speed as 117 knots (217 km/h) and the cruising speed as 83 knots (153 km/h) but even the biggest supporters admitted that such a maximum speed was reached only with a strong following wind and that same wind would prove challenging if you were attempting any sort of speed going the other way. Whilst the Seagull was armed with two 303-inch Lewis or Vickers

Launching the aircraft from HMAS Canberra, *c. 1930s.*

machine guns and could load as many as eight 9 kg bombs, serious damage to any target was never a consideration. Where the aircraft was vitally important was for reconnaissance. Though sturdy and even capable of acrobatics, the Seagull proved unnecessarily large. At least the newest amphibian accorded greater protection for the crew, was safer for cargo and passenger transfer as well as for the telegraphist air gunner who clambered above to catch and attach the crane hook to the amphibian.[174]

The RAAF assumed responsibility for the training of aircrew and technical personnel for seaplanes attached to cruisers, but the aircraft remained under the command and control of the Naval Board and the RAN provided its own observers – not entirely a comfortable liaison. *Canberra*'s crew befriended these servicemen wearing a different shade of blue uniform. Though they grumbled about the intrusion and extra work involved with the strange craft, they found it fascinating, nicknamed it 'The Pussar's Duck' or 'Our Old Duck' and, as expressed in this sailor's ode, valued the contact with the wider world that the aircraft provided.[175]

I've seen the Aircraft Carriers
With their slick fast fighters up,
They make a mighty picture
And stir your blood well up.
But I'm not a Carrier
A cruiser, that's my luck,
The only aircraft we can boast
Is the Navy's Pussar Duck.
For me you have your Carriers
With their dive-bombers and pursuits,
For I get quite a thrill,
When the Duck from the catapult shoots,
She makes no pretty picture
As she roars and shakes her tail,
But the boys will shout from the upper deck
Bring back some bloody mail.
She fades slowly in the distance
And life goes on the same
But when we come onto the upper deck,
We look out for the plane.
Then later in the evening
As the sun is going down,
The heavens will be roaring out
For our Duck sure goes to town
She hits the water nearby the ship
And is hoisted by the crane,
Eight bags of mail lie in the Duck
Not bad for a little plane.[176]

John Napier Bell, who catapulted off HMAS *Canberra* in the Seagull, had written 'Clerk' on his RAAF enlistment form. Though born in Adelaide his family had relocated to the outback South Australian township of Farina to take over the general store. Working as a merchant and clerk held little interest for John; it was the world of flying that excited him and conjured up visions of swashbuckling pilots in leather helmets

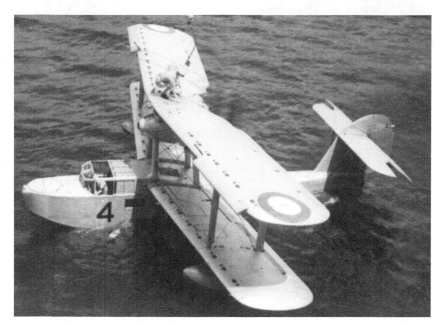

Preparations on Seagull III *at sea, c. 1930s.*

and jackets with white scarves streaming behind them and their open cockpits. Bell was delighted to be accepted as an air cadet on 15 July 1935 and designated pilot material. Even with his overactive imagination, the 19-year-old could never have foreseen his ensuing RAAF career. Pilot Officer Bell was posted to No. 5 (Fleet Cooperation) Squadron, RAAF Richmond, New South Wales, on 1 July 1936. It was a rather rude awakening for someone with grand visions of fighters or bombers flying exhilarating and terrifying operations to be learning about the eccentricities of the Seagull V amphibian. 'Terrifying' at least applied when in February 1938, Bell and his aircraft hurtled off *Canberra* for the first time.

It was a thrilling ride. Those minutes before you were thrust abruptly off the warship and for the seconds after when you prayed the plane would lift and not go straight down into the ocean.

Over the ensuing months, Bell and his terrified and exhilarated observer and his equally terrified wireless operator gunner survived 80 catapult launches. In that time they knew *Canberra* as others did, as

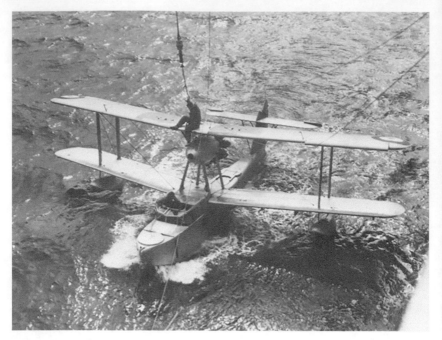

Pilot Officer Napier Bell, RAAF, emerges from the cockpit of the Seagull III, *c. 1939.*

their home, even perfecting the 'legs further apart' stance so as to stay upright in rough weather.

Flight Officer John 'Dinger' Bell was posted off the cruiser in August 1939, reluctant to leave but excited that he was off to England to pilot larger aircraft, in the form of Short Sunderland flying boats. Nonetheless it was Bell's Seagull (Walrus) experience which resulted in his being chosen for a secret operation. At 0255 on 18 June 1940, Walrus L2312 took off from Mount Batten, near Plymouth in the south west of England, with Flight Lieutenant John Bell at the controls. The observer and acting air gunner was 31-year-old Sydneysider, Australian Sergeant Charles 'Chas' William Harris, RAAF (1730). The third crew member was Wireless Electrical Mechanic Corporal Bernard Nowell, RAF. Also onboard was British intelligence officer, Captain Norman Hope, the only person who knew the destination and purpose of the operation. With the capitulation of France to German forces, General Charles De Gaulle, leader of the Free French, was evacuated to England.

Flight Officer John 'Dinger' Bell, in cap, and his crew, c. 1940.

He made a special request of British Prime Minister Winston Churchill for his wife and three children to be rescued from the French coastal town of Carantec.

After flying south in very heavy fog for about an hour, the crew realised the aircraft had strayed off course, 30 kilometres south west of its intended destination. At around 0430 Bell decided to land in a field near Ploudaniel. He saw the fog-concealed embankment too late. The Walrus crashed, broke in two and burst into flames, killing all onboard. Their bodies were recovered and buried by French locals in Ploudaniel cemetery. Madame De Galle and children eventually escaped to England by boat. The deaths of the Walrus crew remained unconfirmed until 1946.[177]

In 1940 news of Bell's presumed death was upsetting for those in *Canberra* who had liked and admired him. It was particularly disturbing for the close-knit Seagull crews for whom much tragedy would follow – within two years three of the five cruisers with Seagull crews were sunk.

It was a time of change as the RAN entered a new chapter with Prime Minister Lyons announcing a three-year defence spending programme in August 1937. At the 1937 Imperial Conference, Australian Defence Minister, Sir Archdale Parkhill, warned officials in London that he doubted that the RN fleet would be sent, as promised, to protect Australia. However, the ACNB had complete faith in this promise and reliance on the 'Singapore Strategy' that the British fortress of Singapore could not be breached. They were convinced that Singapore could only be overwhelmed by 50,000 troops, a feat which would take up to five months in which time the RN would arrive in force.[178] British authorities proclaimed the concern unwarranted stating that in the event of Japanese aggression, regardless of what may occur in Europe, the British Government would 'send to the Far East a fleet which is at least adequate to contain that of the Japanese'.[179] What wasn't said was that, as early as 1935, British Government officials privately accepted that Britain would be unable to protect the dominions, that the priority must be for the dominions to protect Britain as had occurred in World War I.[180] Increasingly, British officials was loathe to admit that RN supremacy was an illusion. The prospect of a grand fleet sailing to protect Australia and New Zealand was 'little more than a fantasy'.[181]

Nevertheless, Australian scepticism increased in line with European and Asian aggression. The 1937–38 estimates allowed for increased stockpiles of fuel, equipment and munitions and long-range navy wireless stations at Darwin (Coonawarra) and Canberra (*Harman*) which would prove critical to the war effort. Money was made available for the armour enhancement of the cruisers *Australia* and *Canberra*. The ACNB finally began to give more than lip-service to Australian fears concerning Japanese aggression by accepting that the priority should be

Ordinary Seaman II William Ross Cowdroy, c. 1938.

the protection of sea communications and trade routes. The new First Naval Member, Vice-Admiral (later Admiral) Sir Ragnar Colvin, RN, was much more responsive to Australia's defence needs than his predecessor and pressured the government to purchase new cruisers. The Modified Leander Class Light Cruiser HMAS *Sydney* II had been commissioned in 1935 and would now be joined by sister ships *Hobart*, commissioned in September 1938, and *Perth*, commissioned on 10 July 1939. However, the emphasis was again on the procurement of ships and material with little priority given to personnel policy. Only in April 1938 did the ACNB agree to a campaign to recruit an additional

2,000 sailors, but the question remained whether the high level of sailor discharges between 1930 and 1937 could be overcome quickly.

RAN training establishments were suddenly expected to pump out trained personnel in large numbers to fill the lower deck chasm, but there were too few instructors. Tensions in Europe had resulted in RN expansion which meant the RN instructors traditionally requested by the ACNB were unavailable and too few Australians were qualified. The ACNB preference to crew RAN ships with RN personnel rather than recruit Australians further compounded the shortfall.

Able Seaman Bill Danswan, c. 1935.

The young sailors who drafted to *Canberra* in 1938 and ensuing years had only the very basic training. The expectation that they could quickly become expert seamen was not realistic.

Sailors fresh out of HMAS *Cerberus* walked slowly into the dockyard weighed down with their rolled-up hammocks and kit bags. The teenage bravado they had felt at the end of their training had all but evaporated. Thoughts turned to HMAS

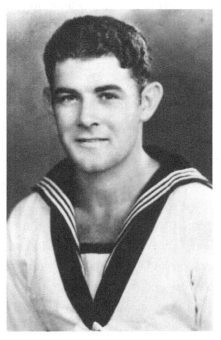

AB Frank Dandridge Johnson, c. 1941.

Canberra. Many had unsettled feelings in their stomachs as they climbed the gangway and observed senior NCOs sternly watching their approach. They were once again the newest, the lowest in the RAN chain of command; they were 'maccas', their fresh, barely bristled faces confirming their age and lack of experience. This was their first ship – it seemed huge, brimming with guns and activity. How would they ever learn their way around, let alone truly become part of the 700-odd crew? The quartermaster looked them up and down when they came to attention as they stepped down off the gangway. He hid his smile as he regarded the narrow-bottomed regulation trousers, perfectly white caps, strong blue collars and khaki hammocks. It wouldn't be long before the salt and grime dulled that brighter-than-bright newness, before these young sailors actually took to scrubbing the colour from their own uniforms so as to be less noticeable, and before they purchased 'tiddley' 32-inch bell-bottoms.

Ordinary Seaman II William Ross Cowdroy (21820) was born in the small farming town of Kilcoy, in the Lake Somerset region of south-east Queensland, 58 miles (94 km) from Brisbane. Kilcoy, named by Evan and Colin MacKenzie, after their Scottish home town, was stained by Aboriginal massacres in the 19th century. It was an unlikely place to foster a 16-year-old who enlisted in the nation's navy. There seemed such a lot for an ordinary seaman II aged 17 to learn. And then there were the officers who appeared so formidable. Cowdroy looked initially to sailors like AB William Leonard Edward (Bill) Danswan (20548) to accustom him to his new home and duties.

Danswan was also a country boy from Temora, north-east of the Riverina area of New South Wales, 260 miles (418 km) from Sydney. Temora was a pastoral station until gold was discovered but the gold had disappeared long before Bill enlisted in the RAN. Cowdroy found it easy to bond with Danswan, not just because they were both from the country and that both enlisted at 16 as ordinary seaman II.

Danswan was an easy-going bloke who was happy to share knowledge of the ship and routine because he had been in *Canberra* since November 1935. Rated as able seaman in March 1937, Danswan was an accomplished trumpeter and the *Canberra* band was better for it.

From Sydney via *Cerberus* recruit training, Frank Dandridge Johnson (22047) followed Cowdroy to *Canberra*. They were typical of the enthusiastic, fit young recruits now allowed to enter the RAN. They met at *Cerberus* but did not realise how hauntingly parallel their lives would be – it was just that Frank was always a few months behind Bill. Both were born in 1921; Cowdroy in April, Johnson in July. Cowdroy enlisted in January 1938, Johnson in May. And so it continued with drafts to *Canberra,* promotion to ordinary seaman and able seaman as both perfected their skills in *Canberra*. Cowdroy spent just shy of three years in *Canberra* and was promoted to Acting Leading Seaman on 1 January 1941. Johnson was promoted seven months later by which time he was onboard the newly-commissioned HMAS *Perth* – and this time Cowdroy followed to *Perth*, in January 1942. New recruits like Cowdroy and Johnson expected to be taught their seaman craft but instead found themselves doing repetitive tasks at the expense of learning vital naval duties.

Henry Albert Longdon Hall was a child of the 1920s. Born to James and Dorothy in Sydney, he found life was an uphill battle as the depression bit deeply. It worsened when Henry's father James simply left. Dorothy remarried and two more children were born. By 1938 Dorothy and the new family had departed for England in search of rosier circumstances and Henry and his brother were alone and struggling. The RAN was one of the few available options and Henry enlisted at 16. The recruitment literature said the RAN would provide free medical and dental care and three meals a day.

> I was told I would receive a feed and a pair of boots ... I got the
> pair of boots but not a feed.[182]

Henry had laboured on a dairy farm to survive but he was astonished at the privations facing the most junior in the RAN as he weathered 'the worst nine months of my life'.[183] The lack of food was of particular concern. Henry thought at least he would have bread and butter but for the first three months he never saw the butter. The rationing system for the lower deck was open to exploitation by those in authority.

Ordinary Seaman Henry Hall, c. 1930s.

'The chiefs and petty officers would take the food (intended for junior sailors) home'.[184] Commissioned ranks were less than interested in what was occurring than they should have been and also some of the less scrupulous syphoned off ration allowances into other RAN areas.

The diminutive 16-year-old was very determined to survive and make the navy his life but he was puzzled by his seniors' priorities. It seemed that it was their whim to change the rig of the day countless times during any given day. Attempts to wash uniforms in laundry tubs were interrupted by commands to 'clear the blocks' for a cross-country, only to find uniforms stolen on return.

The uniforms themselves caused problems. Henry broke out in a rash from the coarse flannel shirt. When the medical officer instructed him to wear an ordinary shirt, the rash disappeared, but he was ordered back into the flannel shirt – the rash returned. Leave offered no relief for Henry because, without next of kin, there was no option but to remain at HMAS *Cerberus*.

It was a bewildering, anxious, strenuous world. Though his hard work was noted and he gained two month's seniority, Henry's RAN time did not commence until he turned 18, a year and a half after he first donned the coarse flannel shirt.

His training had not entirely made a lot of sense and he thought it would improve when he joined the fleet. A draft to HMAS *Adelaide* did little to reinforce this belief. 'I became expert with a chipping hammer, wire scrubber and red lead (paint)'. He spent three months as a scullery hand. Watches on *Adelaide* meant eight hours on and four off or four hours on and four hours off. During the four hours off, sailors were expected to sleep, eat and maintain their uniforms and mess. So it was that when Henry received his first draft to the Kent class cruisers, he was delighted. 'You beaut.' Henry Hall wanted desperately to perfect his seaman duties but it seemed those in charge seemed less enthusiastic about the operational tasks of the RAN.

It was accepted that in a warship, the 'Captain was God' and the crew rarely saw him. There was also a lack of communication between the upper and lower decks. Henry Hall believed you 'needed to keep your men informed'[185] but he struggled to elicit information that would help him to learn his craft. It seemed to be all about routine, cleaning, discipline and officers' social activities. Hall thought it vaguely amusing that during the many officer social functions, junior sailors known as 'side boys' stood either side of the quartermaster at the top of the gangway. As a lady guest arrived, they would assist her up the gangway with white-gloved hands.

An article written by a guest 'civilian observer' travelling onboard *Canberra* wrote of 'a pleasant stay of about 12 days' in Brisbane, of the attractiveness of sailing the Great Barrier Reef, of the annual regatta and the anticipation of being in Melbourne for 'the Cup'.[186]

Procedure needed to be taken more seriously with the accent less on painting and polishing and more on combat skills but senior officers continued to be slow to accept this and operational training continued to suffer at the expense of other activities. *Canberra* was slow to move from being the 'glamour ship' of the early 1930s used primarily to fly the flag and be a platform for entertaining dignitaries, to being truly a training ship preparing RAN personnel for war.

With recruitment sluggish, the ACNB slowly began to integrate the RAN Reserve forces. Though the Royal Naval Reserve (RANR) and the Royal Australian Naval Volunteer Reserve (RANVR) had been created under the *Naval Defence Act, 1910*, RAN administrators had always adopted a somewhat arrogant attitude to reserve personnel.

The view from the bridge –
the 'Captain was God'.

There was little or no place in its senior ranks for the gifted reservists who made such a mark in the First or Second AIF.[187]

Midshipman Kenneth James Hopper was a member of the RAN Reserve (Seaman Branch) and joined *Canberra* on 15 October 1937 relishing the opportunity now offered. His midshipman journal over the ensuing six months articulated great enthusiasm and maturity. Born on 26 November 1919 in Taree in New South Wales, Hopper was 18 and had been employed by Burns Philip Shipping Line when appointed a midshipman (probationary), as distinct from commencing at the RANC at the age of 13. On joining, Hopper was struck by the cleanliness of *Canberra*. He was 'very interested in the various armaments and the way they worked', listened intently to an explanation of the 'various regulations and traditions to be observed' and on day one decided 'I am going to like this ship very much'.[188]

The word 'interesting' appeared over and over as he learned ship gunnery, stores, signals and kept watch. He was disappointed to receive a reprimand, not for any professional slip. It was the result of failing to ferry guests fast enough for the Admiral Lane-Poole's 'at home', a Sunday afternoon function on 25 October 1937. Guests of the Admiral waited at the 'man-o-war steps' to be brought out to *Canberra* at its mooring in Sydney Harbour. Both *Canberra*'s motorboats as well as the motorboats belonging to HMA Ships *Sydney*, *Australia* and *Penguin* were deployed for the social function. Some guests arrived in their private boats. Hopper was less than impressed in 'attending to the guests' and surprised that when motorboats were hauled back onboard, the instruction came to 'clear lower deck' and the retrieval was done

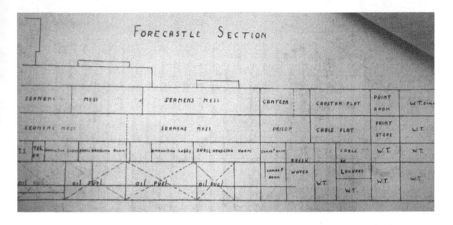

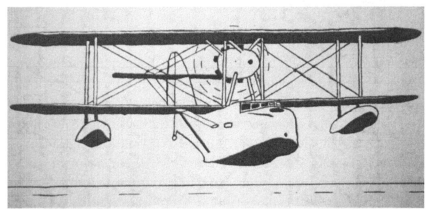

Drawings in Midshipman Kenneth Hopper's journal is a credit to his artistic ability, c. 1940s.

manually whereas 'in the merchant service they were always hoisted by a winch'.[189]

Hopper's enthusiasm returned as the cruiser put to sea and he began to learn more.

> I kept the afternoon watch on the compass platform and I marvelled at the way in which the other ships in the squadron kept formation. ... depth charge practice was carried out by the destroyers ... I was surprised to find that the concussion was felt onboard here although the charges were fired some distance away.[190]

His journal quickly became illustrated with drawings, such as one of the forecastle (fo'c's'le), the section of the upper deck of a ship located at the bow forward of the foremast.

Hooper jumped at the opportunity to fly in the Seagull. Initially he admitted feeling 'peculiar' but then 'I settled down and 'enjoyed the trip very much. We could see for miles'.[191] As the aircraft climbed so too did his enjoyment.

Above the clouds it seemed like a different world of its own. We climbed to 9,000 feet where the temperature on the wing dropped to '4° above zero'.[192]

Hooper was disappointed when *Canberra* went into Cockatoo Dockyard for a refit, then into Sutherland Dockyard. January evaporated in a flurry of paint and maintenance, excruciatingly slowed by rain. His journal showed little of the earlier enthusiasm as pages were filled with social activities and observations from the deck of his land captive cruiser. Finally in February 1938, *Canberra* was released and steaming on exercises again. Midshipman Hooper's excitement returned as drills and exercises prevailed, at least until it was time for the Hobart Regatta and weeks of balls, parties and inter-ship competitions. The most noteworthy event that he recalls was his first swim in Tasmanian waters. 'Intensely cold,' he wrote.

The perils of a life at sea were far more severe than a swim in the cold waters off Hobart. The loss of Leading Seaman Henry Joseph Storer (18383) from Wallsend, NSW highlights the dangers. Storer's career had spanned a decade and most of the Australian fleet. He was 28, a two-badge experienced seaman, yet that did not save him on 15 March 1938. *Canberra* was steaming north towards Jervis Bay in very heavy seas. At 0200, several chests in the chest flat and their contents were dislodged as winds reached gale force. By 0700, the chest flat was a mess of wreckage. With the ship rolling violently sailors attempted to secure spilled contents. There was a vicious roll to port and Storer was jerked off his feet, slid from the starboard side across the torpedo space under the torpedo tube, and was washed overboard. Lifebuoy sentries

Photo taken by Chief Stoker John Radley onboard Canberra *on 15 March 1938.*

dropped a marker and a lifebuoy which Storer grabbed. The seaboat was manned and lowering commenced as *Canberra*'s CO, Captain Wilson, DSO, RN, ordered the ship about. A wild wave crashed the seaboat against the cruiser's hull and Wilson ordered a halt, believing the rescue attempt could result in further loss of life. It was a very difficult decision. The ship zigzagged the ocean and Storer was seen.

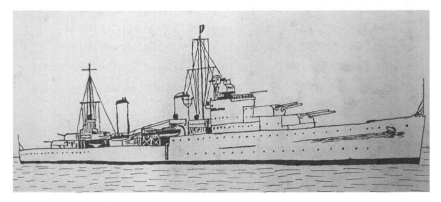

Midshipman Hopper's drawing of Canberra, *c. 1940s.*

Before a deck rescue could be attempted, he was lost in the heavy swell.

Edna Storer and their children, living in Crib Point, Victoria, received a Navy Department notification that Harry had been 'lost overboard presumed drowned' in 'heavy and dark weather at 0825 Tuesday 15 March 1938. Search was conducted till dark without result'.[193] His service certificate was notated 'Discharged DEAD'. Onboard *Canberra* the shock affected all. Midshipman Hooper drew a thick black square around the date 15 March in his journal. Several members of the crew had suffered broken limbs – a sobering warning of the unpredicatability and harshness of the ocean.

All too soon Midshipman Hooper's time on the cruiser was over. He later served in merchant ships and auxiliary minesweepers until finally given his own command of the corvette, HMAS *Burnie*. Hooper was 'mentioned in despatches' for 'gallantry in dangerous waters' in 1943 and again 'for courage and skill in operations in the Far East' in 1945. He reached the rank of Lieutenant Commander. His drawing of HMAS *Canberra* is a testament to the the enthusiasm of an RANR (S) Midshipman who appreciated the opportunities being offered and from whose experience the RAN also profited.

In February 1939, the social columns of the *Sydney Morning Herald* reported on the festivities of naval officers and their guests.

> Hobart's summer season promises to be better and brighter
> than ever this year. With so many socialites dashing across to
> escape Sydney's humid heat, and the Fleet arriving there next
> Friday, the list of forthcoming gaieties grows. Among naval
> officers' wives making the trip is Mrs W. R. Patterson wife of
> Captain Patterson of HMAS *Canberra* who leaves this week.
> This will be her first visit to Tasmania and she says Sydney
> won't be seeing her for at least a month.[194]

On 10 May 1939, the cruiser and sailors were used to host another reception, the 'Welcome to Admiral's Wife'.[195] So blinded to reality were those who controlled Australia's navy that *Canberra*'s sister cruiser *Australia* was paid off into reserve on 24 April 1938. It was not recommissioned at Sydney until 28 August 1939 under the command of Captain Robert R. Stewart RN – three days after the signal 'Increase state of readinesss of ships. The situation as regards now with Germany is considered critical'.[196]

Midshipman MacKenzie Gregory eagerly awaited the end of his final year at RANC. It had been four years of hard work, education, navy and physical drills. 'Mac' was looking forward to leave before he returned to the college for his final term and the stress of facing end-of-year examinations. Not only would these be in the usual secondary school subjects – including the dreaded calculus – but cadets were also required to have a basic understanding of seamanship, naval engineering, naval history and naval signalling, which embraced reading and sending messages by semaphore and morse code. A further requirement was to gain the Life Saving Society's Bronze Medallion. As they prepared to depart for the warm embrace of families and home cooking, Year 4 leave was cancelled. Final year cadet midshipmen would remain at RANC to undertake an additional two weeks of courses before 'joining the fleet'. There would be no final term or passing-out parade.

The mix of emotions was apparent because the word 'war' was on everyone's lips. What would it mean? On 30 August 1939, the 12 RANC midshipmen joined HMAS *Canberra* and wondered how the future would transpire as news came of German forces goose-stepping into Poland two days later. Thoughts deepened when they listened to the sombre tones of Australia's Prime Minister Robert Menzies at 2105 on the evening of 3 September 1939.

Fellow Australians, it is my melancholy duty to inform you officially that, in consequence of the persistence of Germany in her invasion of Poland, Great Britain has declared war upon her, and that, as a result, Australia is also at war ... In the bitter months that are to come, calmness, resoluteness, confidence and hard work will be required as never before ... I know that, in spite of the emotions we are all feeling, you will show that Australia is ready to see it through. May God in His mercy and compassion grant that the world may soon be delivered from this agony.[197]

Cadet Midshipman Gregory realised his life was 'about to be changed forever'. In his midshipman's journal he drew a map of Europe depicting 'Austria and Czechoslovakia as part of Germany'.[198] Within days, he and five other RANC midshipmen from the class of 1936 posted off *Canberra* to *Australia*. Within six months, he had departed from England to undertake the obligatory RN service. By 26 December 1941, Sub Lieutenant Gregory, RAN, was again serving in *Canberra* as Japanese forces advanced rapidly towards Australia.

Left home at 6 o'clock very depressed ... not knowing when I will return to my wife and baby.

Leading Sick Berth Attendant Allan Farquhar, RAN.[199]

Australians attempted to absorb the news that their nation was at war again, the second within living memory for many. For the young, it was exciting but for their fathers and mothers, the thought was horrific. Onboard *Canberra* the news was met with 'pandemonium ... cheering, stamping, whistling, laughing and clapping continued'.[200] The response of veterans of the previous world conflict was more restrained and, after observing the excited reaction of the inexperienced, they retired to ponder how many of these bright young people would survive.

Unlike other British Dominion leaders, the Australian Prime Minister, so imbued with veneration for Britain and in such haste to commit the nation to war, did not first consult Parliament. He sent a telegram to Prime Minister Churchill promising all the nation's resources to achieve a British victory.[201] Churchill replied that this would be a 'splendid episode in the history of the Empire [if Australian troops] defend the Motherland against invasion'.[202] Many Australian people no longer shared such reverence for the mother country and the clarion call to arms for the Empire did not generate the same fervour as it had in 1915. Australia had sacrificed too many in the 'war to end all wars'. Again the enemies and strategic priorities appeared painfully familiar. Whereas 62,786 enlisted in the AIF in the first six months of World War I, only 21,998 enlisted in the second AIF within the first six months of the new war.[203]

Despite the 1938 recruiting drive, it became quickly apparent that there was a shortage of volunteers wishing to enlist in the RAN whereas 4,000 swelled the waiting list for the RAAF. The navy had a poor public image. RAN policy makers had never nurtured Australian recruits and they were poorly equipped to understand how to appeal to potential sailors. There had long been distaste amongst RAN administrators for publicly promoting their service, in part due to a preference for insularity and an avoidance of public interference. In much of Australian society this was interpreted as aloofness or arrogance, and the perceived 'Britishness' of the service tended to confirm this interpretation. The acrimonious debate over 'whose navy was this really?' and public concern over sailor welfare meant that the Australian working and middle classes were 'out of sympathy' with the RAN.[204]

This was compounded by the public address by the Second Naval Member in December 1938 arguing that the role of the RAN was as a 'link in the chain of Empire Defence and [it] must be kept strong enough to prevent that chain from snapping'.[205] This statement is in direct contrast to the one made in 1902 by the 'Father of the Australian Navy', Vice Admiral Sir William Rooke Creswell, RAN, who had cautioned that if the nation's navy was controlled by other than Australians, the nation's defence would be in jeopardy.[206] His words gained relevance with the passing years. Although Menzies declared war on 3 September 1939, RAN commanding officers received a signal at 0341 on 1 September reporting that:

> Australia has placed her naval forces at the disposal of Great
> Britain ... Imperial War Telegram is to be obeyed if received
> prior to receipt of Australia War Telegraph.[207]

The ACNB and the British Admiralty had agreed how to deploy RAN

With war came the urgent need for RAN recruitment and training, c. 1939.

ships in the war against Germany, in the Mediterranean and the Atlantic.

In 1939 the RAN was small. The fleet was made up of two heavy cruisers, *Australia* and *Canberra*, which both carried 8-inch (203-mm) guns; three modern light cruisers, *Hobart*, *Perth*, and *Sydney*, which mounted 6-inch (152-mm) guns; the older cruiser *Adelaide*; four sloops, *Parramatta*, *Swan*, *Warrego*, and *Yarra*, although only *Swan* and *Yarra* were in commission; and five V class destroyers, *Stuart*, *Voyager*, *Vendetta* and *Vampire*. RAN permanent personnel numbered 458 officers and 4,593 sailors.[208] The book *HMAS* published by the Australian Government through the Australian War Memorial in 1942 proclaimed that on the declaration of war, the RAN immediately mobilised the Reserve 'in accordance with carefully prepared plans'.[209] This was at best an exaggeration.

Members of the Reserve had always been viewed unfavourably by career RN/RAN officials but in 1939, permanent RAN numbers were so depleted there was no alternative. Commonly, sailors who had accepted free discharges as the ACNB slashed their numbers, enrolled in the Royal Australian Fleet Reserve (RAFR). They were now subject to immediate call-up. This was done in such haste that reservists were not told that the change from part time to full time also meant they were liable for overseas service and many were quickly despatched to the Mediterranean to man destroyers.

The face of the RAN began to transform with the call-up of reservists which increased the RAN force to 9,617. Regular reserve training was suspended during the war with all new entry sailors coming in through the RANR. New recruits signed on for the duration of hostilities instead of the customary 12-year engagement. The first called to service were 86 RANR (Seaman) officers, 222 RANR (Reserve) officers and 3,869 ratings. Wartime officers were distinguished by their crooked (wavy navy) rank stripes. They commonly had their authority limited and reserve seaman officers were generally restricted to positions of authority on small auxiliary vessels. In June 1940, the RAN introduced a separate Yachtsmen Scheme, the Royal Australian Navy Volunteer Reserve (RANVR). Up to September 1941, the RAN also supplied the RN with 96 reserve officers and 172 reserve ratings with their initial anti-submarine qualifications gained at HMAS *Rushcutter*. The RN continued to draw from the ranks of the RANR and RANVR and, as late as June 1944, 500 Australians served overseas with the RN.[210] By war's end, the total RAN reserve force numbered 2,863 officers and 26,956 ratings, comprising 80 per cent of the personnel serving with the RAN.

Between September 1939 and 1945, the RAN expanded from 13 ships to 337 vessels of all types and from 458 officers and 4,593 sailors to 36,976 officers and sailors.[211] Sailors required urgent training, initially training at the New Entry School at *Cerberus,* then going on to perfect their skills at sea. The necessity to expand rapidly and become an operationally-effective RAN was enormous, made ever more difficult by the myopic RAN administration of previous decades.

The demands on senior sailors on *Canberra* and *Australia* particularly were extraordinary as the influx of new sailors rose dramatically and the need for them to instruct and prepare ordinary seamen and stoker IIs became vital – there were simply too few senior sailors.

When stoker IIs, King, Dare and Ridd, joined *Canberra*, they were quickly made aware of the towering presence of Stoker PO Stanley Coates (16294). It was not because Coates was a tall man – he was only 5 ft 7¼ inches (1.70815 m). It was because of his bellowing voice, made all the louder given he had served as a stoker since 1925. His hearing may not have been as acute as it once was or it may have been because men born in Liverpool, England, were naturally full of voice. He made quite an impression on the youthful stokers who fell under his charge.

Coates was a graduate of the old dirty coal-burning warships such as *Melbourne* so for him, these new lads had it easy. Coates had joined *Canberra* as a Leading Stoker in November

Petty Officer Stanley Coates, c. 1938.

1932, was promoted to Acting Stoker PO on 21 February 1935 and was substantiated in that rank a year later. The young stokers quickly learnt to pay attention and, during their years on the cruiser, many learnt the trade in an uncompromising manner.

PO Coates' RAN career between 1937 and 1942 was indicative of the severe shortage of qualified sailors; his drafts numbered 12, mostly four months here and a month or two there. The list of ships he served on is many: *Vendetta*, *Yarra*, *Adelaide*, commissioning crew for *Perth*, back to *Adelaide* until another draft to *Canberra*.

The outbreak of war meant decommissioned ships required hasty recommissioning. Merchant shipping needed to be brought on line to convoy troops and supplies – some required supplementary navy personnel. Most importantly, RAN warship crews needed to increase from peacetime to war complements – the pressure to recruit, train and qualify was titanic. HMAS *Canberra* commonly carried a peacetime crew of 717, with 30 senior sailors as part of the Admiral's 'retinue' when it was the flagship. To be ready for war, *Canberra's* crew grew to 819, which included a seven-man RAAF Seagull detachment.[212]

Whereas pre-war promotions had been slow, now they were rushed through. In April 1933, James Henry Fryirs (19700) enlisted from Newcastle, New South Wales as a Stoker II. Though deemed very good in conduct, his ability was only deemed 'satisfactory', below the classification necessary for promotion. As war broke, he was drafted to *Canberra* as an Acting Leading Stoker. Fryirs was substantiated in the rank of Leading Stoker in April 1940 and in less than nine months, he was an Acting PO Stoker. George Edward Anderson (20385) enlisted as an ordinary seaman in September 1934, the son of a navy family who lived just outside the HMAS *Cerberus* gangway. In April 1940, he was promoted to Leading Seaman. Four months later he was promoted to Acting Petty Officer and was instructing at *Cerberus*. A fortnight after his substantiation as Petty Officer on 1 July 1941, he was demoted to Leading Seaman and drafted to *Canberra*. Within 12 months, Anderson was again an Acting Petty Officer.

Geoffrey Belfield Phillips (20688) entered as an ordinary seaman on 25 February 1935 from Melbourne. Drafted to *Canberra* in June 1939 as Able Seaman, he was promoted to Acting Leading Seaman when war was declared, Leading Seaman the following year, and Acting Petty Officer (Ty) just over a year later. The initials (Ty) were now being scrawled on service certificates – (Ty) for 'Temporary'.

When war was declared, *Canberra* was moored in Sydney Harbour. The ship's company was ashore and was hastily recalled, some with no time to change out of civilian clothes. By dawn on 4 September 1939, the cruiser and *Hobart*, *Vendetta*, *Voyager* and *Vampire* were patrolling Australia's east coast securing trade and communication lanes. *Canberra* the cruiser was no better prepared for war than its crew.

HMAS Canberra *moored in Sydney Harbour, c. 1930s.*

The defect lists for the ship had multiplied over the previous years and had been largely ignored. Clearly Engineering Officer Commander Otto 'Mac' Francis McMahon, RAN, had become increasingly frustrated. McMahon had done everything needed to be taken seriously – his service had been impeccable since he entered the RANC during the year of its inception, 1913. His was the December class and by the end of his four years, his intelligence and technical predilection had been recognised. Born at Mareeba in far-north Queensland,] on 5 January 1900, by November 1921 he was a Lieutenant (E), a Lieutenant Commander (E) by May 1929

HMAS Canberra *Engineer Officer, Commander Otto 'Mac' Francis McMahon, RAN, c. 1950s.*

and a Commander by December 1933. His experience was broadened by extensive service at sea with the RAN and on exchange with the RN. McMahon had served in *Canberra* during 1931 to 1933. His third posting to *Australia* was from 1936 to 1938 then he returned as an engineering officer to *Canberra*. His knowledge of County Class engineering was beyond question. McMahon became increasingly outspoken during 1938 and 1939 with regards to the neglected maintenance and general lack of support to make the ship ready for action. This did little to improve his promotion prospects but as an Engineering Officer McMahon likely realised, promotion above the rank of commander was much less likely than if he had been a seaman officer. Navies were developed around sail, seamanship and gunnery – they were slower to accept the ramifications of technical momentum and appreciate the importance of qualified technicians.[213] The demarcation between seaman officer and non-seaman officers was further signified by the introduction of distinguishing colour on the sleeves of non-seaman officers.[214]

In March 1938, Rear Admiral Richard H.O. Lane-Poole, CB, OBE, inspected *Canberra*. The report sent to the Naval Board was glowing.

The organisation for war is on sound lines and the training of personnel is thoroughly satisfactory. ... The gun armament is in a thoroughly efficient state. ... torpedo equipment – very good. ... The machinery and boilers are in efficient running conditions.[215]

Commander McMahon rejoined the cruiser the following month but was not of the same opinion. Furthermore, by May 1938, the full extent of deficiencies in the Naval Store Armament account of *Canberra* for the period 12 April 1934 to 9 July 1936 were now realised. In June 1938, the Naval Board decided to notify the Admiralty that their commissioned gunner on loan to *Canberra* (who had since returned to England and the RN) had not 'correctly' or 'properly performed' his duties; indeed he had carried these out 'in a most slovenly manner' and had not even conducted a stocktake.[216] Not only did he not deserve the special allowance the RAN had paid for the additional duties but more seriously £284/12/7 worth of guns, side arms, ammunition and equipment – pages upon pages of items – were missing from *Canberra*'s stores.[217] The Admiralty defended the commissioned gunner and simply deducted £15 from his salary. The missing stores were never recovered.

Commander McMahon continued the flow of '*Canberra* supplementary defect' lists.[218]

'List of repairs absolutely required for fighting and seagoing efficiency' he wrote on 6 November 1939. A major refit was absolutely necessary to rectify the 'extensive list hull and miscellaneous, propelling and auxiliary machinery, boilers, gun mountings'. He argued strongly that the refit had to be longer than five days because some items had 'not been tested since 1936'. Too many items were 'rusted through', boiler room valves were 'leaking ... worn thin and corroded', boiler drain valves had 'threads corroded and worn', piston rods needed to be urgently 'renewed', cylinders were worn and had to be 'renewed' while the gun mounting equipment must be 'stripped and refitted'.[219] There were no fewer than 95 items which required urgent attention and others only slightly less so.

Canberra's Executive Officer (second in charge) was Commander William Thomas Alldis Moran, RAN, an RANC entry from Fremantle, Western Australia. Moran had elected to specialise in torpedoes, and served three RN deployments, which included service on the battle cruiser HMS *Repulse*. Moran returned to Australia in January 1938 and was posted to *Canberra*. Having spent years in *Australia* he was familiar with the Australian cruisers and was sympathetic to the engineering officer's concerns. Moran signed his name to the latest defects list as did Gunnery Officer Lieutenant Commander David Maxwell Hole, RAN. Hole, from Sydney, was appointed Cadet Midshipman in January 1919. He served in *Canberra* during 1932 and 1933 before serving in the Northern Hemisphere firstly in destroyer HMS *Codrington* and then undergoing further gunnery training at HMS *Excellent*. On his return to Australia, Hole was posted to *Canberra* in July 1938. At the end of 1939, Australia was at war and these *Canberra* department heads hoped that the ACNB would finally appreciate the urgency. In late December, it was agreed that *Canberra* would undergo a minor refit in Sydney.

Canberra *undocking from Sutherland Dock, Sydney, c. 1930s.*

For most of the crew, 10 days leave allowed families to share a joyous Christmas. They must have wondered when next they would be so fortunate. The future was dark and foreboding. Commander McMahon remained concerned that, although 10 days would permit many minor defects to be fixed, a longer refit was needed, but by now the Australian Government had decided the first Australian military contingent would sail for the Middle East in early January 1940.

Eleven passenger liners were requisitioned to carry 13,500 New Zealand and Australian troops. Communication in the form of a minute from Britain's Prime Minister Winston Churchill to the First Lord of the Admiralty accentuated the fact that as it was unknown how many German raiders might be operating in the Indian Ocean, the Empire required as many RAN warships as were available.[220] The Australian War Cabinet accepted the Admiralty's recommendation.

The convoy gathered in Sydney Harbour and, with *Canberra* as escort, set sail on 10 January 1940. Protective plating had been added to the Canberra's upper works but the plating and hull reinforcement were not completed.

In what became a monotonous programme, *Canberra* and its crew shepherded the slow, fully-loaded requisitioned passenger ships

The Queen Mary, *a former Cunard liner requisitioned for use as a troop ship, escorted by* Canberra, *c. 1940.*

including *Queen Mary*, *Aquitania*, *Empress of Japan* and *Straithaird* across oceans, ever alert for German raiders.

The journalistic description of the departure was typical of the naïve bravado of the day.

> It was an unforgettable sight as the ships slowly steamed past with the brilliant summer sunshine beating down on the calm blue sea. Ferry boats heeled over to one side filled with people cheering the troops bound for the Middle East.[221]

War games of a type were attempted on passage by escorting warships, however, given that the primary charge was protecting troopships, these were not particularly successful.

Captain Wilfred Patterson, CVO, RN, relinquished command of *Canberra* with his promotion to Commodore and Captain Harold B Farncomb, MVO, RAN, assumed command in June 1940. Sailors referred to him as 'Fearless Fred' for his ship-handling skill but they had misgivings concerning this new CO because of his reputation as a very strict disciplinarian. Early in his *Canberra* command, a crime was committed onboard and Farncomb angrily swore that when the sailor responsible was found, he was to be 'hung from the yardarm'. This sailing ship terminology may well have remained in naval jargon but sailors wondered if that type of punishment still applied in 1940.[222]

Leading Sick Berth Attendant Allan Herbert Farquhar (R20418) spent his time below decks assisting with the general health and wellbeing of the crew. He had enlisted in the RAN in 1934. He drafted to *Canberra* not long after completing an eight-week operating theatre course at Prince Alfred Hospital in Sydney, nine days before the ship sailed with another convoy. In his diary, he wrote 'left home at 6 o'clock very depressed ... not knowing when I will return to my wife and baby'. It was an expression of emotions seldom publicly acknowledged by sailors but privately held by most. Typically, families were torn by conflicting sentiments: loyalty to the Empire, concern for the safety of their nation, pride as sons and daughters donned uniforms, and an overwhelming concern about the unknown.

William 'Ross' Cowdroy had joined the navy in January 1938 and joined *Canberra* as an Ordinary Seaman II eight months later. By January 1941, the torpedo specialist was promoted to Acting Leading Seaman and left the cruiser that had been his home and training unit in July 1941 to join HMAS *Perth*. In 1940, he was both proud and apprehensive that his brothers had enlisted in the army. Private (Pte) Charles Noel (Noel) Cowdroy (QX5843) enlisted in June 1940 and was one of the soldiers Ross and *Canberra* escorted to the Middle

East.[223] Their brother Plunkett John Cowdroy, (QX20157) became a Corporal in the 2/121 Australian Brigade Workshop.

Leading Sick Berth Attendant Farquhar found his operating skills were not needed as his cruiser escorted the troop ships in July 1940. What ailed the crew was far more fundamental to a life at sea – seasickness.

AB William 'Ross' Cowdroy and Private Charles Noel Cowdroy, c. 1941.

Most rough passage ... lots of damage to ship during storm ... very treacherous sea ... many of the crew are violently ill. The bight [Great Australian Bight] living up to reputation and heavy sea. Heavy seas all day the old ship is groaning and moaning.[224]

It was with great relief when the convoy approached South Africa on 10 July 1940. 'All excitement aboard today we arrive at Cape Town tomorrow ... everybody is cheerful'.[225]

Escort duties ended when a damaged propeller sent *Canberra* into dry dock at the RN base at Simonstown (also known as Simon's Town) on the east coast of South Africa on 29 July. For the crew this was nonetheless good news because it meant: 'We are leaving for Australia owing to a damaged propeller and shaft'.[226] But yet again as the cruiser ventured into the Indian Ocean, the ocean was so rough 'it was practically impossible to stand up, waves crashing over the upper bridge'.[227]

Seasick crew and ship damage was one thing but the loss of a mascot was another. Most ships had mascots, particularly during peacetime. The size and type of the mascot depended on the indulgence of the Captain and Executive Officer. *Canberra* had its share of big and small, one of the most notable coming onboard when the convoy arrived in South Africa. When the cruiser sailed again for Australia, 'Nuisance' was discovered hidden in a sailor's mess deck. The great dane was deemed a little too large to be a mascot and the cruiser changed course to return 'Nuisance' to South Africa.

His replacement was a more acceptable, size-wise, a cat for which sailors made a miniature hammock. Returning from South Africa, 'Cat' was nearly washed overboard as the

'Nuisance' the great dane mascot, found onboard after stopover in South Africa, 1940.

'Nuisance' was returned to South Africa, replaced by a smaller mascot, 'Cat'.

cruiser surged through heavy seas, and henceforth was secured below. When *Canberra* finally sailed north along the Australian east coast 'everyone onboard is singing and whistling and the atmosphere has changed to what it was about six weeks ago'.[228]

By 31 August, *Canberra* had joined another convoy to the Middle East via Colombo. There were more heavy seas until the ship approached the equator when the ship became 'like an oven, everybody is only wearing shorts'.[229] The 'crossing the line' ceremony was conducted to initiate novices into the Brotherhood of the Seas and as subjects of 'His Oceanic Majesty, King Neptune'. This was an age-old custom whereby King Neptune and his attractive attendants (depending on a person's appreciation of weirdly dressed sailors) some with voluptuous bosoms, held court and dealt with the accused and those who had yet to cross the equator, most of whom ended up being dumped in a makeshift pool covered in a slimy substance.

Farquhar was 'totally unimpressed' with Colombo and 'the poverty'.

> The filthiest place I have ever visited. They eat sleep and
> wash on the streets constantly begging. I returned onboard
> thoroughly disgusted.[230]

He was also disgusted by how Australian soldiers 'wrecked Colombo'. Onwards further north to India, the 'heat [is] unbearable'. On 10 November, Farquhar was down-hearted. It was his twenty-ninth birthday and he was 1,000 miles south east of Bombay, India. 'Next Year I wonder? Where? Our hopes of seeing Aussie are pretty vague'.[231]

Crossing the line ceremony, HMAS Canberra, *c. 1940.*

This was war but somehow not as war was imagined to be.

The German merchant cruiser *Pinguin*, armed with six 5.9-inch guns, four torpedo tubes and a cargo of mines, was in the Indian Ocean targeting shipping and then mining the sea approaches to Newcastle, Sydney, Hobart, Port Phillip and Adelaide. On 12 November, *Canberra* was on the way home from escorting convoy US6 to Bombay when there was a report of a raider, probably *Pinguin*, operating off Sumatra. The

SS Port Brisbane, *c. 1930s.*

crew was called to action stations, course changed, speed increased and the seaplane was catapulted. 'Everyone is as keen as mustard to hear the thunder of the guns' wrote one sailor.[232] Alas, the enemy again proved elusive.

Canberra arrived back in Fremantle on 20 November and the crew was delighted to step onto Australian soil before their warship was required to escort US7 in two days time on 22 November. No sooner were the crew ashore than a distress call was received from the British steamer, *Maimoa*. They were under attack. Captain Farncomb pre-empted the signal from the ACNB, ordered the crew recalled and steam was raised. *Canberra* left in such haste some crew never made it back onboard. Those who did were excited by the prospect of real war. Another British steamer, SS *Port Brisbane*, had answered the distress call from *Maimoa* and was also heading north. On the dark night of 21 November, *Port Brisbane* was surprised by the unlit German raider and *Pinguin* opened fire at point blank range.

Allan Farquhar scanned the broad horizon on 22 November and recorded the findings.

At 0800 this morning we came upon a lifeboat empty. We sunk it by gunfire and first angry shot of the war. Nothing else

The rescued SS Port Brisbane *crew onboard HMAS* Canberra, *1940.*

happened until 6 pm. This evening when we sighted on the horizon three boats with sail. They were survivors from the *Port Brisbane* who had managed to escape from the raider. There were twenty there; all told the Huns had captured about 60 others. They had many varied stories to tell. They are all safe onboard now and are happy. So off we go again on our chase all hope to get her in a couple of days.[233]

Over the ensuing days *Canberra* chased a ghost ship, the German raider showing tactical superiority even with *Canberra*'s aircraft being catapulted each morning on reconnaissance. When the Seagull cracked a valve, *Canberra* returned to Fremantle on 27 November. The following day, *Canberra* was to escort another convoy north. Life returned to boring routine.

In the second week of December, the scuttlebutt was according to Farquhar 'we expect to make contact with a raider today or tomorrow'.[234] *Canberra*'s port propeller broke again. The German ship continued to range unhindered. For the *Canberra* crew, there was some consolation. 'Great excitement because that means Cockatoo island'.[235]

On Friday 20 December, 'at 0530 that very welcome sight, Sydney. Home after four months'.[236] The cruiser had spent 92 days at sea, crossed the equator 10 times and sailed 42,523 miles (68,434 km). Since the beginning of the war, *Canberra* had spent 298 days at sea and travelled 101,756 miles (163,760 km).[237]

The unexpected Christmas at home was wonderful before *Canberra* was required to escort yet another convoy to Colombo. The year 1941 opened as 1940 had concluded. Sister cruiser *Australia* had been experiencing a different war in the Mediterranean, fighting off enemy bombers, patrolling off Norway with the RN First

Canberra's *AB Percy Alexander Tipper (left) and Ord Seaman Cecil Dobell (right) in front of their 4-inch gun mount, c. 1940.*

Cruiser Squadron, and engaged in the search for the German battleship, *Gneisenau*.

It was then to Dakar, French West Africa, and the bombardment of Vichy French installations whilst being subjected to high-level bombing attacks. *Australia* was hit and her aircraft was shot down. Repairs were undertaken in Liverpool, England during a December of heavy air raids. Those in *Canberra,* itching for action, envied the men who had been

Duty stations, HMAS Canberra *c. 1940.*

drafted to *Australia* and wondered if they would ever have an opportunity to witness first hand such excitement because their cruiser seemed doomed to being a training ship and convoy escort.

In an effort to attract more RAN recruits, the public relations machine cranked up another gear and *Canberra* was featured in a series of media photographs. Like the ship's programme itself, there was little which could inspire those with a taste for action and adventure. One photograph showed Sydney-born AB Percy Alexander Tipper (S3207) and Ord Seaman Cecil

Harold Ireland, c. 1940.

Dobell (23424) posing beside one of the cruiser's 4-inch (101.6-mm) guns. Tipper (left) had joined *Canberra* in September 1939, Dobell (right) a month later. Similarly other posed photographs were taken in an attempt to attract more recruits.

With *Canberra* to and fro in home waters, the training of new recruits was a constant. For some sailors there was a sharp learning curve – almost a change in career – from the peacetime cruises and carefree RAN lifestyle, to a rushed, stressful training regimen.

Harold Needham Ireland (16853) had joined as a Boy Seaman 2nd grade in August 1925. For the next 15 years there were plenty of drafts, including two years in *Canberra* from 1931 to 1933, but he had only risen to Able Seaman. With war and his next draft to *Canberra*, Ireland was promoted to Acting Leading Seaman in August 1940, then straight to Acting Petty Officer five months later then substantiated to Petty Officer on 1 February 1942 while still on the cruiser. Although Ireland was a thoroughly seasoned and experienced sailor, to be promoted from AB to substantiated PO within an 18-month period was very unusual and it was demanding to shoulder the additional responsibilities so rapidly.

Within *Canberra* there were senior sailors whose knowledge and experience were truly inspiring – men like Commissioned Gunner

Harold Hardiman, Chief ERA's Arthur Allen and James Kidd, Chief Stokers Malcolm De Espline Stafford and Stanley Coates, PO Herbert Sidney Roy Wilkinson and Chief Shipwright Henry Ewart Shepherd. Some were born in another century and another nation but, for the most part, they epitomised the classic jack tar (sailor).

New recruits could be forgiven for regarding Commissioned Gunner Harold Hardiman (10493) as an old man of the sea. He was short and nuggety with a loud voice. After his many years in RN and RAN gunnery, he had just enough hearing to avoid a medical discharge. The Englishman had been loaned to the RAN in 1927 as a gunner and member of the *Canberra* commissioning crew. He quickly decided Australia was a better place to live and sent for wife, Lily. Ten years later, he was promoted to Commissioned Gunner and, except for a couple of years at *Cerberus,* continued to alternate between Australia's two heavy cruisers. Hardiman rejoined *Canberra* on 13 June 1938 aged 43. He was well respected by officers and sailors.

Another senior sailor born in England and originally loaned by the RN was Chief Shipwright Henry Ewart Shepherd (10637). Shipwrights had always been valuable members of a crew since sailing clippers swept the oceans; their carpentry skills were crucial. Clippers were fewer in number with the advent of iron and steel ships; the new skills required were now largely carried out by electrical and ordnance trained artificers. Shepherd had joined the RAN in January 1923 from London and was awarded a superior aptitude grade every year. In 1928, he returned to England to be part of the commissioning crew of *Australia.* He married in England and when the warship returned to the nation whose name it bore, sent for his wife, Eva, and his son to settle in Sydney. From 1935 the 38-year-old Shepherd was drafted to *Canberra* to supervise the training of new recruits in skills old and new.

James Arthur Kidd (13821) was born in Newcastle, New South Wales in May of the last year of the nineteenth century. He was a fitter and turner and his decision to sign RAN enlistment forms in 1923 was influenced by the availability of further trade training as an electrical artificer (EA). Electricity was still a relatively new phenomenon. It was 8 July 1904 when electric streetlights were switched on for the first time in Australia's largest city, Sydney. The *Sydney Morning Herald* reported on this new wonder.

> There is no comparison between the old and the new style of lighting [because] gaslights have been completely overshadowed by the brilliance of the new electric arcs'.[238]

The dangers of navy training became brightly obvious the following year when Kidd suffered a scalp wound, and concussion but remaining in service meant a trip around the world to fetch the new RAN heavy cruisers in January 1928. He was drafted to *Australia* but served in its sister cruiser in 1930 and 1931 before further time at *Cerberus*. His next draft to *Canberra* was 1932 to 1936 as a highly respected three-badge, Chief EA II. Kidd was redrafted to *Canberra* in 1938. Kidd and the amicable Henry Shepherd were joined in the chief's mess in October 1941 by Chief Petty Officer John Kelly (16130). Born in Melbourne, Kelly, a former bricklayer, was seven years younger and two years junior in rank to Kidd; he too had served on *Canberra* during 1930 and 1931. Indeed, there was scarcely an Australian ship Kelly had not served

A different breed, Canberra *stokers relishing a breath of fresh air, c. 1940.*

on. Regardless of their birthright and backgrounds the duties of these senior sailors were closely intertwined and pivotal to the operation of the cruiser.

The next tier down, that of petty officer (PO), arguably had more direct interaction with juniors than chiefs. *Canberra* had POs who were 'recruiting poster' sailors, such as Herbert Wilkinson (14782). Wilkinson was another who was born in an era of large families and financial hardship. His salary as an RAN boy seaman was crucial for the wellbeing of his parents and sibling. He survived the harsh training in 1924 and 1925 onboard the training hulk *Tingira* which languished awkwardly off Sydney's exclusive Rose Bay. Wilkinson progressed without blemish through ships in the fleet and ranks: Boy 2, Boy 1, Ordinary Seaman II, Ordinary Seaman, Able Seaman, Leading Seaman and Petty Officer. From the age of 14 to 31, the navy was his life.

Stokers, those who were closeted away between decks in boiler and engine rooms, were seen as a different breed; the headstrong, recalcitrant men of any navy. Some like Laurence Mervyn Peck did little to discourage this reputation. Peck was born in Lithgow, a Blue Mountains town in New South Wales renowned for coal mining. In 1900, Lithgow produced the first steel manufactured in Australia. Copper smelting, brickworks, pipe and pottery works and breweries followed but the region's industry began to wane with the Depression of the early 1930s. Laurence Peck wasn't cut out for coal mining or industry and as a 17-year-old salesman, he did not flourish. The RAN was his ticket out of town but he wasn't really sure he wanted to go to sea or be a stoker. Peck wasn't entirely sure what he wanted but in January 1936 he was wearing naval uniform and classified as Stoker III (20980). After five months *Cerberus* training, he drafted to *Canberra*. Age determined that he became a Stoker II and then time served saw him promoted to Stoker but he struggled. The RAN kept him onboard *Canberra* from June 1936 but his behaviour deteriorated. Shortage of leading stokers saw him promoted to Acting Leading Stoker or A/Ldg Stoker (Ty) but it only lasted two months before he was demoted to Stoker for unsuitability. Still he remained on the cruiser throughout 1941 and into 1942.

Stokers believed theirs was a worthwhile career and a vitally important job, because without combustion, warships stopped dead in the water. No matter how good the gunnery, or how true the torpedoes ran, power is the no. 1 requirement. This opinion was nonetheless not shared by those in authority within the RAN,

Chief Stoker Malcolm De Espline Stafford (16090) joined the RAN within a month of John Kelly. They served together in *Canberra* in 1930 and 1932. Being a seaman, Kelly was promoted to Acting Petty Officer (A/PO) in 1932. Regardless of the same divisional officers' aptitude and conduct ratings, Stafford had to wait another two years. Stafford rejoined *Canberra* in May 1937 and waited until January 1942 before he wore the chief's insignias – Kelly wore his from April 1940. The disparity in promotion was not unusual.

For some recruits, the reality of being in the Navy did not match their expectations as in the case of Russell Keats. *Canberra* was Keats' first deployment at sea, something he had eagerly looked forward to – now he wasn't too sure. The rolling of the ship and keeping his balance was something that he had trouble with. What made things worse for Keats was that his mess was forward which took the brunt of the warship fronting heavy swells.

Keats was a good writer and decided to write to his family without the naval parlance of 'bulkheads, deck-head or deck' preferring the terms they were familiar with. 'We tossed and pitched, heaved and rolled till I didn't know whether I was walking on the walls, ceiling or floor'.[239] Despite the unease he felt, unlike most first timers, Keats managed to avoid seasickness.

Since leaving Sydney on New Year's eve 1940, Keats had to 'work like fury' to keep a handle on the stores which were packed into every conceivable space that he had 'been sorting out and straightening ... and look[ed] like doing to the end of time'.[240] Horace 'Russell'

Supply Assistant Horace Russell Keats, RAN, c. 1940.

Keats was not the stereotypical bronzed Aussie. Born into an educated and musical family, he was a talented musician who had mastered the flute, piano and organ. He was an ardent reader and was fluent in French. Russell nonetheless was fascinated by the military which embodied other virtues he aspired to. His parents were less than happy and much persuasion was required before they agreed that their sensitive son could join militia signals in 1938. He begged them to allow him to enlist in the army or air force. Perhaps they believed he would be safer in the navy and finally agreed to his enlisting in the RAN on 29 November 1939. According to his brother, Brennan, 'it was a very joyous Russell Keats who now gave his address as 6 Mess, B Block, Flinders Naval Base, Victoria'.[241] His enthusiasm was observed by instructors and the RAN rewarded his intellect with his classification as a probationary Supply Assistant (23768). Many photos were taken of him proudly in uniform; he joined *Canberra* on Christmas Day 1940.

His new life was exciting and he so wished to share this with his family but the RAN had introduced very strict censorship since 20 November 1940. On that fateful day at 2030, HMAS *Goorangai* (223 tons) was steaming from Queenscliff to Portsea when it collided with the troopship *Duntroon* (10,346 tons gross). *Goorangai*, crewed mainly by members of the RANVR, was cut in two and sank killing the entire

Shortly after this photograph was taken at Beachport, Adelaide, a wave lifted the German mine onto the beach where it fell on its detonators and exploded, killing Danswan and Todd, 14 July 1941.

crew of 24. Due to wartime security regulations, *Duntroon* was unable to stop or turn on searchlights. Only six bodies were recovered.

The RAN had ordered the minesweepers *Goorangai*, *Orana* and *Durraween* into Bass Strait to destroy minefields around major Australian ports that had been set by German ships *Pinguin* and *Passat*. The strategy was to block sea approaches to Newcastle, Sydney, Hobart, Port Phillip and Adelaide.

The blatant enemy mine-laying of Australian coastal waters had commenced a debate on competency that the tragic collision did little to assuage. Newspaper articles made much of the fact that 'the first Australian warship to be lost during World War II was lost in local waters in Port Phillip Bay, Victoria'.[242] It was an ignominious start to the war for the Australian Navy and the inevitable question 'how could this happen?'

During the same year, these mines took the life of popular trumpeter, Able Seaman William (Bill) Danswan. Bill had joined *Canberra* in 1935 and remained when he sewed on his good conduct

HMAS Goorangai *sunk off Victoria on 20 November 1940 – an ignominious start to the war for the RAN.*

badge in March 1939. But in March 1941, Bill was subjected to a naval medical survey as authorities considered he should be discharged from the RAN for 'defective vision'. Bill was devastated. *Canberra* had long been his home – now he was to be discharged from the navy. However, he convinced authorities not to discharge him. Deemed unfit for sea duty, he was drafted ashore.

The RAN attached Bill to the South Australia base of *Torrens*. On 14 July 1941, a partially submerged massive metal sphere was seen near the shore at Beachport. It was a live sea mine filled with up to 300 kilograms of explosives. An inquisitive, if not particularly well-informed, fisherman hauled the mine to the Beachport jetty. Alarmed community leaders called naval authorities. As members of the Rendering Mines Safe (REMS) unit Able Seamen Bill Danswan and Thomas Todd (PA439) were left with the difficult task of overseeing the mine's removal and detonation.

The German raider *Pinguin* had proven to be a successful and illusive raider and the search continued into 1941. The crew of *Canberra* were ever hopeful that they would be the ones to track and challenge the raider or, if not, perhaps the German pocket battleship, *Admiral Scheer*. *Admiral Scheer* had entered the Indian Ocean and sunk a number of ships triggering a massive hunt from February 1941. Given the poor armaments of the Australian cruiser, it was fortunate that *Canberra* did not interact with the heavily-armed 11-inch gun pocket battleship. Russell Keats wrote home about how the German ships proved to be elusive.

> We had a great time for a while but mutual excitement ceased after a very short time. They're a sullen pair of blighters.[243]

The German ships continued to outmanoeuvre the British and Australian attempts to find them. Searching for them became as disappointing and monotonous as convoy escorting. It became clear that the 15,420 ton 610ft 3in (186 m) *Admiral Scheer* had simply disappeared from the Indian Ocean as effortlessly as it had entered.

On 4 March, *Canberra*'s aircraft reported 'two unknown types of ships bearing 117 degrees 45 miles from position'.[244] *Canberra*'s masthead lookout reported smoke on the starboard side and then two masts and a funnel. Captain Farncomb ordered a change of course and increase in speed to 25 knots. *Canberra* looked a splendid sight cutting through the ocean, crew at action stations ready for a first test in battle. The foreign ships were signalled but failed to answer, warning shots were fired and still they failed to comply. Captain Farncomb ordered his gunners to open fire. Below deck Russell Keats scribbled.

> Nerve racking ... we would hear shell after shell leave us with a mighty crash and waited. Waited! The suspense was terrific! Was she going to hit us? ... Wonder if any of our pals would collect one? ... Panic! Nerves! Bravado talk! Callous talk! Clean jokes! Dirty jokes! Passing around personal addresses and instructions should anyone be killed.[245]

Russell Keats braced himself HMAS *Canberra*'s 8-inch guns roared.

HMAS Canberra's *8-inch guns, c. 1941.*

It was not very exciting.

Supply Assistant Russell Keats, RAN.[246]

On 4 March 1941, shells from *Canberra*'s 8-inch guns thundered from the extreme range of 2100 yards. Captain Farncomb was of the belief that one of the enemy ships was an armed raider and kept *Canberra* at a distance of not less than 19,000 yards (1.7 km) and therefore out of torpedo range. *Canberra* fired 215 rounds. It was later described as 'an extraordinary expedition considering both enemy ships promptly took scuttling action'.[247] For those who could not watch from the upper deck, a running commentary was piped below. Commander McMahon believed this held the ratings' interest 'more than a broadcast description of a Test Match with Bradman batting against Larwood'.[248]

There was an explosion and the enemy vessel caught fire. Having scuttled their ship, the crew lowered lifeboats and cast adrift. The crew of the other ship, an oil tanker, followed suit.

It was discovered that, what was believed to be a raider, was the German supply ship, *Coburg*, and the other, the ex-Norwegian tanker, *Ketty Brovig,* which had been taken the previous month by the German raider, *Atlantis*. The grand visions of a sea battle with *Pinguin* evaporated – there had been no fight at all. 'Our small action. It was not very exciting for us'.[249]

The scuttled *Ketty Brovig* was slow to sink so Captain Farncomb ordered gunfire to hasten its demise. Able Seaman Stephen Stewart St George (20222) on the fore end of the 4-inch gun deck was ordered to open fire. His captain was unimpressed with his expertise and announced that though it was an excellent rehearsal for 'the real thing', it was good 'the enemy was unable to profit by our error ... Bloody bad gunnery'.[250]

Stephen Stewart St George was born in Onslow in the harsh Pilbara region of Western Australia on 26 September 1916. His background is somewhat vague. Next of kin, place of enlistment and home port are unknown; his previous occupation was believed to be stockman. Following his enlistment in July 1934, there was a surname change and a change of religion from Church of England to Roman Catholic. There was a fair bit of mystery about the new Ordinary Seaman II physically described as 'dark brown' – long before the term 'stolen generation' was coined. The journey from Onslow to the precincts of Melbourne and then to Sydney and ships in between was a huge adjustment and one St George did not always manage well. Easy access to alcohol affected his service. He was gregarious and likable which resulted in a flawless 'very good' character assessment from his divisional officers even though under 'ability' they marked him only 'satisfactory' or 'moderate'. His progression through the ranks was almost surprising. He joined *Canberra* in January 1938 and was promoted to acting leading seaman in January 1940. Unfortunately, his larrikin qualities prevailed and a year later, after incurring eight days punishment, he was demoted to

A scuttled Coburg – *photo taken from the* Seagull, *4 March 1941.*

Ex-Norweigan tanker, a scuttled Ketty Brovig – *the crew were rescued in lifeboats by Canberra, 4 March, 1941.*

131

Canberra's *crew pose for a photograph after first engagement in war that took less than 30 minutes, c. 1941.*

The starboard forecastle deck framed by a turret 8-inch gun barrel, c. 1940s.

able seaman. Then his captain and gunnery officer chastised him for his half-hearted gunnery. The following year, the resilience and harshness instilled by the Pilbara ensured that this wayward sailor proved an unlikely hero when it came to 'the real thing'.

Following the engagement with German ships, questions were asked concerning the main 8-inch shoot against *Coburg*, and the expending of so much ammunition and 'that delayed action shells were used in error'.[251] Captain Farncomb himself received some criticism. In a letter between Admiral Ralph Leatham, RN, Commander-in-Chief, East Indies, to Rear Admiral John Crace, RN, Rear Admiral Commanding H.M. Australian Squadron:

> it was correct that *Canberra* should have taken precautions against the possibility of the supposed raider firing torpedoes, but I think it was being over cautious to avoid approaching nearer than 19,000 yards on this account. Had a more effective range been attained quickly, the enemy might have been identified sooner and much ammunition saved.[252]

Australia was at war – the need to save ammunition due to the cost of ammunition was strange. Furthermore, the opinion of Rear Admiral Crace, RN, with regards to *Canberra*'s CO choosing to retain a significant distance from the enemy ships, emanated from Crace's adherence to textbook and traditional tactics, rather than from a consideration of appropriate action concerning a particular era, enemy and region. This criticism echoed throughout the Australian fleet, and come November 1941, likely influenced the tactics of another cruiser CO with dire consequences.

The headline 'Cruisers Sink Two Ships' was an exaggeration but was intended to make more pleasant reading on the pages of the *Sydney Morning Herald* dominated by news of the German bombing blitz of London and AIF losses in the failed Greek campaign. Though the sinking had taken place in the first week in March, the news was not released to the media until two months later as public information was increasingly controlled by authorities. The first to know of the naval exchange was the ACNB, which reported to the Admiralty in London. The Australian Minister for the Navy, the Right Honourable William Morris 'Billy' Hughes, was unimpressed that he had been informed of the incident after the British media.[253]

Stores Assistant Russell Keats believed he could now write of new concerns which arose during the first case of his ship firing shots in the war.

Don't worry about anything happening to me as it won't for a start and should it. I have made all arrangements for someone to let you know in case the Navy, in its usual fashion is slow, if ever! Do, however remember this much, should the worst happen, apply for my deferred pay immediately. Will be a fight to get it, but even at the moment its worth quite a bit.[254]

From such comments, the lower deck were well aware of the issues of payment entitlements or lack there of for them. Even so, there was a war on and that was their main concern.

Russell Keats tells his version of what it was like onboard.

Sea, Sea! Water, water, all around! Hot oppressive weather, tepid nights, stars by the million, stars we never dream of at home. Skies as rich a blue as 'tis possible to imagine. Sunsets with every colour of the spectrum. Sunsets that would give the average artist the horrors, when he thought of painting them. Beauty that only God can create. Moons, each night as big as mountains. Glassy oceans – fixed and glazed as 'twere. And yet in the midst of it all, we search to kill. Blood lust! Still, I suppose it is necessary as those at home must be preserved. Must not depress you with this attitude anyhow as you probably still listen to every news session and hear enough of it.[255]

Keats was already struggling with the void between his romanticised vision of war and the reality. How could he and others within the cruiser derive a comfortable compromise between the desire to survive and the appeal of more? In the short term, for this crew there was little choice, because after the mere 30 minutes of excitement, it was back to routine and constant escort duties and patrols, and days, weeks and months of oppressive tropical Indian Ocean weather.

'There's absolutely nothing to write about.' Even the food was poor. 'Biscuits weevilly, no more spuds and on bully beef, no fresh vegetables for some time, meals terrible.' Worst still, they were 'drinking semi-salty water' wrote Leading Sick Berth Attendant (LSBA) Farquhar.[256] Naval morale was thoroughly affected by food.

The ship docked at Mauritius for a medical emergency and finally fresh supplies could be replenished. Unfortunately it was a bitter-sweet situation for the crew because popular Bandsman Arnold Pearce Partington (22132) had acute appendicitis. Partington, like Russell Keats, came from a musical family.[257] Partinton's condition deteriorated and he died in the Royal Military Hospital, Mauritius on 6 April 1941. His family was informed that he was buried with full military honours in Phoenix Cemetery, a large civil cemetery near the capital city of Port Louis. The 25-year-old 'fine trumpeter' was a long way from his home in Glenorchy, Tasmania, Australia.

Canberra steamed yet again to Colombo to collect another convoy of young Australians bound for combat in the Middle East. The heat had been a struggle but it became worse as the cruiser steamed into the

Gulf of Aden and headed for the Red Sea. 'Heat sweltering ... the crew were suffering prickly heat and other forms of heat rashes'.[258]

Aden was stifling and the inhabitants were not to everyone's taste. 'They are a blood thirsty lot and did not receive us too enthusiastically' wrote LSBA Farquhar. He was assisting in the care of AB Reginald Charles Bryant (PM2227) who was struggling with high fever. Bryant was a 24-year-old lad from Launceston, Tasmania, who had entered the RAN in February 1939. The cruiser was the only ship in which he served. As *Canberra* steamed towards Colombo, Bryant's condition deteriorated and he entered the Military Hospital as soon as the ship docked. There was nothing more that could be done. Bryant died of malignant malaria on 29 June 1941 and was buried in Colombo General Cemetery.

Canberra returned to Australia during the last week of July. The second half of 1941 saw the warship operating in the eastern Indian Ocean escorting convoys from Australia to Singapore and Ceylon. The pure monotony was as challenging for the crew. For Engineer Commander McMahon and his staff, the constant running of the ship was equally challenging as they struggled to resolve mounting defects. By 3 October 1941, the cruiser was finally secured to No. 1 buoy in Sydney Harbour but again the long leave and ship refit did not materialise. After just three days, a recall was sent to crew ashore and the ship sailed again. *Canberra* was back in harbour on 24 October and a week's leave was granted. Escorting US13 convoy followed. Since the convoys had commenced in 1940 over 180,000 troops were transported overseas – *Canberra* had accompanied most of them.[259]

In the Middle East around 14,000 Australian soldiers were besieged in Tobruk between April and August 1941. Lord Haw Haw (William Joyce), the German propagandist, derided the Australians as 'rats' for their tenacious defence. It was intended as a term of contempt but instead was embraced by the Australians and the term 'Rats of Tobruk' entered military folklore.

Nonetheless between early October and late October Australian 9th Division casualties numbered 749 killed, 1,996 wounded and 604 prisoners.[260] Australians were becoming increasingly concerned.

Mr A. H. Walker of Epping New South Wales wrote to Minister 'Billy' Hughes on 3 October 1941.

> It has been brought under my notice from a reliable source that a full-blooded German is stationed on HMAS *Canberra* as a wireless operator. His surname is Von Bock, and his Christian name Lyle (I understand that he has given his name as Bock, omitting 'von'). It seems to me to be out of order to have a German in such a position.[261]

Navy investigators resolved that the sailor was a chief petty officer writer employed in the Admiral's Office. Lyell Adolphe Bock (14608) had joined the RAN from Tasmania as a boy seaman in 1924 at the age of 16. His service had been exemplary and he was a member of the *Canberra* commissioning crew as well as further serving on *Canberra* during 1939 and 1940. At the commencement of the war Bock, like all with German heritage, had faced great scrutiny but authorities found 'no question about his loyalty'.[262] Bock retired from the RAN in 1957 with the rank of Lieutenant Commander. Unbeknown to the Mr Walker of Epping, *Canberra*'s butcher was Karl Klein[263] and his fluency in German proved most useful when *Coburg* and *Ketty Brovig* prisoners were brought onboard.

There were no casualties when the RAN lost its first warship to enemy action. Following an attack by dive bombers off Tobruk, Libya on 29 June 1941, the destroyer HMAS *Waterhen*, affectionately known by her crew as 'Old Chook', sank to the depths of the Mediterranean – fortunately after being abandoned. Five months later on 19 November 1941, the RAN suffered its worst naval tragedy. The light cruiser HMAS *Sydney* was sunk by the German raider HSK *Kormoran* in the Indian Ocean off the coast of Western Australia. None of the 645 crew survived – they and their warship just disappeared. At point-blank range, the first German salvos devastated *Sydney*'s bridge and fire control systems. Torpedoes punctured the hull and fires raged. Why had Captain Joseph Burnett, RAN, CO of *Sydney*, and his immediate subordinate officers on the bridge been surprised, been underprepared, outsmarted and outmanoeuvred? Why did *Sydney* approach the suspicious ship so closely? At the beginning of the war, Burnett was recalled from England to become Deputy Chief of Naval Staff (DCNS) at Navy Office, Melbourne. His first direct command was *Sydney* from May 1941. Captain Burnett would have been well aware of the correspondence between flag officers and the criticism directed at *Canberra*'s CO for standing off 19,000 yards.

The loss of so many officers and sailors destroyed families around the nation. It greatly diminished the number of trained RAN personnel and deeply affected the morale of those who remained. Many of those in *Canberra* had served in *Sydney*; many who died had served in *Canberra* – sailors like ERA Frederick Reville, the sailor who wrote to his fiancée how he missed being home but realised he needed to work hard at his navy career so that they, as a couple, would 'be able to benefit later'.[264] The Partington family, struggling with the death of *Canberra* bandsman and son Arnold, now needed to accept that Leslie had died. A few months later, there was to be further bad news concerning their third son, Perce, and HMAS *Perth*.

For 12 days after *Sydney* disappeared, the Australian Government maintained the strictest secrecy. When Prime Minister John Curtin made the first of two public announcements on 1 December 1941, he did little more than confirm rumours. The Government, the RAN and the Australian people were stunned. Just months earlier *Sydney*'s crew, resplendent in summer dress whites, had marched through the centre of the city after which their ship was named. The crew were all justifiably proud of their courageous Mediterranean war service. For the public, there was bewilderment, which was deepened by the lack of official information. This shocking loss had occurred, not overseas, but off the nation's coastline. Australians had not only lost a major warship and crew but also an innocence derived from being physically removed from the horrors faced by those in the Northern Hemisphere. The loss of *Sydney* remained one of Australia's biggest mysteries. How had *Kormoran*, from which 317 of the 397 crew survive, destroy such a superior warship from which there were no survivors? The questions remained and in 1997 a Parliamentary Joint Committee Enquiry was held. The enquiry could offer no further explanation. The wreck of *Sydney* was not found until 2008.

The officers and sailors of *Canberra* were deeply affected by the loss of friends and shipmates. There was to be many a discussion around 'what if' in relation to the demise of *Sydney*. If it had been their cruiser which had sighted *Kormoran* during one of the numerous forays into the Indian Ocean, would the resulting battle have been different? Having escorted convoy US13 until relieved near Cocos Islands, Canberra arrived back in Fremantle on 15 November. Whilst coming alongside the dock *Canberra* collided with the troopship *Katoomba* and sustained damage to the stern. Running repairs meant the cruiser could escort *Katoomba* to Victoria before steaming home to Sydney and arriving on 24 November for a short refit. It was wonderful to be home again in safe waters; perhaps they could enjoy a break from the bad news and from the emotional and physical strain of the last months.

On 27 November, just eight days after HMAS *Sydney* disappeared, 138 officers and men died when the Grimsby class sloop HMAS *Parramatta* was torn apart by a torpedo from German submarine U559 off Tobruk. There was barely time for the order 'abandon ship' before the Australian warship rolled rapidly to starboard and sank leaving only 24 survivors. This was just one more tragic and destabilising event for a nation and its navy.

In May 1941 Admiral Sir Ragnar Musgrave Colvin KCB, had been replaced by the 5th Sea Lord of the Admiralty, Vice Admiral Sir Guy Charles Cecil Royle, RN, KCB, CMG as Australia's First Naval Member and Chief of Naval Staff (CNS).

Prime Minister Robert Menzies had nurtured a close working relationship with Colvin, who had been forced to resign on medical advice. Menzies was not impressed with Royle. In Menzies' opinion, Royle was not 'clever' and had difficulty 'comprehending large issues'.[265] Nor did Royle enjoy the same confidence of the Australian Cabinet as Colvin.[266] Royle was a naval officer of wide experience but he came to Australia an exhausted and sick man who failed to inspire the RAN or to enhance the prestige of the service.[267]

Lacking Colvin's experience in the Australian political field, and the status he had held as an advisor ... Royle, in his tired condition, was handicapped in combating fallacious arguments ... also handicapped in upholding the navy's prestige with the Government.[268]

Admiral Colvin with Prime Minister Menzies and dockyard official, c. 1941.

For the individual chosen by the Admiralty and seconded by the Australian Government to direct RAN operations as well as be Commander of the southwest Pacific in 1941, this was ominous.[269]

At the same time, there was a lack of harmony within the Australian Government when the Australian people were in dire need of strong government. Menzies had taken the leadership of the United Australia Party

The new Labor Minister for Navy the Hon. Norman Oswald Makin with Vice Admiral Royle, c. 1941.

(UAP) on the death of Prime Minister Joseph Lyons on 7 April 1939. Unwisely, Menzies was overseas for four months of 1941 at a time when it was increasingly obvious a new enemy threatened. During his absence, the Leader of the Australian Labor Party, John Curtin, and Acting

Prime Minister and Country Party Leader Arthur Fadden, issued a joint statement warning of deteriorating security in the Pacific. On his return to Australia, beset by dissension within his own party, Menzies resigned on 28 August. The balance of power was lost when two independent members crossed the floor, and a general election was necessary. On 7 October 1941, John Curtin was sworn in as Prime Minister and Minister for Defence Coordination (later Defence).

Australians who served in the nation's navy struggled to cope with the political crisis, change of government, a change of Minister for the Navy (to the Hon. Norman Oswald Makin), a change in the Chief of Naval Staff (CNS), the loss of ships and shipmates unmitigated by compensating triumph.

For Australian sailors their very social standing at home was challenged when in Sydney and Melbourne, certain hotels and dance halls refused them entry. When RAN authorities visited the offending proprietors specious explanations were given, such as a sailor's uniform with no collar and tie did not conform to dress code. Another excuse was that managers had deduced that sailors were uncomfortable socially in the presence of RAN officers.[270] That these same establishments allowed the entry of airmen and soldiers was unfair and clearly deprived 'volunteers in the naval service of their citizen rights'.[271]

Other issues loomed large. Although pay rates increased slightly in 1941, they had not kept pace with inflation. Sailors had 'little money to spend on necessities when on weekend leave'[272] and married men found their families could no longer make ends meet. It was salt on the wounds that members of the RN serving in the RAN had the additional benefit of being paid in pounds sterling at a higher exchange rate. Supply Assistant Russell Keats was unsure of the true value of a pay rise he received, called the Action Plot Allowance. Keats was now keeping duty in the plot office and because the plot was so close to the bridge, which was the enemy's prime target on a warship.

Keats had entered the RAN with the great enthusiasm of the naïve and uninitiated. The actual experience had been less than fulfilling. He retreated into his musical comfort zone whenever he could. In a letter to his father, Horace, he wrote about his musical exploits.

I'm doing a lot of work with the Bandmaster, Harry Blackett. ... Loves music ... Thinks 'She Walks in Beauty' [setting of Lord Byron's poem by Horace Keats] perfect. Assisting me to form a choir. Please do me 4 parts for above. I can manage orchestration for combination we have 2 tenors, 2 basses.[273]

Days later Keats was horrified to find that another sailor, while cleaning, had disposed of every sheet of music he possessed including some of his own compositions. When questioned about the missing music, the sailor had replied 'Oh, you mean the paper with the funny writing on it. I ditched that'.[274] Keats wondered if things could get any worse, and then they did.

Douglas Grenfell Hazelton straightened his uniform and pushed his cap further down on his head to resist the wind blowing off Sydney Harbour. The uniform still felt foreign and its pristine condition was in marked contrast to those of sailors who looked him up and down as they raised their right hand to salute. He knew they saluted the officer's cap crown rather than him; he needed to earn respect as an officer and a man. Hazelton was one of the new breed of naval officers; even he was hard-pressed to find a longer new rank title than his own; Probationary Temporary Engineer Lieutenant RANR. It was now the end of November 1941 and he paused to regard the warship in front of him. *Canberra* was impressive, magnificent as warships went, even with his limited knowledge.

The last month had been nothing short of insane. It had been less than four weeks since his service enlistment papers were signed and endorsed by the RAN Surgeon Lieutenant who found him fit to serve. The rapid uniform fit, a rushed seven-day course at HMAS *Cerberus*, a bit of marching and drill, a brief return to his Sydney home to farewell wife, Josephine, and their two children and here he was standing looking up at this steely grey-white majestic cruiser. Hazelton was 33 and an experienced engineer, but there was so much to learn before he could feel comfortable in navy uniform and with his engineering duties. He reported to Engineer Commander McMahon, a man exceedingly preoccupied and busy directing a large number of personnel. Hazelton was immediately plunged into a frantic routine to become familiar with the mechanisms of the cruiser but he also needed to appreciate the refit dilemma facing his superior.

With little Government and private investment, Australia had already been desperately short of shipping of all kinds when war broke out. In short order, a shipbuilding programme was initiated and 17 corvettes, seven for the RAN and 10 for the Admiralty, became a priority in June 1940. This programme rapidly escalated and included orders for 10 more RN corvettes and four corvettes for the Royal Indian Navy (RIN). The building of eight 9,300-ton merchant ships were also underway by July 1941.

> The combined naval and merchant shipbuilding programme as they stood in July 1941 were then estimated to absorb all building facilities available in Australia until around the end of 1943.[275]

Australian dockyards also fitted 214 ships with defensive armament, 216 with paravanes, and degaussed 198 vessels.[276] Australian shipyards were overstretched and the ACNB was forced to inform the Admiralty that it was impossible to undertake further construction for the RN or RIN.

Canberra's Engineer Commander McMahon was no stranger to defect lists; he had bombarded Navy Office with over 100 lists in less than two years and continued to implore the authorities to give them priority so that his ship could become seaworthy. McMahon also had concerns about unfinished modernisation. With *Canberra* finally docked in Garden Island dockyard from 24 November 1941 for a very overdue refit – after more than 175,000 miles of wartime operational steaming,– McMahon was intent on rectifying faults during the month of December. His frustration increased because the shipbuilding and auxiliary war programme had resulted in an acute shortage of available dockyard personnel and maintenance materials. Corners had already been cut. Supply problems in the United Kingdom meant 'bulletproof plating and D1 heat treated plating' could not now be completed. In addition, and modernisation and protective work completed on

HMAS Canberra
entering dock
for refit, c. 1941.

Australia was now 'under review'.[277] The Admiralty then decided that the additional 'non-magnetic and bulletproof plating' should not now be fitted to *Canberra* because 'they do not consider it desirable to adopt this in view of the excessive weight involved'.[278] Further alterations and improvements were now 'to be carried out as opportunity arises' including 'improvements to boilers and the 8-inch fire control system'. Other works were cancelled including the fireproofing of timber work.[279]

Timber had become a major issue during the building of Australia's two Kent sub class County Class cruisers.[280] Discussion had escalated into argument during 1925 and 1926 when Australian business lobbied their government to ensure 'Australian timber' was used to manufacture 'as much of the cabin furniture as possible'.[281] The Admiralty preferred mahogany but submitted to pressure from the Commonwealth Government. Assessment of the different woods, availability and shipment were considered until it was settled that Queensland maple be utilised as soon as the large shipment arrived. During the building process, it was found that Queensland maple could not be fireproofed. The RAN representative in London advised the Admiralty that 'there is no objection to the use of Queensland maple not fireproofed for certain portions of the cabin furniture'.[282] When supplies of the timber were exhausted, it was decided the remaining maple was to be used for the 'visible' parts of cabin furniture whilst mahogany plywood, stained to appear like maple, would supplement. Only 'the latter will be fireproofed'.[283]

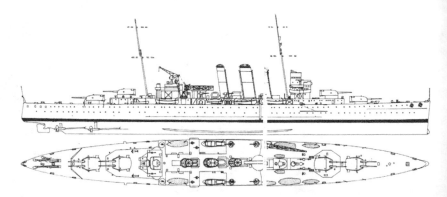

Drawings of Kent (County) class heavy cruisers, c. 1930s.

In February 1933, there had been a fire in *Canberra*'s sick bay. Surgeon Lieutenant (D) Leonard Malcolm Shugg, RAN, suffered third-degree burns to much of his body. Whilst Shugg was found culpable for incorrect procedure with a flammable substance, a rapid acceleration of the fire was only averted due to the 'prompt action and initiative shown by the chief petty officers from the adjoining mess and other ratings'.[284]

McMahon conferred extensively with his staff and decided that the threat of fire was a priority and the boiler rooms and fan flats urgently needed to be covered 'with flatting in order to reduce the fire risk'. He wanted all wood lining to enclosed messes to be removed and 'sheet steel to be substituted'.[285] *Canberra* had been a show boat and flagship with more and more coats of paint applied since she commissioned.[286] McMahon believed this needed to be removed as quickly as possible. This was a huge and time-consuming task but all flats and spaces needed to be chipped away and then just 'one coat of flat paint' applied. There was so much work to be completed during December 1941.

Throughout 1941, prolonged discourse continued between nations concerning the deteriorating situation in the Pacific but a preoccupation with the war in Europe had been exacerbated by British arrogance and underestimation. From the highest imperial authority to the lowest ranked RAN recruit, there was the firm belief that Britain, the RN and fortress Singapore would reign supreme should Japanese forces have the audacity to threaten British dominions.

> British Chiefs of Staff maintained that the security of Singapore
> and of Indian Ocean communications was the main defence of
> the whole British Commonwealth in the Far East.[287]

In 1939, British Prime Minister Winston Churchill had declared the Japanese 'would not embark upon such a mad enterprise'.[288] A large part of the Australian defence budget had been given to Britain during the previous decade for the naval base build-up at Singapore in return for the gentleman's agreement that a British fleet would arrive in time to save the day. This promise was now threatened despite urging from successive Australian Governments. In spite of blatant Japanese

Less imperial loyalty was now being depicted in newspaper political cartoons, c. 1941.[289]

military aggression, Britain continued to gamble that Japan would not attack British dominions. Anglo-Australian relationships were marred by Churchill's antipathy and the paternalism of British chiefs of staff. Churchill debated the idea of the abandonment of Singapore in a secret message to his chiefs of staff on 21 January 1941. When a copy was revealed to the newly-installed Australian Labor Government, the reaction was predictable and a strongly-worded telegram warned Churchill that such an evacuation would be an 'inexcusable betrayal'.[290]

The assumption of British racial superiority compounded a perilous situation as Japanese military boots marched ever closer. British General Robert Brooke-Popham, Commander-in-Chief of British Forces in the Far East, offered the observation that the Japanese soldier was a 'sub-human specimen' incapable of forming 'an intelligent fighting force'.[291] One of his battalion commanders lamented that British soldiers could be called upon to face such an inferior opposition whilst another thought it a pity that the Japanese would be so inhibited by British Far East military strength that they would never attack. A senior Royal Air Force officer espoused the belief that Japanese aircraft were not only few in number but given they were 'tied together with bits of string and bamboo', Japanese air war capability could only be considered 'a joke'.[292] The sentiment imbued every aspect of RAN training.

> [At Recruitment School] we were told that our purpose in life was to serve the British cause. That the British navy was the most powerful force for good in the world. The Japanese barely got a mention. It was well known that they were not far removed from monkeys ... it was obvious that one of us was worth at least ten Japs ... We were also told that aircraft posed no threat to well-armed warships. If the ships under attack aimed their anti-aircraft guns and laid a barrage ... it stood to reason that they would be shot down before they could drop their bombs.[293]

Churchill ordered 'our newest battleship, *Prince of Wales*, to join *Repulse*' and be sent to the Indian Ocean. On 10 November 1941, Churchill delivered a warning to Japan that the British were now 'strong enough to provide a powerful naval force' having stretched 'the long arm of brotherhood and motherhood to the Australian and New Zealand peoples'.[294] Confidence and complacency abounded when the RN's Z Force, *Repulse* and *Prince of Wales*, with Admiral Sir Tom Phillips, RN, the newly-appointed Commander-in-Chief, Eastern Fleet, arrived

Crew leaving Canberra *for shore leave, Sydney, c. 1940s.*

at Singapore to much fanfare on 2 December 1941. The Commander of the RAN, Vice Admiral Royle, sailed for Singapore on 29 November, arriving on 5 December, for strategic talks with Phillips.

Canberra was undergoing a refit with the cruiser's engineer and staff pushing slowly through a challenging list of defects and unfinished modernisation work. This came to an abrupt halt when the United States air forces were decimated in Hawaii's Pearl Harbour and in the Philippines on 7 and 8 December. The ferocity and extent of the Japanese attack was stunning at sea, on land, and in the air. An estimated 17,000 troops landed at Kota Bharu, Malaya, and Singora and Patani in Thailand. The Japanese conquest of Shanghai was completed; Wake Island, Hong Kong and Singapore were bombed. Within two days, British, US and Australian vulnerability was totally exposed. Admiral Phillips took his fleet to sea to make a pre-dawn surprise attack at Singora and intercept the Japanese 7th Cruiser Squadron.

On 10 December, the British fleet was attacked. The strike came from the air, 88 bombers and torpedo bombers 'with complete disregard for anti-aircraft fire' dived repeatedly until *Repulse* and *Prince of Wales*, were destroyed and sunk. Of the *Repulse*'s crew of 1309, 513 were killed. Of the 1612 onboard one of Britain's newest and most imposing battleships, *Prince of Wales*, 327 died, including Admiral Phillips.[295]

At 0130 on 10 December, the *Canberra* crew were recalled. There was confusion as those onboard were told they could go ashore again while other recalled crew members continued to arrive.

The following day Australians tried to comprehend what had happened. Information was scarce. The Government and Defence chiefs were only marginally better informed. What did this mean? How could the invincible be so vulnerable? Chief of the RAN, Vice Admiral Royle, was still in Singapore. Orders came again for *Canberra* to proceed to sea for an 8-inch full calibre gunnery exercise, before returning to harbour on the morning of 12 December. Another hasty order was received to sail with the light cruiser *Perth* at speed for Brisbane that afternoon. On negotiating a sharp bend in the Brisbane River on 15 December, *Canberra*'s steering motors failed. Full steam astern and a rapid drop of anchor averted catastrophe. More harried investigation

HMAS Canberra *in Sydney Harbour, c. 1940s.*

from engineering staff meant that the cruiser could proceed towards New Caledonia hours later, again with *Perth*, to rendezvous with the first American convoy to travel to Australia.

The significance of this convoy and the American troops within was not lost on the Australians nor was the impressiveness of the 9,100-ton, 10x8 inch gun, 1,200 crewed Pensacola-class heavy cruiser, USS *Pensacola*. The 'Pensacola Convoy' had departed Pearl Harbour bound for Manila in the Philippines on 29 November 1941. Fortuitously, they had escaped the destruction and the convoy was diverted to Australia. For the *Canberra* crew, this was their first interaction with the United States Navy (USN), the first of many.

Russell Keats wrote another letter to his family, filled with the contradictions he struggled with between his intellectual and religious upbringing and beliefs, and where and what he was in December 1941.

You know, when the Lord made the world, everything was perfect with one exception – the lords of the earth. I look out from where I sit on the bridge and see an eternity of heavenly, divinely deep blue sea sparkling as a never ending bed of diamonds ... most peaceful ... Yet the oceans are littered with battle-wagons spitting fire and the lands are split asunder by man-made volcanoes hurling thunder hell and destruction. Queer, isn't it, that the pride and glory of Creation should be so childishly destructive.[296]

With the convoy safely ensconced in Brisbane, Keats and his shipmates were delighted that *Canberra* turned south along the stunning New South Wales coastline to Sydney.

On 24 December, Rear Admiral Grace reallocated from *Canberra* to sister ship, *Australia*, which had been recalled from duty in the Northern Hemisphere. Captain Farncomb, in a direct exchange with Captain George Dunbar Moore, RAN (later Rear Admiral), gave up his command of *Canberra* for the newly designated flagship. Born at Springsure in country Queensland, Moore had transferred to the RAN from the English Merchant Navy when the RANC was founded, entering as a Midshipman in July 1913. It was a further disruption for the *Canberra* crew. On 28 December 1941, *Canberra* sailed to escort 4000 Australian soldiers to another war zone – to Port Moresby, Papua New Guinea.

During his visit in England in 1941, Menzies had been asked by the British Government for the RAN to man a further three N-class destroyers in the Mediterranean. Menzies agreed because the ACNB had informed him that the RAN were accepting 400 new recruits each month, more than enough to meet both RN and RAN requirements. By September 1941, the RAN had 68 ships in commission with more due to be completed. Mobilised personnel now numbered 19,740, of whom 8,640 were in HMA Ships on the Australia station, a further 3,500 on HMA Ships overseas and 6,400 engaged in land-based duties.[297] About 900 RAN personnel were serving with the RN and an additional 300 in HM-armed merchant, *Kanimbla*.[298] The ACNB had grossly underestimated. Sailor recruitment stalled whilst new accommodation blocks were built at *Cerberus* and a new naval base was established at Fremantle, Western Australia. It was also blatantly clear that personnel expansion was severely hampered due primarily to the 'lack of experienced instructors and of accommodation in seagoing ships for the practical training of recruits'.[299]

Australia had paid dearly in 'the war to end all wars', World War I. Of the Allies, only New Zealand suffered more military casualties per head of population than its larger neighbour. In 1914, war was seen as a grand adventure especially to the bushies – the country boys whose skin was burnished by the strong Australian sunlight. Grand recruitment drives through country towns and along dirt tracks swelled the ranks of the Australian New Zealand Army Corps (ANZAC) who fell on the blood-soaked beach at Gallipoli in 1915 and then in the mud of the Western Front in Europe until 1918.

Life between the wars was not easy for many. The Australian bush was romanticised by many a poet and balladeer, but the reality was often much harsher. Small country towns filled with modest weatherboard houses with paint blistered by the relentless Australian sun were home to many a family who found life a struggle as employment ceased during the Depression. AIF WWI service meant little after return to Australia when it came to caring for a growing family. Soldier farm settlements, planned to provide a living for many, were too often unsustainable. The WWI legacy of poor health – physical and mental – haunted returned soldiers and denied fulfilled lives.

In this the Stephens family were typical. Stanley 'Roy' Stephens was born on the second day of 1923 in Corryong, Victoria – his father a WWI veteran. When the rains came and seasons were good Corryong, 75 miles (120 km) east of Albury-Wodonga, was nourishing. When the rains failed, the Murray River stopped flowing and the crops failed. The Stephens family needed to move on, to Ballan on the Werribee River, 48 miles (78 km) north-west of Melbourne, but employment remained scarce. Characteristic of his generation, Roy left school to help his family survive. Before long he moved to Melbourne and at 17 joined Victorian Railways.

At Christmas 1940, Roy returned home and told his mother Ada that he was going to enlist. She implored him not to join the army – the

Stoker Roy Stephens, c. 1942.

family had felt the brunt of AIF WWI service. Honouring his widowed mother's wishes, Roy attempted to enlist in the RAAF. When told no more airmen were required, he approached RAN recruiters. Roy was told there was a waiting list and even then the navy was only looking for stokers. Having worked in a railways workshop, Roy signed on enthusiastically. Then he waited, and waited, until May 1941 when he commenced three months training at Williamstown Drill Hall 'while waiting for accommodation at HMAS *Cerberus*'.[300] Finally on 28 July 1941, Stoker II Roy Stephens (W/2119) arrived at *Cerberus* to begin his technical training. He delighted in the intricacies of engine mechanics, repairs and operation. The day Pearl Harbour was attacked Roy was one of a dozen young sailors drafted to the cruiser *Canberra*. Stoker II Stephens commenced his sea-going career on 2 January 1942, his nineteenth birthday, with not the slightest idea of what he would face before he turned 20. Neither did his navy. 1942 turned out to be the blackest of years, with the loss of five major ships, a number of smaller vessels and too many lives.

CONVOY DUTY

Immediately ahead, laying across our bows ... was one of the largest submarines I had ever seen.

Able Seaman Stephen St George[301]

The sailor from Australia's Pilbara with the vague ancestry, whose gunnery had been criticised by *Canberra*'s former CO, thought his eyes were deceiving him. Dead ahead in the late afternoon sunshine of 4 February 1942 was 'one of the largest submarines I had ever seen'.[302] AB Stephen St George felt his stomach leap into his throat and for once he was lost for words, almost. The black sinister shape with its sloping conning tower and forward deck gun, appeared to be stopped dead. 'I could see no crew members on her decks, nor notice any movement around her conning tower.'[303]

On 4 February, *Canberra* was on convoy duty – a journey which had already been eventful. The cruiser was to escort the troop ship *Aquitania* north when Australian soldiers decided they would take leave in Fremantle regardless of orders to the contrary, and helped themselves to every manner of boat to get ashore. For this reason, sailing was delayed while police rounded up the soldiers. Then *Canberra*'s turbines broke down and the cruiser was forced to continue on three shafts. Orders were changed. One high command said the destination was Singapore and another said the southern end of Sumatra.

Complicating matters further, they were joined by ships of other nations which made up the hastily-organised American-British-Dutch-Australian (ABDA) Command, or Allied forces in South-East Asia. The main objective of ABDA under the command of British General Sir Archibald Wavell was to maintain control of the 'Malay Barrier' – the Malayan Peninsula, Singapore, the Dutch East Indies, the Indian Ocean and Australian sea lanes. While Japanese troops were efficiently transforming their leaders' strategic priorities into reality, the Allied response was rhetoric and debate far from the din of battle. ABDA was the cumbersome result, doomed to fail and fail dramatically. Co-ordinating the forces of four nations with different training and equipment proved difficult. Conflicting priorities made agreement impossible. British leaders were primarily interested in Singapore and the Dutch Administration was focused on defending the Dutch East Indies. The United States, still stunned from Pearl Harbour, was preoccupied with the US Commonwealth territory of the Philippines. The Australian Government was faced with a large defence deployment in Europe and the Middle East and Imperial Japanese Navy (IJN) supremacy in the western Pacific. Wavell arrived in Singapore on 7 January 1942 and on 18 January needed to move his headquarters to Java.

Japan's next priority was to capture oil deposits. Although a US navy attack on Borneo on January 24 cost the Japanese six transport ships, Japanese progress was relentless. At the same time, ABDA Command became further divided. Most nations wanted a single command based in Washington, DC, but the British wished to retain control and a Far Eastern Council (later known as the Pacific War Council) was established in London on 9 February – with another council in Washington. During the first months of 1942, Allied resistance to Japanese attacks in Malaya, Singapore, the Dutch East Indies and the Philippines crumpled.

The next pieces on Japan's board of conquest were the Bismarck Archipelago and the Solomon Island group. The capital of New Britain was Rabaul. On the north-east shore of Simpson Harbour, Blanche Bay, modest colonial structures stood comfortably with the crowded bustling shacks and shops of Chinatown – but all were diminished by the backdrop of towering volcanic peaks. Rabaul was bombed for the first time on 4 January 1942.

By the end of the month the light defence of New Britain was overpowered. Military forces and the people of Rabaul and surrounding regions faced a grim future. About 1400 Australian military personnel were in Rabaul before the attack. Approximately 400 escaped to Australia, while the rest and about 200 civilians became prisoners of war (POWs). In addition, over 200 civilians in the area were interned. 1,045 were placed on the *Montevideo Maru* on 22 June 1942 to be transported to Japan. On 1 July, when off the southern coast of China, the ship was torpedoed and sunk by the submarine, USS *Sturgeon*. There were no survivors. Rabaul had been a central Japanese objective. It was perceived as a very suitable stepping stone to the largest island in the Archipelago, New Guinea – the doorway to Australia but more importantly offered the Japanese the opportunity to disrupt Allied supplies and reinforcements.

As Rabaul succumbed, *Canberra* was passing through the increasingly treacherous, narrow waters of Banka Strait that separates

Liberty men alight at Man O' War steps, Sydney. For engineering staff, there was no long leave as their ship faced a long refit, c. 1940s.

Sumatra from Banka Island in the Java Sea. It had left the convoy to retire to the Dutch Naval Base at Tanjong Priok (now Jakarta) for turbine repair. *Canberra* arrived at the conclusion of an air raid. Many of the crew were eager to leave this part of a besieged world as quickly as possible. Russell Keats hoped 'we're coming home'. *Canberra* steamed south to Australia but the turn-around at Fremantle was all too rapid. They arrived on 29 January and departed the next day with convoy MS3 of four cargo ships and seven oil tankers bound for the Dutch East Indies. The convoy optimistically hoped to load last minute supplies of Dutch oil and rubber before these too fell to the enemy.

It was now 4 February and the menacing shape of a Japanese submarine was directly ahead. With a mixture of fear and excitement, Able Seaman Stephen St George watched as:

> a flurry around her stern indicated that we had at last been
> sighted, and before we could swing to bring armament to bear,
> she submerged.[304]

Canberra had neither radar nor sonar to detect submarines and without any sort of launch device, the crew could only dump depth charges over the quarterdeck rails at the position of last sighting. The Seagull was launched but with light failing, it was useless. The following day, the aircraft was catapulted again but the submarine was long gone. Relieved of its convoy duty, the cruiser returned to Australia and this time to Sydney on 17 February. Much to the relief of Commander McMahon and his engineering staff, RAN authorities had no alternative but to allow *Canberra* to commence a very overdue refit.

The news about the war continued to go from bad to worse and Australians struggled to grasp how the situation had so quickly deteriorated. The 'Singapore strategy', the cornerstone of British imperial defence policy, had evolved from 1919. It was believed that fortress Singapore was impregnable, able to deter any aggression, particularly when an RN fleet was based there. It was believed that any force heading south to India or Australia would be intercepted and defeated. Britain had convinced successive Australian governments to

LEFT: *The doomed Australian 8th Divisional landing in Singapore in August* RIGHT: *1941 Singapore surrenders, February 1942.*

devote a sizeable percentage of defence budgets on the establishment of the naval base at the eastern end of the Strait of Malacca. This would avert any attack that was expected to come from the sea with enough warning for reinforcements to arrive from Britain. The strategy had led to the despatch of Force Z to Singapore and the subsequent sinking of the *Prince of Wales* and *Repulse* by Japanese air attack on 10 December 1941. The attack from the sea never eventuated; it came from the mainland and on 15 February 1942, the supposedly impregnable fortress Singapore succumbed to the Japanese. British Commander Lieutenant General Arthur Percival called for a ceasefire and surrendered. Despite instructing his soldiers to remain at their posts and fight, General Henry Gordon Bennett, the Australian Commander, and two staff officers escaped to Australia. More than 100,000 troops and hundreds of European civilians became prisoners of war (POW) – thousands did not survive captivity. Britain's Prime Minister Winston Churchill described the ignominious fall of Singapore as 'the worst disaster and largest capitulation in British history'.[305] For Australia's defence, the collapse of Singapore was critical: the Australian mainland was now exposed.

At 0958 on 19 February 1942, Australia came under attack when 54 land-based bombers and approximately 188 attack aircraft, launched from four Japanese aircraft carriers in the Timor Sea, bombed the Northern Territory capital, Darwin. In the first 40-minute attack, Darwin Harbour and the city was pattern-bombed while dive bombers and Zero fighters attacked shipping in the harbour, civil and military airfields, and military and industrial areas at Berrimah. An hour later the Parap RAAF base was subjected to high altitude bombing. The raids killed at least 243 people and wounded between 300 and 400. Eight ships at anchor were sunk, 20 military aircraft were destroyed and military and civil facilities in Darwin were demolished. With the fall of Singapore just days earlier, an Australian Government concerned about national morale, announced that the attacks had been minor with only 17 people killed. In total there were 64 air attacks on Darwin with the last in November 1943.

With Malaya lost and the Allied position in the Dutch East Indies precarious, General Wavell resigned on 23 February 1942 and ABDA Command was closed down. Wavell evacuated to India to resume his position as Commander-in-Chief India and lead the unsuccessful defence of Burma. Dutch Rear Admiral Karel Doorman assumed control of the remaining naval ships, one of which was the light cruiser HMAS *Perth*. Doorman was totally inexperienced in battle but retained command on the grounds of seniority. Overlooked for the position was the highly experienced Australian Captain Hector 'Fighting Hec' Macdonald Laws Waller, RAN, DSO (and Bar).

There had been ample time for ACNB to recall *Perth* as it journeyed north after the fall of Singapore but the order to proceed was the only one sent. In the Battle of the Java Sea on 27 February 1942 the Doorman-led Allied naval force was outgunned and out-manoeuvred by the Japanese fleet. Allied casualties were heavy. Admiral Doorman, his Dutch cruisers, five Dutch and RN destroyers and almost all of their crews were destroyed. The only ships to escape the carnage were *Perth* and USS *Houston*, due to the expertise of Waller. Unfortunately, whilst attempting escape to Australia through the Sunda Strait the following day, they encountered the Japanese 'Western Invasion Force'. Both crews fought valiantly but were vastly outnumbered and were sunk in the early hours of 1 March 1942. Those who survived became POW and were sent to labour and die on the infamous Burma-Thai railway and in Japanese coal mines. Of the 1008 in *Houston*, only 266 returned to the United States at war's end. Of *Perth*'s crew of 681, just 214 were repatriated to Australia in 1945.

The Australian cruiser *Perth* was the last-minute pawn in a belated attempt to appease the Dutch. Those who dictated British Dutch East Indies strategy, due to arrogance or ignorance, or a combination of both, completely misjudged the capability of the Japanese and had forsaken *Perth* and crew to a deadly fate.[306]

This was yet another shock for officers and sailors of the RAN – they had lost friends, shipmates, classmates – way too many. For years *Canberra* was used as a training ship; sailors and midshipmen came, qualified, were promoted and took their expertise into the rest of the fleet, but that fleet was shrinking and these officers and sailors were dying and disappearing too fast. For those in the Australian Navy, this was very personal as men from different ships had trained together or worked together. Throughout the cruiser, officers and sailors mourned the loss and this was not limited to the seaman and engineering branches. The *Canberra* band had entertained thousands during open days. Their brass instruments and marching had caused children to mimic them and adults to fill with the pride that only a precision military band could muster. Unknown to the general public was that bandsmen had far more hazardous duties in times of war. Commonly it was the treacherous undertaking of resupplying ammunition to seaman gunners or tending the wounded. *Canberra* had lost a fine trumpeter in Arnold Partington. His brother Leslie died with *Sydney* and now the last of the RAN Partington

Bandsman Harry William Freestone, enjoyed his service in Canberra, *c. 1941.*

 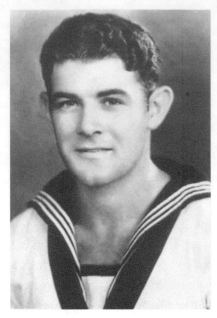

Ordinary Seaman II, Ross Cowdroy (LEFT) *and Ordinary Seaman II Frank Johnson* (RIGHT), *c. 1940s.*

bandsmen, Perc, was missing in *Perth*.

Bandsman Harry William Freestone (19182) had amused many in *Canberra* with his London cockney twang, sense of humour, and photographic and musical talents during his time in the warship, 1933–1935 and 1939–1940. Freestone was then drafted to *Perth*. His 'dits' (stories) were well worth listening to because he had entered the RAN in 1928 after serving in World War I with the British 1st Battalion South Staffordshire Regiment.

Perc Partington eventually returned to his family after years as a POW but Harry Freestone did not return to his wife, Jean and 12-year-old son, Harry. He was a casualty of the Battle of Sunda Strait on 1 March 1942.

Ross Cowdroy and Frank Johnson were both born in 1921 and enlisted in the RAN the same year. Both underwent recruit training at *Cerberus*, not realising how hauntingly similar their careers and lives would be. The new Ordinary Seamen IIs drafted to *Canberra* for sea training.

Years later, as well-qualified leading seamen, they joined *Perth*. Both survived the battle and sinking but became POWs and worked as slave labour on the Burma-Thai railway. Ross Cowdroy suffered a tropical ulcer and a camp doctor amputated the leg. Due to malnutrition, his immune system collapsed and he died on 1 February 1944 aged 22. Johnson watched Ross die, survived the railway and was placed on the *Rakuyo Maru* with 1,317 other Australian and British POW. On 12 September 1944, the US submarine *Sealion II* torpedoed the transport and 23-year-old Frank Johnson was one of the 1,159 who did not survive.

MacKenzie 'Mac' Gregory was concerned for classmates Jack Steel Lester and Norman Harold Stephen White. They were innocent 13-year-olds when they all joined the RANC in January 1936. Their graduation was hastened by the start of a war and they found themselves midshipmen in training in *Canberra* in September 1939 before being shipped overseas to the RN for the obligatory training to turn them into true naval officers. It was a steep learning curve at a time when England was undergoing a vicious German bombing campaign. The youngsters had mixed feeling about returning to Australia believing their duty lay in the protection of a Britain in need.

Their arrival home after two years away coincided with the destruction at Pearl Harbour and left little doubt as to where they were truly needed. There was some relief in now being sub lieutenants as that promotion, according to 'Mac', was 'probably the largest one makes in a career as a naval officer' because a midshipman was regularly described as 'the lowest form of animal life in the Navy'.[307] It helped also that the salary increased from 6 shillings a day (60 cents) to 11 shillings a day ($1.10). The young men wearing their bright gold single strip were spread out through the RAN. 'Mac' Gregory was posted to *Canberra* on Boxing Day 1941. It was January and February when Jack Lester and Norm White joined *Perth*. Word of the sinking of *Perth* caused ongoing consternation because it was not until the end of the war that families learned the individual fate of *Perth* crew. Only then 'Mac' discovered Jack Lester had died the night his ship was sunk, and that Norm White had survived three and a half years as a Japanese POW.

The fate of the crew of HMAS *Yarra* II was known sooner. The

HMA Ships Perth (LEFT) *and* Yarra (RIGHT) *c. 1941.*

destroyer lost a battle against superior Japanese ships and was sunk on 4 March 1942 not far from where *Perth* was lost. Of the 151 *Yarra* crew 138 were killed in the action or died subsequently. The shock reverberated through a nation and a navy now severely diminished in ships and personnel – *Waterhen, Sydney, Parramatta, Perth* and *Yarra* and an estimated 1,583 officers and sailors gone.

Everything was moving too quickly. Old loyalties were now in question with even the most loyal Anglophile realising the motherland could not rescue Australia in its time of greatest need. Prime Minister John Curtin shocked fellow Australians in his address which headlined newspapers on 27 December 1941.

> Without any inhibitions of any kind, I make it clear that
> Australia looks to America, free of any pangs as to our
> traditional links or kinship with the United Kingdom.[308]

Curtin's government had become increasingly concerned with British strategy and the competency of senior British officers. This was compounded by the loss of so much of the RAN, the capitulation of Singapore and the capture of thousands of Australian servicemen. It was a catastrophe Curtin described as 'Australia's Dunkirk'.[309]

Curtin's resolve strengthened. He wanted the return of Australian forces from the Middle East, despite Churchill's determination that a division be diverted to Burma, and Churchill's threat that a very 'grave effect will be produced upon the President and the Washington circle, on whom you are so largely dependent'.[310] In a cable to Churchill on 17 February 1942, Curtin demanded the immediate return of Australian troops and made it clear that no more would be diverted. Churchill remained unconvinced and Curtin was 'greatly shocked' as the angry discourse between the two Prime Ministers continued.[311] Burma fell on 8 March as quickly as Singapore but the Australian soldiers were spared the same fate as their brethren in Singapore. Curtin finally agreed that two 6th Division brigades would make up a temporary garrison in Ceylon but that the vast bulk of Australians should return home.

When Japan attacked, Curtin had declared that Australia had entered its 'darkest hour'. As Australians turned the volume up on their wirelesses, their Prime Minister spoke to the people. He made the situation very clear.

> The call is to you for your courage, your physical and mental ability, your inflexible determination that we as a nation of free people shall survive.[312]

War was no longer a distant reality. Australians needed to depend on their own enterprise and American assistance because their very nation was now 'the stake in this conflict'. In February 1942, Curtin called for 'total war', total mobilisation of manpower, primary resources and industry. Public attention on the home front now focussed on domestic precautions and stringencies. Restrictions on resources such as petrol were widened and austerity was encouraged. Street lighting was reduced and a partial blackout was implemented. A prohibition on the manufacture of many non-essential goods was announced, 'from bath heaters and lawn mowers to fur coats and men's evening dress'.[313] Identity cards were introduced for all British subjects over 16. Clothing coupons were initiated as Curtin broadcast to the nation.

> I say quite flatly that regard will be given only to the minimum requirements of the civilian population.[314]

For the first time Australian women's defence force auxiliaries were formed. Over 70,000 women eagerly donned military uniform and gave crucial war service in the Women's Royal Australian Naval Service

Not until 1943 were posters circulated to encourage the full enlistment of Australian women in the defence of Australia.

LEFT: *Prime Minister Curtin welcoming US General Douglas to Australia in 1942.*

RIGHT: *Illustration from* The Argus, *14 February 1942.*

(WRANS), the Australian Women's Army Service (AWAS), and the Women's Auxiliary Australian Air Force (WAAAF). More joined the Women's Land Army (AWLA) and were essential to farm production. Others undertook traditional male occupations as well as labour in war industry. Never before had so much been expected from, and so much responsibility given to, Australian women, and they relished the opportunities.

In March 1942 Prime Minister Curtin warmly welcomed US General Douglas MacArthur to Australia and announced MacArthur's appointment as Supreme Commander of the South-West Pacific. Photographs of the General who many hoped might be their nation's saviour appeared everywhere even above the front doors of Brisbane's Myer emporium. What had started with a trickle of American servicemen with the Pensacola Convoy which *Canberra* had escorted from New Caledonia to Brisbane just before Christmas 1941, became a flood. More than a million US servicemen gradually arrived to mount a counter offensive against the Japanese and Australians were asked to welcome them.

The loss of Australian warships and the total mobilisation of manpower, primary resources and industry all added stress and complications for Commander 'Mac' McMahon and his staff during *Canberra's* refit. The very defence of Australia was now crucial. The loss of so many warships and their crews had depleted the operational effectiveness of the RAN dramatically and the pressure to finish the refit and get the cruiser back into the front line of defence was enormous. Shortages of materials and dockyard personnel meant that some of the refit needed to be cut, even some of the most fundamental mechanical and electrical work. Serious shortcomings in RAN infrastructure and technical innovation made the task at hand even more difficult.

The material superiority of the Americans came as a shock to the RAN ... Much of this was due to the general technological superiority of American industry over the British, more ... the Americans had been spending much greater amounts on the modernisation of their navy than the British ... American units were far better suited to Pacific conditions than those of the RAN. In particular USN engineering practices were markedly better.[315]

Fireproofing remained urgent. McMahon asked that all wood lining to enclosed messes be removed and sheet steel substituted. He was told 'either through shortage of labour or for other reasons this work could not be carried out'.[316] This was unacceptable.

'I then obtained the sheet steel from the Naval Stores' and 'we carried out as much work as possible with the ship's staff'.[317] Similarly on other issues, the initiative of the *Canberra* crew was paramount to 'appropriate' even absolute necessities. A great deal of timber was removed from the upper deck stowage and they were 'gradually' chipping through the layers and layers of paint in all flats and spaces and replacing them with only one coat of flat paint – but everything was taking so long even with round-the-clock shifts. McMahon rarely took time off and, while they respected his commitment, even the younger engineering officers struggled to keep up.

The popular image promoted by the RAN between the wars, c. 1930s.

The name Brynmor Wheatley Mussared lent itself to a vision of navy dress whites, cravat, and sword. The man himself with the finely chiselled beard and moustache was the very model of a modern naval officer. But this was where the similarities between Lieutenant (E) Mussared, RAN, and the image the Naval Board promoted during the 1930s ended.

Mussared was born on the South Australian coast in January 1917, in a pleasant northern seaside suburb of Adelaide, the salty ocean always just a

Brynmor Wheatley Mussared, c. 1945.

breath away. Appointment as an RANC Cadet Midshipman in September 1932 wasn't unusual and at 15 he was just a little more mature than the normal 13-year-old entries. On graduation in 1936, he took second and third prizes in most of his subjects and demonstrated a prowess for the technical side of the navy. After his six months in *Canberra*, he was sent to England to study at the Royal Naval Engineering College (RNEC) Keyham, Plymouth, England.

It was a struggle in the beginning, adjusting to what he had believed was the same culture and being one of the few Australian students. His intermediate examinations saw him finish twenty third and he studied harder. He was exempted from the preliminary exam because of his intermediate results – even if it was due to his fluency in French. In his large RNEC class, Mussared finished sixteenth and was delighted to be not only promoted to Sub Lieutenant (E) but also to be on his way home after four long years. Promotion to Lieutenant came in September 1940 by which time he was serving in *Canberra* with grease under his fingernails and the noise of diesel engines ringing in his ears.

In 1942 even the most junior *Canberra* stoker, such as 19-year-old Stoker II Roy Stephens, did not escape the frenetic pace of the refit. He was given the labour-intensive task of scrubbing the cruiser's screws with wire brushes to remove shell fish and all other manner of material which had adhered to *Canberra*'s propellers over the many thousands of miles.

From the youngest to the oldest, from the least experienced to the most seasoned, all realised the seriousness and urgency of their tasks. Few were immune to the increased propaganda exhorting Australians

HE'S COMING SOUTH

It's fight
work or perish

Propaganda poster, c. 1942.

to give more or face dire consequences. But it was now April and then May and *Canberra* was still not ready regardless of defence plans being devised in cigarette smoke-filled bunkers to include the warship in 'Force 44' and the defence of New Guinea's Port Moresby.

By April 1942 the Japanese had formed a defensive perimeter which stretched from the Kuriles Islands southward through the Marshall Islands to New Britain, westwards to Java, Sumatra, the Andaman Islands and Burma. Within that huge perimeter Japanese authority was unchallenged and outposts were held at Lae and Salamaua in northern New Guinea. Buoyed by the ease of their conquests, Japan's leaders decided to extend the perimeter and the first amphibious attack on Port Moresby took place on 29 April. On 3 May 1942, Japanese forces landed at Tulagi, an island in the Solomons Island group.

Commander-in-Chief Pacific Ocean Areas, Admiral Chester William Nimitz, USN assembled 'Task Force 44' south of Guadalcanal in the Solomon Islands and on 7 May, Japanese troop transports bound for Port Moresby were attacked – the Battle of the Coral Sea had commenced. By 8 May opposing forces had suffered losses of ships and men. Each had lost carriers, but the Japanese aircraft losses were particularly severe and their landing at Port Moresby was abandoned. This was the first time that the Imperial Japanese Navy (IJN) had met concerted opposition.

News of the Battle of the Coral Sea was enthusiastically received and Prime Minister Curtin launched into his most powerful oratory.

I ask the people of Australia, having regard to the grave consequences implicit in this engagement, to take a sober and realistic estimate of their duty to the nation. I put it to every

Canberra in the foreground of an unfinished Sydney Harbour Bridge in 1930.

man whom these words may reach ... that he owes it to those
men and to the future of the country to be unstinting in what he
will now do for Australia.[318]

The words resonated strongly with officers and sailors of *Canberra* who
had again missed out on an important chapter in the war and on the
action that had seen the Japanese retreat. And of course, *Canberra's*
sister cruiser *Australia* had been at the centre of the offensive again.
Finally, an end was made to the refit but there was no time for work-up
sea trials.

On the night of 31 May 1942 *Canberra* was at number 1 Buoy Farm
Cove, in Sydney Harbour. It was a relief to be deemed operational again
but it remained in sheltered and safe waters, the crew able to go ashore
and seek refuge in homes and familiar surroundings. Some of the
oldest hands carried a photo of *Canberra* anchored near the unfinished
Sydney Harbour Bridge. *Canberra* had been present at the opening in
1932 as well.

The photographs and postcards were nonetheless unsettling. So
much had changed; so much innocence lost. In 1932 so many of the
families had eagerly crowded on the bridge to walk the span which
finally connected the shores of their magnificent harbour. Those who
had participated in the joyous harbour celebrations, were now torn
apart by the losses in the war and the prospect of invasion by Japan.

481 *Illuminations — Bridge & H.M.A.S. "Canberra" Sydney.*

Postcard from 1932 of the Sydney Harbour Bridge opening celebrations with HMAS Canberra *illuminated in the foreground.*

While it was rare for a citizen of Sydney not to be related to someone wearing military uniform or engaged in the war industry, the city had not been directly touched. Cautionary measures and limited supply of basic items had led to lifestyle alterations. City buildings were sandbagged and windows taped. Air raid shelters, perhaps many of dubious value, had been dug and built in suburban backyards and vegetables flourished where lawn had once been. Still, the people felt comforted for once by the tyranny of distance between Australia and the rest of the world.

HMAS *Canberra* was a very familiar sight in Sydney Harbour. Once starkly white and grand, it was now painted dark matt sea grey. The war camouflage paintwork used on *Perth* and *Yarra* was now of questionable value. Another recent change had been the addition of two 20 mm Oberlikon Mk1 guns, one atop of the aft 8-inch B turret and one midships. A air/surface warning radar (Type 271) had been fitted on top of the bridge. On the evening of 31 May 1942, warships flying the flags of several nations moved gently at their moorings in Sydney Harbour. *Canberra* was nestled off Farm Cove again close to the iconic bridge. From *Canberra*'s decks the US heavy cruiser *Chicago* was visible in the approaching dark, so too USN ships *Perkins* and *Dobbin*. Spread out across the harbour were other HMA Ships: the minelayer *Bungaree*, the armed merchant ships *Westralia* and *Kanimbla*, minesweepers *Whyalla* and *Geelong*, the old cruiser *Adelaide*, as well as the Indian corvette HMIS *Bombay*. The Dutch submarine *K9* was moored next to HMAS *Kuttabul*. There was also a Sydney ferry, converted to accommodate RAN sailors. The peaceful scene was about to change abruptly.

At dusk on 31 May 1942, five large Japanese I class submarines had rendezvoused 35 miles (56 km) north of Sydney. In the pre-dawn light of the following morning, submarine *I21* launched a single float-plane which flew a daring reconnaissance mission over the harbour circling *Chicago* twice before flying away eastwards. The duty RAN officer at Garden Island travelled to *Chicago* to query the origin of the aircraft. He was told that it was an American cruiser aircraft. Though it was agreed there was no other US cruiser in the region, no further action was taken.

About 9 miles (15 km) east of Sydney Heads, the Japanese submarines, *I27*, *I22* and *I24* released three two-crew Type A midget submarines. Each displaced 46 tons submerged, were capable of a submerged speed of 19 knots and were armed with two torpedoes. On the dark and cloudy night of 31 May the first midget submarine, from *I27*, crewed by Lieutenant Kenshi Chuman and Petty Officer Takeshi Omori, entered the harbour at 2000 but its propellers became entangled in anti-submarine nets near the harbour's western boom gate. A vigilant boatman thought he saw a large shark close enough to the surface for him to use an oar to prod it – it made a metallic sound. He immediately reported it to authorities but was told he was drunk. He persisted and HMAS patrol boats *Yarroma* and *Lolita* were despatched to investigate. Unable to free their propellers from the net, the Japanese crew set off demolition charges to destroy their submarine but in so doing, they raised the general alarm. It was 2237.

Meanwhile, the second midget submarine, from *I24*, with crew Sub Lieutenant Katsuhisa Ban and Petty Officer Mamoru Ashibe, had successfully entered the harbour at 2148. Being moored furthest from the

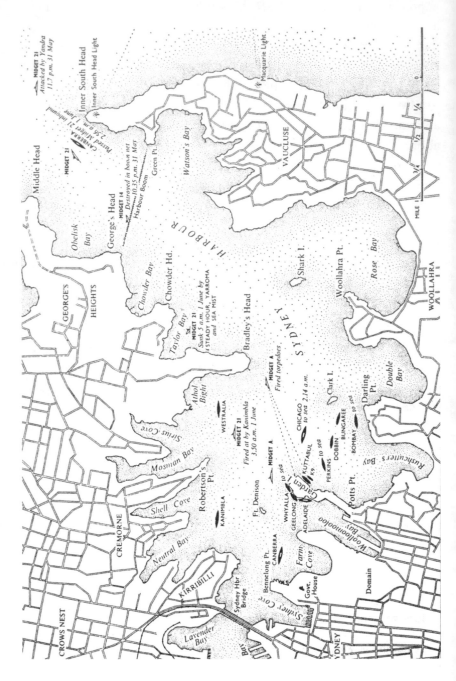

Position of naval shipping in Sydney Harbour the night of 29 May 1942.[319]

harbour entrance, *Canberra* duty personnel remained unaware of the imminent danger. However, *Chicago* lookouts sighted the submarine's periscope. Searchlights were illuminated and shots were fired but with guns unable to be depressed low enough, this was ineffective. Half an hour later the second midget submarine fired two torpedoes at *Chicago*. One torpedo ran ashore at Garden Island but failed to explode. The second torpedo passed under Dutch submarine *K9*, struck a sea wall and exploded on impact beneath *Kuttabul*.

The RAN accommodation ship sank immediately killing 19 Australian and two British sailors. Ten others were injured, some trapped in the wreckage. West Australian bandsman Melville Neilson Cumming (20501) had been enjoying some leave from *Australia* and had just returned from an enjoyable day ashore when *Kuttabul* exploded and disintegrated around him. Sustaining only cuts, he hurriedly removed his boots and dived into the black bitterly cold harbour frantically searching the shattered hull for survivors. Again and again he submerged and managed to rescue three injured men.

Retrieval of the midget submarine, c. 1942.

Ban and Ashibe evaded detection and withdrew from the harbour. The wreck of their submarine was not found until the year 2006, off a northern Sydney beach. The midget submarine launched from *I22*, with Lieutenant Kieu Matsuo and Petty Officer Masao Tsuzuku, entered the harbour in the early hours of 1st June but was detected in the waters of Taylors Point and depth charges were dropped by patrol boats. Their submarine crippled, the two-man crew committed suicide.

Pandemonium reigned as shrill warship alarms pierced the night. Smaller ships quickly began to traverse harbour waters with an unprecedented urgency. The heavy cruisers *Canberra* and *Chicago* were the most desirable enemy targets. *Chicago* proceeded to sea before daylight. *Canberra* was only manned by a skeleton crew with two thirds of the ship's company on night leave. All that could be done for *Canberra* was to raise enough steam to slowly swing the warship so that it was not silhouetted against city lights.

Supply Assistant Russell Keats was spending the night at the Mosman home of a shipmate. They were woken by the sound of gunfire. Realising it was the guns of *Chicago*, they quickly prepared to return to their own cruiser. While in transit Keats 'lit three cigarettes, considered a harbinger of bad luck'.[320] Commander McMahon was enjoying one of his rare overnight stays with his family on Sydney's north shore. His 12-year-old son, John remembers being woken by a hammering on the front door of his home. A policeman spoke solemnly to his father who dressed hastily and disappeared into the dark night. By the time McMahon was back onboard *Canberra*, it was a new day, harbour defence craft had undertaken a full-scale hunt and no further enemy craft had been found. *Canberra* had been fortunate. Within hours *Canberra* sailed from Sydney as part of Task Force 44. The cruiser would never return.

Australians were disturbed by how close the enemy had advanced to their largest city. The bodies of the four Japanese crewmen were recovered, cremated with full military honours and their ashes returned to Japan. This caused some dissent amongst the city's citizens but Rear Admiral Gerard Charles Muirhead-Gould, DSC, RN, Flag Officer-in-Charge Sydney believed it was honourable and perhaps believed it would indicate to the Japanese that combatants could retain civility to those who fell into the hands of the other side. Unfortunately, the Japanese were not listening.

*I reported to my Captains on many occasions
that the efficiency of the ship had been lowered by
frequent drafting changes.*

Commander Otto McMahon, RAN.[321]

For two months *Canberra* conducted exercises with the other ships of
Task Force 44 off the coast from the Queensland capital, Brisbane. Due
to the refit, the cruiser had missed the Battle of the Coral Sea. Half the
crew were bursting for action and the other half were more restrained in
their ambitions. Joint exercises were not entirely without hazard as USN
ships and their Australian counterparts attempted to perfect language
and manoeuvres. US technology, particularly in communications, was
extremely different and improved compatibility only slightly when
ships exchanged a few personnel. Worse still, Australian ships were not
equipped with Talk Between Ships (TBS), the radio network American
warships used to communicate with each other using a standard
encoded terminology.

The lack of experience working together was exposed in one serious
situation when *Australia*, *Canberra* and *Chicago* returned from
exercises off the seaside resort of Caloundra, north of Brisbane. Those
on *Chicago* were somewhat familiar with the Australians but not so
the personnel on USS *Salt Lake City*, a Pensacola-class heavy cruiser

nicknamed for reasons not known to the Australians as 'Swayback Maru' or 'Old Swayback'.

As the warships approached their anchorage, the usual anchor signals were flashed down the line (by blinker tube in USN language). *Canberra*'s navigator was Lieutenant Commander Jack Statton Mesley, RAN. Studious and clear thinking, Mesley had entered RANC from Melbourne at 13 in January 1924. He excelled at the Royal Naval College, Greenwich, England, finishing with first class passes in gunnery, navigation and torpedo. Chosing to be a navigator, he spent much of his career bouncing back and forth to England on exchange or in the cruiser HMAS *Hobart* before taking up his new post in February 1942.

Mesley was watching from the bridge as signals for 'prepare to come to starboard anchor; speed 10; stop engine; let go' were flashed. Unfortunately, *Salt Lake City* missed the 'stop engines' signal and was still moving at 10 knots when the captain did see the 'let go or anchor instantly' order. Not wishing to be shown up on seamanship, he retorted 'Well, if the gord damned Limees can do it, so can I. Let go, back terrific'.[322] The *Salt Lake City* was a 10,826 ton, 585 ft 6 in (178.46

Left to right: Canberra, Chicago, Salt Lake City *and two Curtiss SOC Seagull float planes, c. 1942.*

metres), 4 shaft, 10 × 8 inch (203 mm) armed, 6 × 21 inch (533 mm) torpedo tube, heavy cruiser carrying four float planes and a crew of 1,200. This was not the recommended method of bringing such a warship to anchorage. There was a very distinctive inhaling of breath throughout Task Force 44 and colourful utterances from Australians and Americans alike, as 'Old Swayback' pulled up without tail-ending any other ship, or crashing into unsuspecting shore side dwellings. Mesley was as dumbfounded as he was impressed but simply muttered, 'remarkable'.[323]

Lieutenant Commander Jack Statton Mesley, RAN, c. 1945.

Mesley was far from being the only 'newish' crew arrival. *Canberra* had been inundated with new personnel, from the captain down. Captain Frank Edmond Getting, RAN, assumed command on 17 June 1942 with the promotion of Captain Moore to Commodore and his appointment as Second Naval Member.

Born in Sydney in 1899, Getting had attended the Sydney Technical High School. It may have been this which made him even more determined to prove himself in the ranks of navy officers who were mostly graduates of expensive private colleges. Since entering the RANC on the last day of December 1912, Getting had impressed his superiors.

He has so favourably impressed me with his ability, keenness and power of command ... he has a fine physique and a good manner and appearance. His whole heart seems to be in the Service and I am sure he will do very well.[324]

An excellent sportsman, particularly in the art of boxing, after extensive service with the RN, Getting posted to *Canberra* from 1935 to 1937 and then as the cruiser's Executive Officer in 1938 and 1939. On promotion to Captain, Getting assumed command of the armed merchant ship,

Lieutenant Commander Frank Edmond Getting, RAN, c. 1930s.

Kanimbla. From May 1941 until May 1942 he served as deputy chief of naval staff. Getting may not have rated highly in some circles for the finer social graces of many officers, but he quickly impressed the *Canberra* ship's company with his ship handling skills. Nonetheless their nickname for their CO reflected his aloofness, 'Von'.

Commander-in-Chief of the Imperial Japanese Navy, Admiral Isoroku Yamamoto, was concerned that despite the crushing blow dealt at Pearl Harbor, the strike had missed US aircraft carriers. The carriers had now enabled raids on Japanese bases in the Pacific. Worse still was the attack, codenamed 'Doolitte Raid', by medium bombers launched from the aircraft carrier USS *Hornet* on Tokyo on 18 April 1942. This first, brazen US air raid strike on Japan by the US, while causing little loss of life, incurred significant loss of face and Yamamoto vowed to fight a decisive battle to complete the destruction of the US Pacific Fleet off the island of Midway. The ensuing battle fought between 4 and 7 June 1942 demonstrated a new chapter in the war at sea and the power of aircraft carriers and their aircraft.

Statistically the Americans won with the sinking of four fleet carriers *Akagi*, *Kaga*, *Soryu*, and *Hiryu* and the cruiser *Mikuma* and the destruction of 292 Japanese aircraft and 2,500 men. The USS *Yorktown* and the destroyer *Hammann* were sunk, 145 aircraft were shot down and 307 US servicemen died. Japan retained a formidable carrier force despite the huge losses, but the Battle of Midway had shown the US and its allies that the Imperial Japanese Navy (IJN) was not invincible.

While the IJN still outnumbered the US Pacific and Australian naval forces, the latter remained confident in their operational superiority. In

Map of the Solomon Islands, c. 1940s.[325]

fact, no alteration was made to Allied strategic objectives. Eighty-five per cent of US military production, supplies and shipping were still devoted to the war against Germany and Italy and to helping Britain. The US priority in the Pacific during 1942 was to protect their own west coast and secondly to protect the shipping lanes from Australia to that coast. Protection of the Australian mainland was a priority for its citizens but such protection was not considered important in the delicate balance of combined operations of US and Australian naval forces.

The Solomon Islands, about 1,200 miles (1,931 km) from Australia, consist of eight main islands and a number of smaller islands spread over a distance of 700 miles (1,127 km). Running from Bougainville to the northwest to Guadalcanal in the south east with New Georgia midway, the island group offered Japanese forces the essential stepping stones to New Guinea and even Australia. Consequently, the Japanese occupied Tulagi Island on 3 May 1942 and constructed a seaplane base. When Allied intelligence revealed a larger airfield being constructed at Lunga Point, on the island of Guadalcanal, this was of greater concern. Allied command had agreed it was crucial to deny the Japanese strategic advantage in the Solomons. This airfield would allow the deployment of fighters and bombers to provide air cover for Japanese naval forces advancing throughout the South Pacific. Long-range bombers could threaten not only the sea lanes but the east coast of Australia. On 10 July Vice Admiral Robert Lee Ghormley, USN, received operational orders from Commander-in-Chief, Pacific Fleet and Pacific Ocean Areas, Rear Admiral Chester Nimitz, USN, to reclaim the Solomon Islands group as soon as possible. Ghormley designed the offensive plan, code named 'Operation Watchtower' by 16 July. More time was needed to prepare a major offensive but time was of the essence.

Task Force 44 left Brisbane on 14 July. On 19 July they anchored off Wellington, New Zealand. More and more ships began to gather. In *Canberra,* the mess deck admirals were coming up with all sorts of scenarios as to their final destination. The sailors loved 'the buzz' (gossip) and some, it seemed, could resolve the war in a matter of days.

Russell Keats wondered if he had had some premonition because, for the first time in his life, prior to leaving Brisbane, he had 'succumbed

Task Force 44 steaming away from Australia, c. 1942.

to drink'.[326] The headache and nausea the next day was not welcomed. Keats needed clear thinking because the impetus had definitely picked up. His action station, the small plot space close to the bridge – already crowded with its whirring wheels, dials and clocks – now had a wireless which sometimes broke from navy transmission into an American 'swing number', much to the annoyance of bridge officers. Clearly, there were still a few technical glitches to clear up. The plotting staff had more responsibilities and felt like a 'squad of chronometers' whenever the ship assumed a zig zag course, having to shout to the bridge the time and alteration of course, enough to 'drive you crazy'. Keats wrote how at times 'I'm very happy on this ship, but [sometimes] I'd give ten years of my life to get off it'.[327]

His sentiments were clearly affected by his failure to be promoted. The paymaster was 'exceptionally pleased with my work' but had denied promotion for the reason 'I'm not the type to lead or be in charge of men', a criticism Keats clearly believed unfounded: 'most extraordinary since whenever we have a working party either aboard or ashore, I'm in charge of it'.[328] The sensitive intellectual supply assistant had failed to fit the classic mould of a tough sailor.

There was concern amongst senior members of the crew that there should have been more time to train the least experienced ordinary seamen and stokers who had arrived in large numbers when the *Canberra* refit concluded. Although it was previously known as the glamour ship and a training ship, when the cruiser was readied for front line combat, priority should have been given to continuity and efficiency within gun crews, engine rooms and other teams. Delays and interruptions within the recruiting and training regimes, and the loss of so many ships and crews, had destabilised the RAN and *Canberra*'s combat readiness. An outspoken critic was Engineer Commander Otto 'Mac' McMahon; it was something he felt very strongly about.

> I reported to my Captains on many occasions that the efficiency of the ship had been lowered by frequent drafting changes ... After representations had been made to the Naval Board, matters improved considerably. At one time in the first two years of the war I felt that every time we came near an Australian port we would lose a large number of trained men .... But after the Japanese came into the war we felt that the ship should have been stabilised as regards drafting. There were drafts of between 10 and 20 second class stokers periodically right up to the last time the ship was in port.[329]

As *Canberra* prepared for action, McMahon was worried. He had lost so many of his most experienced engineering staff only to be sent youngsters whose time in the RAN was minimal, whose training had been rushed and whose first sea posting was the cruiser for which he was responsible. The dangers involved with being a stoker had again been underlined with the sinking just two months earlier of another Australian ship, the destroyer *Nestor* on 15 June 1942. Those killed were four boiler room stokers. Boiler rooms and engine rooms are the heart and lungs of a ship and his had some very trustworthy men like Chief Stoker Malcolm De Espline Stafford (16090) and Chief Stoker Stanley Coates (16294) but they also had too many stoker IIs. He was still learning their names: Harold James Tilling (F3963), Rex Robert Dare Oliver (H2000), George Jones (W2121), Douglas Fentiman (S5832), John Walton Foulkes (F3660), and John Hough Gaston (S5767). All had drafted to *Canberra* since February – Tilling and Oliver as late as July – before the ship sailed the last time from Australia. All were between 18 and 20 and McMahon was fairly certain the fair-haired, fresh-faced 18-year-old Fentiman wasn't even shaving yet.

The air of expectation increased onboard as *Canberra* set sail from Wellington on 22 July 1942 and on 26 July rendezvoused with the larger Task Force 61, led by Vice Admiral Frank Fletcher, USN, off the Fiji Islands. Fletcher had been the commander of the American task force at the Battle of Coral Sea and had fought at the Battle of Midway. He was now given command of a combined task force, numbering 75 warships and transports that was to attack Guadalcanal in the Solomons. Fletcher arrived in the carrier USS *Saratoga* 'looking tired and drawn' and 'not really believing in the viability of the offensive[330] which he predicted would 'be a failure'.[331] Others nicknamed the plan as 'Operation Shoestring' a 'bitter reference to the lack of planning and lack of warships and transports'.[332]

Sub Lieutenant MacKenzie 'Mac' Gregory had been on a steep learning curve to achieve his bridge watch-keeping certificate since his return from overseas just months before. This attained, he stood on the bridge casting his eyes over this breathtaking fleet of 75 warships and transports (48 combat). It also included USS *North Carolina* fresh from the Battle of Midway. This massive battleship with its crew of 2,339; nine 16-inch (410 mm), 20 x 5 inch (130 mm) guns and 16 x 1.1 inch (28 mm) anti-aircraft guns could not fail to impress the *Canberra*'s company

HMAS Canberra *leaving Auckland Harbour in July 1942.*

who were thoroughly pleased they were on the same side. The crew of their own HMAS *Australia* had fought in both hemispheres, against all adversaries and most recently in the Battle of the Coral Sea. It seemed strange that *Australia* had faced so much and the closest *Canberra* had been to action was chasing ghostly German raiders and firing in anger at a supply ship and oil tanker in the process of scuttling. This time it would be the real thing

Sub Lieutenant 'Mac' Gregory, middle without hat, with his men onboard Canberra *in 1942.*[333]

and their ship looked proud and defiant amongst the eleven 8-inch cruisers.[334]

There was just time for the screening and amphibious forces to conduct a landing rehearsal on Koro Island with a conference of group commanders prior to departure for the Solomon Islands on 31 July. The rehearsal was not a success; it was rushed and radio silence ordered for security reasons, prevented imperative land-sea-air communications practice. Whilst tactical command was held by Fletcher, the Commander of the Amphibious Forces was Rear Admiral Richmond Kelly Turner, USN. Major General Alexander Archer Vandegrift, USMC, commanded the 16,000 Allied troops, primarily marines on shore. Approximately 670 carrier and land-based aircraft were to offer air cover. Unusually, the architect of 'Watchtower', Vice Admiral Ghormley, was not present but aboard his flagship USS *Argonne* near Noumea.

Also present at the meeting was Vice Admiral Victor Alexander

HMAS Canberra *(foreground), c. 1940s.*

Charles Crutchley, VC, DSC, RN. Crutchley had only assumed command of the Australian Squadron the previous month and was now placed in charge of the group designated 'Task Force 62.2', protecting the transports. As a Lieutenant during World War I, he had won the Victoria Cross (VC) and the Distinguished Service Cross (DSC). With typical impudence, sailors (when not in hearing) called him 'old goat whiskers'.

There was no time for Crutchley to confer with the cruiser captains hastily placed under his command. He did, however, have time to distribute the operational memorandum throughout the fleet. Entitled 'Special instructions to screening group and vessels assigned', this memorandum offered operational instructions for the captains of the

LEFT: *Rear Admiral Richmond Kelly Turner, USN and Major General Alexander Archer Vandegrift, USMC, confer.* RIGHT: *Vice Admiral Victor Alexander Charles Crutchley, VC, DSC, RN, c. 1942.*[335]

warships within Force 62.2.

The ships involved in Task Force 44 had operated together previously but the vast majority of the USN ships had never operated with another nationality. This was to be the first American amphibious operation since 1898 and the first land-based counter attack of the war in the Pacific.

While the Japanese were aware of the gathering fleet, they believed it was to reinforce New Guinea and the Australian coastline. Critical to the success of protecting the coast line and ensuing operations in the region were the coast watchers, a motley bunch of men and one woman, Ruby Boyle. Throughout the Solomons, along the New Guinea coast, on New Britain and New Ireland, these brave individuals, intent on aiding the Allies, scrambled up to high points on islands lugging heavy radio sets with the help of loyal Melanesian native assistants, to report on Japanese movements. So important were their activities that if captured they were immediately put to death.[336]

Commander Eric Augustas Feldt, RAN, had entered as a cadet midshipman in January 1913. He fell victim to RAN 1920 financial stringencies and became a clerk in the public service of the mandated

Jack Read (LEFT) *and Paul Mason* (RIGHT) *in RANR Lieutenant uniforms, c. 1944.*

Coastwatcher Headquarters, Guadalcanal, c. 1942.[340]

Territory of New Guinea. By 1924 he was a patrol officer and, after rising to district officer, was stationed in different parts of the territory. By 1939 Feldt was back in uniform making his presence felt in the intelligence world and was appointed Supervising Intelligence Officer. Feldt was born in Cardwell, North Queensland, and his knowledge of the tropics and New Guinea proved invaluable. Travelling by sea, air and on foot, he visited mainly British and Australian expatriates who refused to evacuate as the Japanese shadow lengthened throughout the Pacific.[337]

Jack Read and Paul Mason were two coast watchers who proved invaluable to the Solomons campaign. Lieutenant Read, RANVR, 'was blunt and straightforward, rather firm than tactful' with a deep voice and explosive laugh.[338] He was based on Sohana Island in the narrow Buka Passage off the north-western coast of Bougainville Island. Lieutenant Paul Mason, RANVR, was a plantation manager on the island of Bougainville. Born in Sydney he had been enjoying life in a lazy tropical paradise but now the region was the frontier of a

Landing on Guadalcanal by US marines. Initially the operation went smoothly but the inability to move swiftly off the beaches through thick jungle hampered the operation, c. 1942.[339]

violent war. The coastwatchers had radioed about Japanese interest in Guadalcanal in June. The Japanese attempted to capture Read and Mason but, due to their courage and extensive familiarity with the local terrain, the men escaped and the intelligence they relayed at the beginning of August was vital.

By 5 August the Allied forces were less than two days away from Guadalcanal and, for once, the weather was favourable with leaden skies and severe rain enabling them to arrive unseen into the waters off

Canberra's *Executive Officer (XO) Commander John Anthony Walsh, RAN, c. 1942.*[343]

During the Battle of Savo Island, anti-aircraft gun crews wearing flash protection clothing on the starboard side of Canberra *looking out for high level bombers. In the foreground is an S1 mounting with its twin 4-inch Mk XVI high angle gun, c. 1942.*

Signalman on flag deck of Canberra, *c. 1940s.*

the Solomon Islands, called 'The Slot'. On the night of 6 August, Allied warships bombarded the islands as the 1st Marine unit struggled into their Higgins landing craft and waded ashore in early morning of 7 August. The element of surprise aided easy footholds on the beaches, but on Tulagi, Japanese soldiers were entrenched in caves and fortified posts.

As the landing craft shuttled back and forth to Guadalcanal, it was obvious that although resistance was slight, the immediate adversary was the dense jungle. There was soon chaos as the beach became clogged with men, weaponry and supplies.

In Rabaul nearly 600 miles to the north west, Japanese pilots ran to their aircraft as last minute instructions were relayed. The twin-engine Mitsubishi G4M medium range navy bombers, codenamed 'Betty' by the Allies, were capable of reaching the Allied fleet. It was unknown if the accompanying Mitsubishi A6M Zero fighters would have enough fuel to return.

On Bougainville Paul Mason in his jungle lookout heard the roar of aircraft engines and transmitted '24 torpedo bombers headed yours' providing a window of two or more hours for the fleet to ready.[341] Almost laconically the pipe echoed through *Canberra*'s decks: 'ship will be attacked at noon by twenty-four torpedo bombers. All hands will pipe to dinner at eleven o'clock'.[342] It was hard to believe that finally this was no exercise – it was real. The excitement onboard was palpable.

Surgeon Lieutenant Kenneth Morris (RANR), c. 1944.

Canberra's executive officer (XO) was Commander John Anthony Walsh, RAN. Born in the lush region of Queensland's Darling Downs, in the town of Toowoomba, Walsh had approached his teens during a world war with militarism very much part of his life. As a 13-year-old, Walsh travelled half a continent away to RANC to begin his RAN career as a cadet midshipman on 1 January 1919. His experience at sea with the RN and RAN had been extensive and had included being a member of the commissioning crew of *Canberra*. His predisposition favoured naval intelligence and his commands had been restricted to destroyers, *Vampire* and *Waterhen*. The loss of so many experienced cruiser officers in *Sydney* and *Perth* saw him posted to *Canberra* at the end of 1941 but the XO and CO complemented each other in demeanour and experience.

The XO warned the ship's company that they needed to take all items necessary to their action stations. They would remain 'closed up' as long as required, perhaps for days. Alert gun crews dressed in heavy anti-flash gear, gloves, overalls, goggles and helmets crowded the upper deck. The 4-inch, Oberlikon and machine gun crews felt exposed but so much a part of the action, each wondering if their nerve would hold as a deep drumming sound became distinguishable.

PO James Arthur Haining (19561) was the director of the after fire control to which guns were connected. He cast his eyes on all

The power of Canberra's *8-inch guns* (ABOVE) *and the 'Y' turret 8-inch gun crew* (BELOW), *c. 1940s.*

the youthful faces gathering on the upper deck; one never knew how men would react in action. He wasn't entirely sure about himself but felt confident his professionalism would kick in. Haining had always demonstrated a high degree of that since he entered the RAN during the Depression in 1932. As the drone of aircraft engines grew louder, and *Australia* and other ships in the northern sector fired into the heavens, Haining thought of wife Freda, his little girl, Carmen and the new baby yet to be born. He waited for the command from the Gunnery Officer, Lieutenant Commander Hole, for *Canberra* to open fire.

The air attack was almost an anti-climax because as the 27 'Betty' medium bombers and 17 Japanese fighters approached they were attacked by the Grumman F4F Wildcat fighters from US carriers. The excitement was in the battle above as aircraft dived and exploded and although *Canberra*'s guns belched fire and lead into the sky, the cruiser was never in danger. The Bagley class destroyer USS *Mugford* downed two aircraft before a bomb killed eight sailors and wounded 17. A further 10 crew were designated 'missing' but it was the American pilots who saved the invasion force.

Canberra remained closed up which meant meals were commonly sandwiches as the cooks were themselves at their action stations around the ship. Some of the more prepared had ensured they had procured canteen snacks prior to taking up their positions. For Signaller Francis William Salisbury Pickup (23143) it was a long way from his civilian occupation as a 'milk carter' in Brisbane to standing on the flagdeck of a cruiser with guns going off. He had entered as an ordinary seaman II but the flag, flash and Morse code skills did not come easily. There were four fails and 18 months before he could sew on his signalman rate (insignia). *Canberra* was the only ship he had known. Pickup had prepared his emergency bag to accompany him to action stations. Tightly bound with rubber bands was a pair of socks, handkerchief, singlet, underpants, shirt, torch (capable of being used for Morse signals), comb, piece of soap, small hand towel, mirror, toothbrush and paste, seaman's knife, a few bandaids, the inflatable life jacket, a tin of peaches and, most importantly 'a small pot of Vegemite'.[344]

A restless night had left crews weary and they stretched stiff muscles and joints and longed for bunks and hammocks; nerves were frayed through the strain, lack of sleep and the tropical heat and humidity. It was 8 August and crews were now on their third successive day at action stations. Coast watcher Jack Read signalled from Bougainville, '40 heavy bombers proceeding south east'. The air-raid alarm startled men out of their tropical lethargy and the fleet rapidly formed air defence disposition, adopting a bow first silhouette, pointing ships toward enemy aircraft. Ears strained to hear the whining of aircraft engines, eyes struggled to define cloud and birds from wings of a more threatening type.

For those below decks, the waiting and the temperature bordered on unbearable. There was no opportunity to actively participate in the action, no chance to see what was taking place in the air and on the ocean. Each time the alarm sounded, they struggled into overalls, gloves, helmets and goggles, and attempted to lie in the most sheltered spot they could find. The silence was tense as they waited and listened until they felt and heard the succession of *Canberra*'s armament discharge, the thump thump of the 8-inch, the rapid firing 4-inch pom poms, the chatter of the Oerlikon 20 mm and the rattle of the machine guns.

The cacophony increased to a barely bearable pitch. You 'sweat in real earnest because you know that they are just starting to let go their bombs or torpedoes', wrote Surgeon Lieutenant Kenneth Newman Morris (RANR), 'imagination left to itself ... If one could only see what was going on things wouldn't be so bad'.[345]

Morris had dressed in naval uniform for the first time on 9 February and arrived in *Canberra* a mere fortnight later.

The Victorian had thought his life plans were settled when he did well in his medical studies and had his eyes set on a small, quiet suburban general practice. Those plans had evaporated and here he was on an Australian heavy cruiser listening to gunfire.

Swimming out of the pool of perspiration that you have been
lying in (relieved always to find that it is only perspiration) and
going up on deck to find out if there are any wrecked planes to
be seen.[346]

It was after noon when high-level bombers dropped their bombs but they were too high to accomplish precision bombing and damage. Then a second wave roared in. 'Betty' torpedo bombers almost skimming the water before releasing their charges. The crew of another Bagley Class destroyer USS *Jarvis* could do nothing as anti-aircraft fire consumed one incoming aircraft and its torpedo exploded against the starboard side killing 14. Another bomber was hit and, on fire, deliberately flew into the transport USS *George F Elliott* disintegrating on impact. A massive blaze destroyed the ship which was abandoned. Seventeen Japanese aircraft were brought down and a cheer went up as the remainder retired. It was another minor victory, and the landings could continue.

For those on *Canberra*'s upper deck, it was a massive adrenalin rush as 'a magnificent curtain of bursting high explosive was put up and enemy aircraft were everywhere crashing in flames.'[347] Gun crews on the 4-inch had a great view as their gun turned and elevated to fire at one then another. The 8-inch gun crews were not so fortunate, shut away in armoured enclosed turrets, stuck in what they referred to as 'this greasy hole'. They had been closed up for two days and had yet to fire. The gunhouse was the size of a small civilian dining room, crammed with operating gear, levers, buttons, gadgets, miles of steel piping for the hydraulic system and the men who had polished the breeches until they gleamed. Each man was highly trained because being member of an 8-inch crew was seen as the ultimate for gunnery seamen. Each of the four *Canberra* turret captains was hunched over the loading levers – their No. 2 ready by the breeches, their No. 4 by the elevating wheel which faced the receiving dials, their No. 3 ready to ram the cordite charge into the breech. The gunhouse was like an oven – no sea breeze, no sound, no ray of sunlight penetrated here. There was just the smell of cordite, oil and human sweat. Then the order came from the bridge.

Stand by for bombardment ... all left guns load with H.E. fused to 600 yards, all right guns with H.E. fused to 800 yards.[348]

Turret teams jumped almost in surprise before following the well-practised routine. 'Barrage, torpedo bombers. We're going to fire broadsides and bracket them'[349]. Twin breeches swung effortlessly open, 256 pound steel and high explosive shells appeared from below to the top of the hoist, 65 pounds of cordite were rammed into each breech and as the breech blocks closed, the turret captains reported 'Both guns loaded, ready.' The crews crouched and waited for the command, 'Fire' and the thunderous roar that caused the cruiser to convulse. USN officers witnessing the barrage were astounded that the Australians were using 8-inch against aircraft and were thoroughly impressed by their effectiveness.[350]

Bruce Hamilton Loxton had entered the RANC in January 1938 after an education at Sydney's Newington and Scots Colleges. After war was declared, he and his class were anxious to be part of it. Cadet Midshipman Loxton gained four months seniority with first class passes in physics and chemistry and won the 'Otto Albert' prize for seamanship. There were no long winded graduation speeches at the end of four years, no real graduation celebrations, just a rapid posting to *Canberra* before Christmas 1941 and promotion on 1 January 1942.

On the afternoon of 8 August, Midshipman Loxton, standing on the bridge, had an bird's eye view of the action.

Canberra opened fire as they came down close to the water. They passed down our port side out of range of the Oerlikons, but the port 4-inch had an excellent target. We fired an 8-inch barrage, but the results were not seen. Two bombers sheered out of line and headed towards our bow ... We succeeded in bringing down one if not both of them.[351]

Having just witnessed the destruction of a second Japanese air attack in two days, like the rest of *Canberra*'s officers and sailors, Loxton was relieved and elated. Within hours, the 18-year-old midshipman would suffer shocking wounds and be struggling to stay alive.

Once you gave a poor devil a shot of morphine you would write an 'M' on their forehead in blood, there was no shortage of it.

Able Seaman Henry Longdon Hall, RAN.[352]

As the excitement and adrenalin dissipated, exhaustion seeped into every muscle; it was difficult to decide if hunger and thirst dominated the mind more than sleep. Clothes stuck to bodies and men scratched at three-day-old beards. Perhaps a shave and wash would be good too. Japanese aircraft had come and been shot down. Surely now they could rest, surely now the Japanese would struggle to send another air attack tomorrow on 9 August 1942. Men looked to their superiors for the answers.

At 1830, Admiral Crutchley ordered his screening fleet to adopt night disposition and patrols commenced. It was such a relief to hear second degree of readiness piped. Half the crew remained closed up at action stations, part of the damage control crews were in place, 8-inch turrets 'A' and 'X' were manned as were single port and starboard 4-inch gun crews, though the guns were not loaded.[353] The more fortunate could submit to the fatigue and sleep at or near their stations. A quiet stillness enveloped the cruiser, with just the noise of the wash to be heard. The phosphorescence of the ship's wake shone in the moonlight before dark and heavy clouds heralded the arrival of more tropical rain squalls.

Captain Getting was in his cabin immediately below the bridge, fully dressed, sitting in a chair. Finally he was able to close his eyes. The gunnery and torpedo officers, Lieutenant Commanders Hole and Plunkett-Cole, also fully dressed, were asleep on bunks in the Admiral's sea cabin. On the bridge stood duty staff looking seaward, slightly envious of those able to relax. Just as 8 August became 9 August, Sub Lieutenant MacKenzie 'Mac' Gregory climbed to the bridge and took over as Officer of the Watch (OOW) for the 2400–0400 watch. He familiarised himself with the course: '130 deg, speed 12 knots, reversing that course on the hour by turning to starboard without signal'. USS *Chicago* was stationed three cables (600 yards) astern, the escorting destroyers USS *Patterson* and *Bagley* were 45 degrees on *Canberra*'s port and starboard bow respectively, five cables (1,000 yards) distance.

The duty principal control officer (PCO) was Lieutenant Commander Ewan James Byam Wight, RAN, a mature officer who had fallen victim to governmental and RAN personnel cuts in 1930. He was brought back into the RAN on temporary service in 1940 because there were too few officers. Navigator, Lieutenant Commander Mesley, left the bridge to sleep, though instructing the young OOW to wake him in time for the 0145 course change. In the earliest hour of the morning of 9 August, more US marines, weighed down with weapons and equipment, splashed onto white tropical beaches which before the war had been idyllic. 'Mac' was pleased to have dry feet. Though weary, he was comfortably attired with ready access to hot sustenance. Who in their right mind would not choose to fight this war at sea! Lightning flashes broke the darkness and rain reduced visibility once again to as little as 100 yards (91 metres). Conversation was sparse as each man on the bridge engaged in interconnected duties. The mood was calm but there were two concerns. When 'Mac' had relieved Acting Sub Lieutenant Royston Miller Dawborn, RANR, Dawborn had mentioned that 'aircraft engines had been heard' and the captain had been informed.[354] More unsettling was that the comforting bulk of the sister ship, the heavy cruiser flagship *Australia*, had vanished from the front of the column.

At 2045 Rear Admiral Turner had summoned Crutchley and

Vandegrift to his command ship, the transport *McCawley*, off Guadalcanal, to discuss the implications of the hasty and unexpected decision by Vice Admiral Fletcher to withdraw his carriers. Fletcher was anxious. He was charged with three of four US aircraft carriers in the Pacific and believed a Japanese submarine attack was imminent. His carrier fighter strength had been reduced from 99 aircraft to 78 during the last days defending the invasion fleet. He also cited a lack of fuel but this was without foundation. Fletcher had signalled Vice Admiral Ghormley at 1807 on 8 August that he wished to withdraw his carriers immediately, a day earlier than planned. Fletcher did not wait for confirmation from the South-West Pacific Commander and Admiral Fletcher and his carriers headed south. The implications for the invasion force were grave. Three days of air defence had been promised, not two. Other than the obvious vulnerability to ships and men, it could result in a shortfall of supplies for the marines as the Guadalcanal runway was not expected to be operational until 17 August at the earliest. Turner later described Fletcher's withdrawal as 'desertion'.[355]

The departure of *Australia* meant that not only was the flag officer not present, but the southern force was considerably weakened. Prior to his departure, Crutchley signalled Captain Howard D. Bode, USN, CO of *Chicago* that, as Senior Captain, he should take charge of the patrol and *Chicago* should assume a position at the head of the column. Crutchley

USS Chicago (LEFT) *and its Commanding Officer, Captain Howard D. Bode, USN* (RIGHT), *c. 1942.*[357]

failed to inform the commanders of the other screening cruiser groups of his departure. Captain 'Bing' Bode was 'an aloof man, lacking a knack for friendship'. He 'possessed supreme self-confidence and in his mind there was no doubt that he would achieve flag rank' but he 'was rarely one to consult his officers and this case was no exception'.[356] Bode decided Crutchley was likely to return early morning and, to avoid the dangers involved in night manoeuvres, decided to remain astern of *Canberra*. Bode chose not to actively take command, retired to his night cabin and went to sleep.

The conference on Turner's flagship concluded around midnight. The superior officers discussed intelligence received concerning Japanese ships, believed to be 'three cruisers, three destroyers and two seaplane tenders or gunboats east of Bougainville Island, steering south east'.[358] Turner believed the enemy was destined for Rekata Bay possibly to operate floatplanes against the invasion force the following day. The meeting broke up and the commanders returned to their flagships. Crutchley, a product of his generation imbued with British racial superiority and the belief that the Japanese were unable to 'see' and attack at night, was comfortable with his decision not to return *Australia* to the southern group before morning. This was not communicated and *Canberra* remained at the head of the patrol.

Vice Admiral Gunichi Mikawa of the Imperial Japanese Navy (ABOVE) *and his flagship,* Chokai (BELOW), *c. 1942.*[359]

Commander of the Rabaul-based Japanese Eighth Fleet, Vice Admiral Gunichi Mikawa, IJN, knew air attacks on the invasion force had not been successful and ordered his squadron of seven cruisers – his flagship *Chokai, Aoba, Kako, Kinugasa, Furutaka, Tenryu, Yubari* and the destroyer *Yunagi* – to raise steam. By 1930 on 8 August his fleet had proceeded north of Buka Island and then down the east coast of Bougainville. Shortly after midday, the Japanese sighted a Hudson bomber shadowing the fleet. Mikawa ordered an alteration of course hoping to confuse the Allied pilot. Shortly after the aircraft disappeared and the fleet had re-grouped, a second Hudson was seen. *Chokai* opened fire and the aircraft flew away. Believing his ships would come under air attack from US carrier-based fighters, Mikawa paused the fleet east of Kieta for six hours. Surprisingly, no air attack came. He was confident in the extensive training his officers and sailors had undergone in night attacks and equally convinced the Allies did not expect a sea attack at night. But they may have lost the element of surprise as Allied reconnaissance aircraft had spotted them. Mikawa wondered if his ships were now sailing into an ambush.

Five RAAF Hudson reconnaissance aircraft had recently moved from Horn Island in the Torres Strait to the completed Papuan Milne Bay Fall River strip. The crews were not briefed on 'Operation Watchtower' and the invasion landings. At 1025, the Japanese ships were spotted by a Hudson crew. Though told to retain radio silence, the crew decided that the size of the Japanese fleet and the direction in which it was sailing was vital information and pilot Flight Sergeant William Stutt ordered his radio operator/gunner Sergeant Eric Geddes to transmit the intelligence immediately to Fall River. The crew realised that breaking radio silence would place them in immediate danger and quickly two Japanese fighters climbed into the sky. 'We thought we can't stand and fiddle around with these people – we've got to deliver this intelligence.'[360]

Stutt managed to bring his crew back alive and debriefed immediately. It is unclear if the fleet was misidentified by the crew as 'three destroyers, two seaplane tenders and three cruisers' or the report was altered by Milne Bay intelligence officers. A second Hudson spotted the Japanese fleet at just after 1100. The crew reported the disposition and that they had been fired on when they returned to Fall River at 1500. Neither report was relayed to the Allied fleet off Guadalcanal until 1845 and 2130 on 8 August.

Mikawa launched floatplanes for his own reconnaissance and they returned with Allied fleet displacement reports – formidable in one way but strangely not in another. Mikawa's fleet was outgunned but with the Allied ships so divided and dispersed, and apparently still unaware, the Japanese Admiral remained confident. His fleet entered 'The Slot' close to 1600 unchallenged.

Admiral Turner requested Rear Admiral John Sidney 'Slew' McCain Sr, USN, Commander of Allied Air Forces, South Pacific, to conduct reconnaissance missions over 'The Slot' during the afternoon of the 8 August but McCain did not, nor did he relay to Turner that these flights would not take place.

As light faded on 8 August, Japanese warships steamed at 24 knots line-ahead through 'The Slot' and as speed was increased to 30 knots in St George Channel, the fleet almost ran over USN submarine *S38*. The enemy was too close for the submarine CO, Commander Henry Glass Munson, USN, to fire torpedoes but his crew immediately radioed a warning. Again the warning was not heeded. Mikawa launched

Eric Geddes far right and the Hudson crew who broke radio silence to report the Japanese fleet, c. 1942.

floatplanes and these were heard at around 2345. On the seaward side of Savo, USS *Ralph Talbot* reported sighting the aircraft to *Canberra* via TBS radio but the Australian warships were not fitted with TBS and never received the report. Mikawa, leading the 2 mile (3 km) column in *Chokai*, hoped his luck would last as he entered the narrow gap separating Savo Island from Guadalcanal, when his lookouts sighted the USN destroyer *Blue* at a distance of around 5.5 miles (9 km) ahead.

Vice Admiral Crutchley had ordered radar-equipped *Ralph Talbot* and *Blue* to patrol west of Savo Island. Radar range of both was believed to be about 10 miles (16 km) but from Crutchley down to those who operated the primitive radar systems, all were unacquainted with the limitations of these systems particularly with how badly radar effectiveness was degraded by nearby landmasses.

Mikawa altered course to north of Savo Island and ordered his warships to slow to 22 knots (41 km) so that ships' wakes were less visible. All guns were directed towards *Blue*. The radar picket reached the end of its patrol track, less than one mile (2 km) from the enemy. Oblivious, *Blue* simply reversed course and steamed away. The Japanese

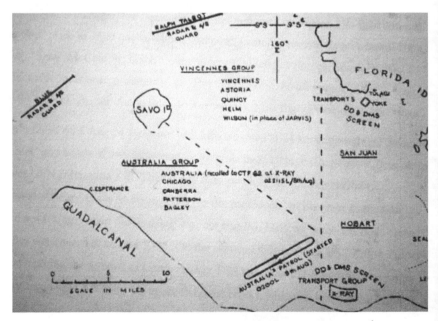

Disposition of ships in 'The Slot' on the night of 8 August 1942.[362]

Admiral could scarcely believe his good fortune and, again turning his fleet southward, increased speed to 26 knots (48 km) and then 30 knots (56 km) as his ships entered the Sealark Channel south of Savo Island.

Admiral Mikawa and his fleet had seemingly infinite luck – the Allies appeared asleep, 'the American look-outs apparently blind and their ships' radar not functioning'.[361] It was the look-outs on his flagship *Chokai* who sighted *Canberra* and *Chicago* dead ahead.

A parachute flare dropped from one of the same aircraft starkly silhouetted all directly before them. The Japanese released the first of 61 'Long Lance' torpedoes to be fired on 9 August 1942 and commenced a barrage of withering fire on the cruiser steaming at the front, HMAS *Canberra*.

Sub Lieutenant 'Mac' Gregory nervously checked his watch as he was very aware he must wake Lieutenant Commander Mesley at 0145 so the navigator could fix the cruiser's position prior to the 0200 scheduled course alteration. It was 0143, two minutes to go. There was an explosion almost due north and *Canberra*'s port look-out reported a ship ahead. Lieutenant Commander Wight could see nothing, nor the Yeoman of Signals, nor 'Mac'. USS *Patterson* on the port bow signalled 'Warning, warning. Strange ships entering harbour', increased speed and changed course rapidly. Wight hit the action alarm and the *Canberra* crew rushed to assume first-degree readiness. Out of the wet, dark gloom, three ships appeared on the starboard bow and Wight ordered the 8-inch turrets loaded. In seconds Captain Getting, the navigator, and gunnery and torpedo officers arrived on the bridge.

The gunnery officer took over from Wight and Wight moved to aft of 'X' turret. Hole ordered 'Port 35 degrees' and 'Load, Load, Load'.[363] As the cruiser swung to port torpedo, tracks were sighted approaching the starboard side. Captain Getting shouted 'Hard a'starboard, full ahead'. As the ship began to swing, Plunkett-Cole crossed to the port torpedo control to fire the port tubes and Hole moved quickly to the port enemy bearing indicator and shouted 'open fire'. Mesley had taken over from the youthful OOW so 'Mac' hurried to his action station in the fore control above the bridge for his regular duties of estimating the course and speed of enemy warships for the transmitting station.

Flares and star shells lit up the sky – the Australian cruiser was silhouetted in glaring illumination. 'Mac' looked through his binoculars only to have the lenses fill with six Japanese cruisers and a destroyer approaching rapidly in attack formation. His loud utterance surprised even him: 'My God, this is bloody awful'.[364] 'Mac' was enveloped by deafening noise which crushed the mind and riveted the body. Shrapnel strafed the space. The sailor beside him was killed by a large piece of shrapnel to the back of the head.

Torpedo Officer Lieutenant Punkett-Cole, c. 1944.

Hole was standing on the port side of the compass platform passing orders to his gunnery control. Getting was standing next to him. There was an explosion amidships, on the 4-inch gundeck. One shell exploded in the vicinity of the forward funnel spraying shrapnel into men in the vicinity of No. 7 and No. 3 Oerlikon and the Flag Deck. The Seagull aircraft resting on its catapult burst into flames. Midshipman Loxton, roused from a deep sleep, ran out of the charthouse and up two ladders to his action station on the port side of the bridge. The ship was swinging rapidly to starboard and 'accelerating, with the funnels vibrating'.[365] Hole crossed to the same position and ordered Loxton out of his way. 'I stepped back ... there was an explosion ... Thrown backwards ... I ended up on the deck'.[366] Loxton had been peppered with pieces of metal and was losing blood rapidly.

The shell which exploded on the port side just below the compass platform decapitated Lieutenant Commander Hole. Plunkett-Cole at the bridge port torpedo control position was knocked off his feet. As he stood a shell ploughed into the bridge. Struggling to get upright again he became aware that his clothes were on fire. 'The torpedo officer arrived

Captain Frank Getting, c. 1940s.

on the platform smouldering quite fiercely – we put him out, and only learned later that he had been well spotted with shrapnel'.[367] Mesley was temporarily blinded by the explosion that wrecked the plot office. As his sight cleared, he realised the gunnery officer was dead and the compass platform was littered with bodies.

Captain Getting was struggling to sit up and asking about the state of his ship. He had horrible injuries – his right leg from the knee down was almost shot away, both his hands were damaged, shell fragments were imbedded in his face and his head wounds were bleeding badly.

Surgeon Commander Downward was summoned to what was left of the bridge. Scrambling over wreckage and the maimed, he examined Getting. The captain insisted others should be treated first and told the doctor he was all right – both men probably realised the injuries were fatal. Downward began to leave the bridge stepping over Midshipman Loxton whom he believed was dead. Loxton was unimpressed. As he wrote later, I 'assured him that I was not'.[368] Downward administered morphia and hurried back to the sick bay flat which had received a direct hit – so many men injured, so many terrible injuries.

Commander Charles Anthony Downward, RAN, had been in the RAN since 1925 when he was 27. He had found civilian medicine unexciting. By August 1942, there was barely an Australian ship he had not served in – but nothing had prepared him for this.

The screams of wounded ... the first casualty appeared with his left arm shot away. A tourniquet had just been adjusted and morphia injected to him and three other casualties, when the lights failed and all water supplies were cut off. From then on it became necessary for members of the first-aid party to use their initiative.[369]

These thoughts fleetingly crossed the mind of Surgeon Lieutenant Ken Morris also. Morris had been asleep on a mess table when abruptly woken by the ship's alarm. He tugged on a pair of overalls and was already moving as he pulled on shoes. 'Some casualties came staggering in much to my surprise as I didn't even know that we had been hit'.[370] He began to work frantically, applying tourniquets as his medical party arrived. Power, light and water were cut. Morris fastened a torch to a headband and continued as best he could to assess and instruct the stewards, cooks and any volunteers – none had trained for this.

Shells continued to penetrate the Australian cruiser with such ferocity and speed that it was impossible to know their exact sequence. A shell ploughed into the port side of the torpedomen's mess deck, another on the port side foretopmen's mess deck exploding against 'B' turret, another into the port side of the stokers' mess deck, another to the port side of the seaman's lower mess deck, another into the vicinity of the main galley and into the sick bay flat, another into the sick bay dispensary, another into the seaman petty officers' mess bursting into 'A' boiler fan flat, another in the after director, another in the gunroom flat, another penetrated through the cypher office to the shell handling room. One hit the warrant officer's flat and another hit the ERA mess bursting into 'B' boiler room. Between 24 and 28 shells hit *Canberra* in less than three minutes and the crew was unable to fire a shot.

Engineer Command McMahon hit the deck running and arrived in the main engine room half a minute after full speed was run through and machinery was being worked up to full power. Then the pressures dropped to nothing and the cruiser stopped dead in the water. McMahon was on the move and approached first one and then the second boiler room fan flat. All was a shambles – ladders crushed, gratings wrecked, fan engine casings scattered, steam pipes fractured – everything blackened by fire before being doused with steam. He climbed to the bridge, found his seriously wounded CO propped up and conscious.

Feeling inadequate, he apologised for the complete loss of power. In a painful splutter Getting replied, 'Do your best, Mac'.[371]

McMahon returned to the dead innards of his cruiser knowing there was nothing he could do but order those who remained in engine rooms to evacuate before they died of asphyxiation and to help supervise the flooding of compartments. He had lost good men including Temporary Engineer Lieutenant Douglas Grenfell Hazelton, RANR, who had climbed *Canberra*'s gangway in his brand new naval uniform during the recent refit. Also lost were all those stoker IIs whose names he was still learning: Harold James Tilling (F3963) Rex Robert Dare Oliver (H2000), George Jones (W2121), Douglas Fentiman (S5832), John Walton Foulkes (F3660), John Hough Gaston (S5767). All had recently joined the RAN; all were aged between 18 and 20.

Mechanician Frederick Keith Gorham (17329) had moved rapidly to his action station in the 'A' boiler room fan flat.[372] Gorham stood near the port airlock door with two young sailors whose names he didn't know. A shell pierced the fan flat from the port side and exploded near the chief stokers mess between bulkheads 118 and 127. Gorham thought 'how easily the shell had penetrated the armour plating'.[373] Dust and smoke smothered those in the fan flat and less than a second later, another shell cut through hitting the port fan, projecting pieces in all directions. A dull explosion and all the fans stopped and the lights went out. Gorham was thrown backward against a bulkhead. 'Briefly it was dead quiet'.[374] Regaining his feet, he grabbed one shocked sailor and pushed him up the port door of bulkhead 105 into the sick bay flat. He knew he must go back. He found the second young sailor badly cut on the head and dazed. 'Smoke and fumes of a strong sweetish smell'[375] made Gorham vomit. Smoke, steam, dust and fumes pushed him backwards. Gorham shouted below into the 'A' boiler room 'but heard no reply ... no one could possibly be alive'. Feeling 'rather shaken and about finished' he dragged the injured sailor to a medical centre.[376]

Stoker II Percival Charles Ackerman (S5651), another of those very green stoker IIs, had been in 'B' boiler room most of the day. Acting Chief Stoker Stanley Coates told him 'to get a couple of hours sleep'. Instead Ackerman decided to wash his three pairs of sweaty overalls.

Engineering staff the most vulnerable to torpedo attack.

Dressed in only a pair of shorts, he ran to his locker for his boots when the alarm rang. He had forgotten his life jacket and needed to retrace his steps to

collect it. Just that delay of a few seconds was all it took. He only got as far as the fan flat. 'After that I only remember coming to, it was hot, and I was burnt'.377 The hot grating was imprinted on his back, his boots were blown off and his feet and face were burnt – skin hung from his body. Those few seconds meant he was only as far as the air lock. It seemed surreal; his brain was jumbled and he remembered the chat he had had less than an hour ago with Stoker Cecil O'Rourke and Chief Stoker Stanley Coates who with others in the boiler room were now presumably dead. And then the pain hit.

A shell exploded in the after end of the damage control headquarters (DCHQ) killing many of those best trained to save their ship; people like Chief Electrical Artificer James Kidd (13821) and the legendary Chief Engine Room Artificer Arthur Allen (11535) – both had mentored so many RAN artificers. Lieutenant Engineer Brynmor Mussared was the damage control officer in DCHQ.

> I had the impression of a kick in the back, a great flash and then apparently lost consciousness. I next found myself on my hands and knees in the port for'd corner of DCHQ and had the impression of another explosion and later found myself on my hands and knees in the cross passage.[378]

Mussared struggled to the DCHQ: 'the place was full of rubbish and apparently dead bodies'. He hobbled into the gunroom flat to the secondary DCHQ where there were two bodies on the deck. Chief Stoker Walter Gordon Hunter (7605) was at action station with DCHQ messenger Stoker Roy Stephens when the alarm was sounded at approximately 0150. They heard a very rapid increase in the revs of the main engines, a shouted warning to take cover before two heavy explosions shook the ship. Minor explosions followed along with the noise of escaping steam. Another heavy explosion came from the regulating office flat. All primary lighting failed. Hunter switched on his torch, stepped into the starboard passage and saw fire.

Below decks the enormous amount of flammable material in the regulating and police offices ignited. Furniture made from Australian timber that was unable to be fireproofed burned, and flames curled up bulkheads yet to be stripped of their many coats of glamour paint. Stoker John Strachan (5588), a member of the oil transfer party, fell into Hunter's arms crying that he was dying. 'He was in a bad way and I lay him on the deck of the engineers office'.[379] Strachan died. Hunter stepped into the passage again and heard cries for help forward. He helped another sailor who was unrecognisable. The regulating office was an inferno and flames were pouring out of the after engine room fan flat. By now the ship was listing to starboard. Hunter found Lieutenant Mussared wounded in the leg and back. Only four escaped from DCHQ, Chief Shipwright Henry Shepherd, 41, was not one of them, nor Acting Lieutenant (E) Brabazon Duke Yonge, 22.

Dudley Robin Ross (S6218) was still getting used to a change of uniform from a corporal in the militia to the navy uniform of an ordinary seaman – which had only occurred in January. Ross had joined his first ship, this cruiser, in June. He was 19. Stretched out on the settee and dozing, he heard a dull boom and felt the ship shudder. His inexperience told him the escorting destroyers were depth charging. Just the same he went to his cabin to gather his helmet. The alarm wailed so he climbed up to the main deck, his brain struggling to comprehend. Enemy searchlights lit the deck as if it were daytime and everything seemed to be exploding. Ross began climb up to his action position on the bridge. As he passed the flag deck, a shell tore into the catapult and the aircraft began to burn. More shells exploded on the 4-inch gun deck, one very close to the flag deck and one on or near the compass platform. Eight seconds later another explosion blew him into the chart house.

> I could hear the groans of the wounded all around ... there were
> several badly wounded lying there including one at the foot of
> the ladder below the chart house and another on the main deck
> abreast of the starboard cutter. Signalman 'Snowy' Thurlow
> was on the Flag Deck and he appeared to have been instantly
> killed.[380]

It was a lot to deal with when you are only 19. Signalman William James Thurlow (24364) was 21. Bill Thurlow had enlisted in the RAN from Melbourne with his younger brother Thomas Cecil Thurlow (24365). Tommy was 19. Both trained at *Cerberus* for over a year to qualify as Ordinary Signalmen, both drafted on the same day to *Manoora* to perfect practical skills, both drafted together as Signalmen to *Canberra* on 23 November 1941. In the early hours of 9 August, Tommy learnt his elder brother was dead.[381]

Hugh Edward Wilkinson (PM2891) was an auburn-haired writer from Victoria. *Canberra* was his first ship. There was another Wilkinson in *Canberra*, Herbert Sidney Roy Wilkinson (14782), but in no way were the men similar. Six years younger than Herbert, Hugh would have preferred to be anywhere else and Herbert 'Bert' would have wanted to be nowhere else. The older Wilkinson had entered the

RAN from Sydney in 1924 as a Boy Seaman 2nd grade. He regarded *Canberra* as 'his ship and his home' because other than leave and two months additional *Cerberus* training, he had been attached to the cruiser since July 1933. The three-badge PO took his responsibilities in the after control very seriously.

Writer Wilkinson was look-out on the port side of after control. He heard 'much swishing of water and saw a number of ships moving around'.[382] It was pitch black and he couldn't make out what was going on. The less experienced Wilkinson moved backwards to ask the director of after control, PO James Haining, if this was significant – if anyone could figure this out it would surely be the two-badge career PO. A shell crashed into the vicinity of the aircraft from 'very short range'. The nearby after control was lit up by a star shell and in that instant Wilkinson thought 'destroyer about 200 yards to port' flashing a search light towards the stern of his cruiser before another shell disintegrated the area in front of him.

Flames flashed out from the inner space. 'PO Haining was lying on the floor in a great deal of blood'.[383] There was groaning and Wilkinson observed his senior namesake, PO Wilkinson, 'in his chair and his legs twisted up and in a horrible mess'.[384]

The 20-year-old AB James Coleman Harris (PA2100) was not moving. POs Haining and Wilkinson and AB Harris were three of those who did not leave their ship on 9 August. The question which would forever haunt Hugh Wilkinson was, 'what if I had moved closer to Haining, Harris or Wilkinson?'.[385]

Those in the three medical centres were working at a frenetic pace but still not fast enough to deal with the injured. 'There was no need for stretcher parties to bring in their wounded; we already had as many as we could cope with'.[386] Supplies were running low. A jagged piece of shrapnel had torn away half the chest of 18-year-old Stoker II Raymond Norman Boys (PA2283). Commander Downward was trying to bind it with cellophane. Boys had been standing near Stoker George Stanley Yeates (22892). When the smoke from the explosion cleared, Yeates shouted, 'Look! Someone's arm has been shot off'.[387] He looked down and realised his own was severed just below the elbow. The medical party included the ship's butcher who skilfully tied a ligature to the stump saving the 20-year-old's life. Downward was moving towards Yeates when he slipped in a pool of blood and landed heavily. 'Most of us had a fall that night what with the grease and blood and darkness and slant of the ship'.[388] Now under the pain-relieving effect of morphine, Yeates enquired where the arm was because it had his wristwatch and a ring on it and he would like them back.

Canberra's Roman Catholic Chaplain, Father W. D. Evans was unable to salvage his vestment from his burning cabin to offer the last rites (viaticum) to the dying so he improvised. They didn't mind and he struggled to recognise the Catholics from the non-Catholics anyway. Then shells hit the sick bay and dispensary, medical parties and the wounded again were victims. 'I picked myself up and dimly saw very still figures lying on bloody, greasy decks'.[389] Those who could stand helped the still living up top.

The upper deck was chaotic, indeed every bit as hellish as anyone could imagine. Fires raged everywhere on *Canberra* and the ocean seemed full of warships ablaze. Surgeon Lieutenant Morris found himself tending wounded beneath the burning Seagull in the area of the aircraft workshop. The men who wore a different shade of blue uniform stood little chance with the direct hit to the catapult under which was their mess. Flight Lieutenant Duncan John Murchison (260818), Corporal Joseph Kenneth Croft (21237), Leading Aircraftsmen Geoffrey George Chapman (60224) and Victor Ronald Egginton (20243), 9 Squadron RAAF, would no longer exchange banter as to whose was the better service. Morris looked up to see the flames spreading along

The Battle of Savo Island, 8 and 9 August 1942.[390]

the wings towards the attached four 100 pound bombs. 'The wings fell off and I moved off with rare speed.'[391] Fortunately with such a short fall to the deck, the bombs did not explode. Only three of the seven-strong Seagull detachment were still alive: Leading Aircraftsmen James Ronald Kenneth McCormack (20914), Frederick George Rivers (32088) and Gordon Douglas Poole (25089). Morris did what he could but McCormack died, Rivers struggled to stay alive and Poole somehow escaped with only slight injuries, showing yet again the fickleness of fate.

While they all desperately tried to keep men alive, they played 'hide and seek with our own 4-inch ammunition − a lot of which we stored in ready use lockers on the deck'.[392] As the fire reached a new locker, everyone dived behind the nearest cover'.[393] The fire raged and 'cancer-like, the flames, fuelled by several coats of paint since 1925, spread uncontrollably.'[394]

The shelling then stopped. The Japanese fleet was cutting a deadly swathe now through northern Allied warships so the emphasis was to extinguish the fires, to save *Canberra*. But there was no power and no water pressure. Bucket brigades were organised, almost ridiculous, rows of men heaving buckets of sea water up and along the deck. It seemed futile but the effort continued.

DCHQ messenger Stoker 'Roy' Stephens was instructed by the wounded Lieutenant Mussared to run to the bridge and inform the captain that the DCHQ had been hit with casualties. Mussared refused to give into his own injuries and was now operating from the secondary damage control HQ. Stephens was 19, had been in the RAN for just over a year and *Canberra* since January. He had 'never been to the bridge before'.[396] As he picked his way around damage, he reached the bridge after it had been shelled.

Stoker Roy Stephens, c. 1940s.[395]

He made the report to one of the few officers still standing and returned with the instruction for Mussared to try to 'stabilize the ship by pumping water and/or oil from the starboard to port tanks'.[397] Clearly whoever remained on the bridge failed to comprehend how the loss of power was just that. Stephens was despatched again to the bridge with the message that it was 'impossible as there was no power to pump anything' because the fans had been hit so 'there was no way of generating power'.[398] The only power available was battery that enabled the secondary lighting system to operate. He returned with an equally confused message from the bridge. Chief Stoker Geoffrey Hunter had finally persuaded Mussared to rest. He simply told Stephens 'there was nothing more' that could be done and that the youthful stoker should join a bucket brigade.

'Mac' Gregory was stunned and decided to clamber back up to the fore control to retrieve his cap with its highly-prized Gieves gold embroidered cap badge. The journey was dangerous but the word 'dangerous' had taken on a new meaning. There was a large shell hole where he had tossed his cap prior to the attack. 'Mac' retraced his steps.

> I came across two sailors with a body on a stretcher. They
> were lifting up this person to drain away the trapped blood.
> On investigation I made out Bruce Loxton ... Bruce had
> ghastly wounds and I did not believe he would survive. He was
> conscious and I said 'How are you Bruce?' His response was
> 'I will be alright' and his fighting spirit pulled him through.[399]

'Mac' grabbed sailors and started another fire party.

At 0325 hearts leapt as out of the smoky gloom a destroyer loomed. They were defenceless, there was absolutely nothing they could do. As the destroyer cast over lines never were Australians so pleased to see Yanks – USS *Patterson* had returned to help. Hoses and portable pumps were passed up and pulled onboard the listing cruiser – it might just be possible to save what was left.

There was a great deal of frustration vented through colourful language when it was found that, no matter how hard they tried,

American hoses did not connect to Australian couplings. It was 'futile' and the fires continued. The list increased to about 17 degrees and there were internal explosions and rumbling deep in the hull. Executive Officer, Commander John Walsh, though wounded himself, had assumed control and issued the order to 'abandon ship'.

With just about all *Canberra*'s lifeboats peppered with shrapnel and unseaworthy, the priority was to move the wounded to *Patterson* via planks and lines. It was a difficult process but nothing was more serious and personal and even the most hardened administered the greatest care. Captain Getting was one of the first. Twenty-year-old Stoker George Yeates, in the RAN for just over three years who had lost his left forearm, was carefully assisted by tough three-badge Acting Leading Seaman Sydney Mason (18003) who had enlisted in the RAN in 1926. They had not previously met but Mason needed no urging. 'The poor chap had his arm blown off ... he was conscious but dopey with the morphine'.[400] Although suffering from shrapnel wounds himself, Mason settled Yeates on the deck of the US destroyer just before more panic prevailed.

It was 0430 and lines were cut, the order 'Out all lights' was piped and *Patterson* was underway with the shout to *Canberra* 'We'll be back!' Suddenly a cruiser opened fire and those on the upper deck of *Patterson* ducked for cover. Yeates let out a yelp 'What the hell is happening now!' Mason replied 'We will soon be all right mate', offered a reassuring pat and covered the younger man's face.[401] The same alarm was felt by survivors on *Canberra*'s listing upper deck as another dark shape loomed menacingly. One able seaman referred to the 'awful moments' when the cruiser opened fire and 'we threw ourselves flat on the deck'. He watched in horror as:

> the strangest thing happened in my life ... [the warship] fired
> two big guns ... those shells were red hot ... they burned through
> the dark skies towards us, fast growing into great balls of fire
> coming straight towards us with a roar like express trains.[402]

The cruiser proved to be *Chicago* whose nervous gunners had opened fire without orders. For a brief moment *Chicago* and *Patterson* transmitted emergency signals and *Chicago* ceased firing on its own.

Henry Hall had one of the most spectacular views of 'the battle of Savo Island'. Having joined at the age of 16 in December 1938, he thought he knew a thing or two and after three and a half years in the RAN, he was a confident 20-year-old Able Seaman. He was stuck midway up the ship's mast in an observation post in the collector as the 'rangetaker, height finder and inclinometer operator' to relay enemy ship co-ordinates and range to the 'director' who in turn passed on range information to the guns.

Able Seaman (AB) Henry Hall, RAN, c. 1940s.[403]

The duties sounded very impressive and necessary but, just before 0200 when 'hell on earth' broke following that initial flare from above, the title and duties came to nought because there was no time to do anything. The sailor next to him was killed, and Hall's headset was smashed. Dropping to his knees he admitted to himself he was 'terrified'. As he began to crawl towards greater cover, Hall bumped into a senior who asked 'What are you doing?'. The youthful AB answered, 'the same thing you are'.[404]

It was chaotic. 'There were fires all over the place' and after an explosion 'the 4-inch deck gun crew just disappeared'.[405] By the time he managed to climb down, the wounded lay everywhere, medical staff were struggling so Hall offered to help.

> You had ampoules of morphine. Once you gave a poor devil a shot of morphine you would write an 'M' on their forehead in

HMAS Canberra *unable to steam under its own power is prepared to be scuttled, 9 August 1942.*

blood. There was no shortage of it. This was so somebody else wouldn't come along and give them another dose. You hoped the 'M' wouldn't wash off.[406]

The list of *Canberra* continued to increase but heavy rain at least doused fires and as daylight revealed the doomed Australian cruiser, *Patterson* returned with *Blue* in support to take remaining survivors off the ship. As the American destroyers moved away, there were only grim expressions on those willing to look.

Last photograph taken of a sinking Canberra.

Our once proud ship was but a sinking scrap heap. We had been
hit everywhere. The after control and directors were masses
of twisted steel; the 4-inch gun decks were a shambles; the
amphibian was but a skeleton; the superstructure was only a
tangled mass of twisted steel; all upperworks were merely a
mess of torn steelwork; decks and sides were ripped and torn;
jagged holes everywhere.[407]

Henry Hall had found himself in an extraordinary situation. With no
previous medical experience, he assisted the overwhelmed surgeons.
Onboard *Patterson*, he was present as Commander Downward operated
on the badly wounded *Canberra* CO but even the most inexperienced
realised how critically injured Captain Getting was. Hall was given the
task of digging out pieces of shrapnel from Lieutenant Commander
Mesley's back. The *Canberra* navigator was stoic as 40 pieces were
removed. The AB observed nightmarish scenes no 20-year-old should.
Attached to 'the Surgeon-General aboard USS *Barnett* the American
ship', a doctor who had served in World War I, and, 'a real character',

Hall 'did whatever he told me to do for the next five days'. The surgeons began to rely on him to help when all was lost.

> Son, you see that man over there, he's dying and there's not
> a damned thing we can do for him. You go over there and do
> whatever he wants. ... I'd just hold their hand and talk with
> them, light them a cigarette.[408]

At the end of the five days, the surgeon looked at the young Australian and said, 'son, you done well'.[409] Able Seaman Henry Albert Longdon Hall was honoured with a 'mentioned in despatches'.

At 0630 Admiral Turner ordered the cruiser sunk. The destroyer USS *Selfridge* fired an estimated 263 5-inch shells and four torpedoes but the Australian stubbornly refused to submit. A torpedo from the destroyer USS *Ellet* finally sent *Canberra* and the souls within to the bottom of what henceforth became known as Iron Bottom Sound. *Canberra* had entered the Guadalcanal campaign with a crew of 819; 744 were transferred to US ships. Nine officers (one RAAF) and 65 sailors, as well as two RN ratings and three members of the RAAF and one US Navy officer were killed or missing. Of the 109 wounded, nine sailors succumbed to their wounds as did their Commanding Officer, Captain Frank Getting. Their bodies were committed to the sea with full naval honours.

I regret that I cannot agree to any of their findings.

Rear-Admiral V Crutchley, RN.[410]

Those onboard *Chicago*, observing *Canberra* under attack had the smallest opportunity to fight. *Chicago*'s CO, Captain Bode was woken and ordered the 5-inch guns to fire star shells but they did not function. The order was given to fire main armaments but it was too little too late. At 0147 a torpedo blew away a 16-foot (5 metre) chunk of the *Chicago*'s bow as shells thundered into the upper deck. Though badly damaged, the USN cruiser was still operational but Bode turned his ship hard to port and exited the battle. He did not attempt to assume command of the Southern Force, nor to continue to protect the transports but steamed west for 40 minutes. No one onboard *Chicago* transmitted a warning. It was 0430 when Bode brought his ship back to the column and his gunners, assuming the destroyer tied to the smoking *Canberra* was Japanese, opened fire on USS *Patterson*.

Patterson had earlier engaged in gunfire with Japanese ships and caused damage to *Kinugasa* whilst receiving a shell that killed 10 crew. After rendering the Southern Screening Force ineffective, Mikawa swept his fleet northwards around Savo Island splitting it into two columns and at high speed approached the Northern Screening Force. Again with complete surprise and devastating results, the Japanese opened fire at very close range. The US cruisers *Quincy*, *Vincennes* and *Astoria* struggled to defend but they were simply annihilated. *Quincy* sank at 0235, *Vincennes* sank at 0250 and *Astoria* just after midday whilst under tow.[411]

In terms of Japanese damage, *Chokai* was hit in the operations room and two other Japanese ships suffered minor damage but nothing could stop Mikawa's fleet. The Japanese admiral made the decision to withdraw, believing he needed to hasten back to Rabaul and Kavieng before the Allies attacked his ships with carrier-based aircraft. As his warships retired at high speed into 'The Slot' at 0240, they offered one final insult – USS *Ralph Talbot* felt the wrath of Japanese gunfire.

With withering efficiency, in 32 minutes, Japanese ships fired 1,028 8-inch shells, 768 5-inch or 5½-inch shells, 1,000 rounds of smaller calibre ammunition and 61 24-inch torpedoes, each with a war head carrying 1,200 pounds of explosive.[412]

When Admiral Crutchley returned to his flagship at 0116, he observed naval gunfire near Savo Island and assumed southern ships were firing at aircraft. He decided to leave *Australia* anchored where it was and retired. The flagship did not fire a gun or release a torpedo on 9 August 1942. Dawn revealed the full extent of the massive destruction, of Mikawa's victory and Allied losses. Of the combined Allied fleet of six heavy cruisers, two light cruisers and 15 destroyers, three heavy cruisers sank, another was severely damaged, another later scuttled and two destroyers were damaged. Mikawa lost 58 officers and sailors and the following day, when the cruiser *Kako* was torpedoed by US submarine *S44*, 34 additional Japanese seamen were killed. Within the Allied fleet between 1024 and 1070 officers and sailors were killed during the Battle of Savo Island.[413] Although achieving a copybook victory, Mikawa was later criticised for not pressing his attack and destroying the transports and invasion forces. Gathered intelligence had failed to inform him of their vulnerability and that there was no likelihood of his being attacked by carrier aircraft.

The Australian Navy Office scrambled to catch up with who was actually in *Canberra*. The lack of updated service certificates caused delays in information and anguish for relatives. So too the official

Survivors arriving in Sydney onboard President Grant, *c. 1942.*

language, referring to the 'disposal of survivors' and 'discharged dead'.[414]

Amongst *Canberra* survivors were three exchange USN signal ratings. Liaison Officer Lieutenant (jg) Joseph Williams Vance, Jr., USN, was killed instantly when a shell hit the Cypher Office.[415] *Canberra's* Canteen Assistant Sydney J. Ricardo was seriously wounded but his two fellow workers were uninjured; RN Stoker PO Ronald Alfred Albert Pitcher (PJX134492) and RN Able Seaman William H. Morrow (SSX17845) were killed whereas eight other RN sailors survived. Seriously wounded Leading Aircraftsmen Frederick George Rivers (32088) and slightly wounded Gordon Douglas Poole (25089) survived the Seagull detachment but five did not.[416]

Confusing the situation further, *Canberra* survivors were now spread across different US warships and transports with the seriously injured taken to New Zealand hospitals until fit enough to endure another sea voyage. The bulk of the survivors arrived in Sydney in *President Grant*. They were barely recognisable, dressed in a strange assortment of US military uniforms.

The media response was predictably a combination of triumph and tragedy with newspaper headlines of the day articulating the mixed responses to the battle.

> HMAS *Canberra* Sunk in Solomons Battle Crew's Magnificent Heroism[417] How Cruiser Met Her End: Thrilling Stories of Great Heroism[418] ' Tradition Knows No Greater Glory[419]
> Hit and Run[420] (to describe the cowardly Japanese) Courage and Heroism: All Hell Broke Loose[421]

The Argus editorial of 21 August 1942, under the headline 'A Gallant Ship Gone' eloquently stated that 'pride mingles with the grief with which the people of Australia have learned of the loss'.[422]

The Argus went on to report that *Canberra* was:

> in the thick of the fight from theof this perilous and glorious enterprise ... in the true Anglo-Saxon aggressive tradition. Australian sorrow ... will be assuaged by the knowledge that ship and crew helped to make history in the truest sense.[423]

The article beneath 'HMAS Canberra's Last Fight' told of 'graphic stories' of bravery, of 'men who refused to leave injured mates' and 'of attempts to launch a torpedo at an enemy cruiser'.[424] 'Loss will be avenged' cited survivors.

We are grieved to have lost the ship, but when we are drafted to another unit we will repay the Japs 10-fold for all they did to the *Canberra*.[425]

Central to media reporting was the concerted effort to paint the sinking of *Canberra* not as an Allied defeat but as an example of an unethical, cowardly enemy by using phrases like 'sneaky attack', 'hit and run'.[426]

The sudden demise of one of Australia's two heavy cruisers needed to be justified in a positive manner and hence reports that not only had *Canberra* fired her guns but also that the worst damage was done, not by a surface ship, but by a Japanese submarine. A tiny article in the

etg Petty Off G. Anderson (missing, believed killed) · Flying-Officer D. Murchison (missing, believed killed) · L. G. Martin, ERA · Stk C. T. O'Rour

Unsettling were the smiling faces of Canberra crew killed, c. 1942.

small regional newspaper, the *Newcastle Morning Herald & Miners Advocate*, on 5 September, was the only one to dare to be different. *Canberra's* Executive Officer, Commander John Walsh, RAN, had assumed command of the cruiser after Getting fell. Walsh had suffered flash burns to both eyes, particularly badly damaging the right, and shrapnel wounds to the back. Somehow Walsh took control of fire-fighting and the safe evacuation of the ship and was later awarded an OBE. On 5 September, Walsh offered a truthful analysis to the newspaper.

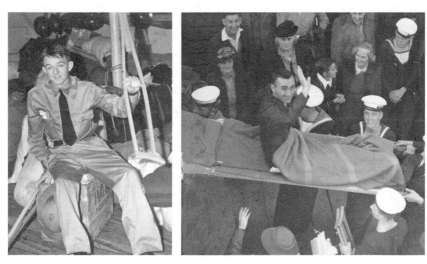

The media featured many photographs of survivors arriving in Sydney, c. 1942.

We are only deluding ourselves by attempting to underrate the Japanese Navy. It is a very efficient and very daring fighting unit.[427]

Another media emphasis, one with which Australian sailors had been versed prior to their return, was praise for the Americans: 'admiration of and gratitude to the US sailors ... The way they treated us was really magnificent'.[428] On a serviceman-to-serviceman level, the praise was truly worthy but Australian officialdom was at great pains not to criticise the Americans in any way and this would distort public information and formal investigations. In the short term, the RAN paid a sizeable USN account for the clothing and messing costs of *Canberra* survivors.[429]

In keeping with RN/RAN tradition, few sailors were singled out for bravery awards. There were many unsung heroes and many more left to comprehend and confront deeds and demons.

Stoker Mervyn Raymond Cowden (S5317), born in Harden in New South Wales, had done little to enhance his RAN career, clearly uncomfortable in navy blue. By 1942, the 19-year-old's service card was noteworthy for the wrong reasons. Cowden was a spare hand in 'A' boiler fan flat taking temperature readings when the action alarm sounded.

When full speed was rung through, Tasmanian Stoker II Rex Robert Dare Oliver (H2000), 20, who had only entered the RAN that March and joined *Canberra* in July, struggled to put on 'A' boiler sprayers so Cowden completed the procedure. Cowden then asked Chief Stoker Malcolm De Espline Stafford (16090) if he should return to the fan flat or remain in the boiler room. Stafford told him to go in the fan flat. 'Chief Stoker Stafford was always a very thorough man, and everyone jumped to it when he gave an order'.[430] Cowden was half way up the air lock when the first thump came. There was an explosion forward and dust flew down from the deck head. Cowden moved to light a secondary oil light and felt another thump below. The air lock doors were shut and the lights extinguished. A large flash was visible through the upper door and red sparks flew in all directions. Cowden was confused. He opened the top air lock door and smoke and fumes made it impossible to focus and he wondered if he should return to the boiler room. Cowden remembered how Chief Stafford cautioned him just the previous day.

He questioned me about my knowledge of the fan flat. He said that all hands in the boiler room would be wiped out by a back flash if the fans were stopped.[431]

Cowden fought fires until ordered to leave the ship. Chief Stoker Stafford had ensured that the inexperienced stoker knew of the dangers. Chief Stoker Stafford died in boiler room 'A'. Cowden went on to serve on the RN gift replacement cruiser re-commissioned HMAS *Shropshire* in the company of many other *Canberra* survivors – there were a few scores to settle with the enemy concerning a ship and mates lost in Ironbottom Sound.[432]

The *Shropshire* crew saw extensive active service in the Pacific and were subjected to many Kamikaze attacks. For Cowden, his war service and survivor guilt took a heavy toll and in 1943 he was discharged from the RAN due to poor health – he was not yet 21.

During the Battle of Savo Island, it was not necessarily the most likely who demonstrated initiative and courage. AB Stephen St George whose background and heritage were as problematic as his RAN service card, had been referred to in many disparaging ways, the least offensive being 'larrikin'. Resilience may have been a way to describe this young man as he aided many in the early hours of 9 August. A member of the 'Y' turret shell handling crew, he was knocked off his feet by an explosion. He then wrenched open the magazine door to allow the men below an exit before struggling with others to lift 'X' turret hatch to free more. Working his way below he found Chief Stoker Hunter with two wounded stokers. He and another AB carried the men to a medical post. St George continued to search for wounded and found the badly wounded PO James Haining. Haining said to St George: 'Don't forget to tell my wife and child, and go and see her'.[433]

Later St George told a board of enquiry administered by high ranking RN and RAN officers that they should ensure 'there was a drastic revision of the type of stretcher' employed on warships because he found assembling a stretcher for PO Haining was 'more difficult' than assembling a radio set. St George ferreted below decks for rope which he sliced up for bucket brigades before helping with the wounded

Canberra *survivors grateful to be back in Australia but soon astounded by criticism of their performance by RAN hierarchy, c. 1942.*

Crew members of HMAS Shropshire, *many survivors of* Canberra *painted shells with messages before these were fired at the enemy, c. 1943.*

on the upper deck. It had started raining so he went below again to find covers. He visited any cabin, including those of senior officers, helping himself to anything which would cover the wounded. Returning to the first medical post, he found the two Stokers he had carried dead. For other wounded he scavenged cigarettes and 'then located the beer and gave them a glass each'. St George offered one of the chaplains a beer 'but he refused. I drank his share'. He was then asked to find blankets so again he picked his way through debris, falling through a hole or two, being burnt by steam, until he could 'raid the Pay Commander's cabin and grabbed an armful'. On the way out he helped himself to a coat because his 'was wet'.[434]

The Battle of Savo Island was far from over and the ensuing months and decades were dogged by controversy and innuendo as high command endeavoured to avoid complicity by deflecting responsibility and blame to juniors. Following a US press outcry as to why US ships 'were under the command of an English Admiral', a formal US Navy Board of Inquiry was conducted by Admiral Arthur Jepy Hepburn, USN. Hepburn travelled extensively including to Australia. He conferred with General MacArthur, Admiral Crutchley and, strangely, some Australian politicians.

Hepburn correctly cited an inadequate readiness and preparation for a sudden night attack, a failure to recognise the implication of the enemy planes overhead the evening of 8 August, a misplaced confidence in radar capabilities, poor communications within the fleet and poor intelligence. Hepburn believed the absence of Rear Admiral Crutchley, RN, had probably affected the outcome and noted 'a contributory cause must be placed on the withdrawal of the carrier group by Fletcher'.[435] This was decidedly an understatement as Admiral Fletcher's withdrawal of his carriers caused a chain of events resulting in not only confusion and severe defensive depletion of the Southern Force, but the loss of air cover. It was alleged by some US authorities that Crutchley failed to prepare, consult and communicate with his warship captains. Crutchley did design and distribute a plan of operations before the fleet reached Guadalcanal but the hasty preparation of the campaign and ensuing air attacks left little time for badly needed collaboration.

Crutchley was certainly guilty of failing to convey his decision not to return with *Australia* at the conclusion of his meeting with Turner. It is also fair to assume in keeping with the tone and tensions of the day, that there was a lack of respect and understanding between the RN Admiral and US Naval officers. The situation was exacerbated because Crutchley had never been involved in combined operations with the Americans and subsequently lacked an appreciation of their culture and operational methods. He was equally unfamiliar with the war in the Pacific and the

Admiral Crutchley, RN attested his lack of responsibility for the destruction of the screening fleet, c. 1940s.

Japanese. His World War I Battle of Jutland mindset favoured old school naval tactics not one geared to modern technology such as the speed and tactics used by the Japanese: 50 knot torpedoes, and IJN advanced surface and carrier tactics were beyond his understanding.

In a secret document addressed to the ACNB, Rear Admiral Crutchley, VC, RN, defended his actions, arguing that at no time did he 'receive a warning' of any imminent enemy surface fleet threat. Crutchley believed the blame lay firmly with inexperienced personnel 'particularly in night fighting' and that crews demonstrated a 'lack of alertness'.[436] While admitting that the lack of TBS on Australian ships made communication difficult between the US and Australian ships and that *Australia*'s absence was regrettable, Crutchley believed the screening fleet had been 'successful' in its duty because the Japanese did not attack the transports and the landing of marines had proceeded. This was despite the death of over 1,000 Allied navy personnel, more than the number of marines killed in the six-month Guadalcanal campaign.

Guadalcanal remained in Allied hands and became the launching pad for their 'island hopping' campaign which proved to be the Allied transition from defensive to offensive. The Guadalcanal campaign continued to rage six months and two days more, until February 1943. It was one of the bloodiest chapters of the war in the Pacific, resulting in the deaths of an estimated 7,100 Allied and 31,000 Japanese military personnel.

Given Crutchley lay the blame firmly on subordinate personnel, he did not endorse Admiral Hepburn's frank statement that the covering fleet was predisposed to defeat because officers in the USN and RAN were:

> still obsessed with a strong feeling of technical and mental superiority over the enemy. In spite of ample evidence as to enemy capabilities, most of our officers and men despised the enemy and felt themselves sure victors in all encounters ... The net result of all this was a fatal lethargy of mind ... I believe that this psychological factor, as a cause of our defeat, was even more important than the element of surprise.[437]

Unstated by both Hepburn and Crutchley was that the vast majority of officers and men were simply following orders and adhering to the standards and values set by those in command. In his report Hepburn failed to censure any fellow admiral and their careers continued unaffected. Crutchley returned to England, was awarded the Legion of Merit (Chief Commander) in September 1944, promoted to full admiral and knighted.

Admiral Hepburn aimed his strongest criticism at Captain Howard Bode on *Chicago*. While Bode demonstrated a lack of professionalism, and *Canberra* and crew would not have suffered as badly had the Australian cruiser been behind *Chicago*, Bode was just one ship captain following a flawed battle plan. Upon learning of this condemnation, Bode committed suicide, shooting himself whilst in his quarters at

Balbo, Panama Canal Zone, on 19 April 1943, and dying the following day.

The Australian Commonwealth Naval Board (ACNB) conducted two boards of enquiry into the loss of *Canberra*. The first board conducted from 21 to 23 August 1942 consisted of Rear Admiral Gerard Charles Muirhead-Gould DSC, RN (President), Captain Arthur Henry Spurgeon, OBE, RAN, Captain W L G Adams, CBE, RN, Captain John Malet Armstrong, RAN, Engineer Captain Leopold James Phillimore Carr, CBE, RAN, and Paymaster Commander Joseph O'Reilly, RAN. The second was made up of Muirhead-Gould as President and Captains Spurgeon and Carr, and was conducted on 21 September 1942.

The 53-year-old Muirhead-Gould was a recipient of the Distinguished Service Cross (DSC) during World War I. A heart condition put an end to his sea-going career but not his appointment from the RN as Naval Officer in Command of Sydney Harbour. Muirhead-Gould was unpopular with RAN officers and sailors alike and critics reflected poorly on his command following the Sydney Harbour midget submarine attack and death of 21 sailors in *Kuttabul*.

As the first *Canberra* survivors returned to Sydney, they were met by Muirhead-Gould who bluntly told them 'we should feel ashamed that our ship had been sunk by gunfire without firing a shot in return'.[438] For traumatised officers and sailors who had lost their ship and shipmates, this was not the sympathetic or morale-boosting response that should have come from a commanding officer who had no direct understanding of the battle. The same aggressive, adversarial approach, lack of finesse and condemnation were adopted during the boards of enquiry he chaired.

The cross-examination of survivors was unrelenting and took an emotional toll. Engineering staff in particular were subjected to disapprobation. Chief Stoker Walter Hunter (7605), who had pulled Lieutenant Mussared and others to safety, was asked by the board why he could not be more precise with times. He replied 'I was too busy to think of it'. Chief Mechanician Walter Weaver (489), who entered the RAN at the beginning of World War I and spent four postings and many years in *Canberra* and *Australia*, had been in charge of the after engine room. Board members asked if he 'appreciated the importance of saving the dynamo in the event of main steam failing to a serious low pressure?' Weaver replied 'Sir, I have been in the Engine Room Department a long time'. The question was repeated and Weaver replied:

Now I am in the after engine room – the steam fails – our orders that have been drummed into us is to shut in throttle valves to keep up steam pressure.[439]

Weaver attempted to explain that once the ship was dead in the water, his concern was to evacuate his sailors and 'my attention was drawn to wounded men'. Board members continued to press and Weaver decided he had little to lose as he had already lost much.

I have always said that the weakness of that type of ship is the boiler room fans. They have no protection and after a hit by anything at all the steam pipes are destroyed and the fans stop. If the fans stop the ship is stopped. Had we not lost the fans we would not have lost the steam. Four distinct lines all cut at once because they are all on one level and at point blank range.[440]

The board then asked Weaver if clothes and personal items in sailor mess decks accelerated the fires. Increasingly frustrated Weaver replied.

You cannot take men's gear or necessary things to live in some sort of comfort and throw them overboard. You cannot have men living on bare decks.[441]

Engineer Commander McMahon was required to testify more than once and did his best to defend his staff. Board members argued that had repair parties 'remained at their action stations' they 'could have made useful repairs that might have affected the final list of the ship'. McMahon was unimpressed and pointed out that most of those within DCHQ were killed or badly injured. He could not speak highly enough of repair party survivors 'who carried on in the way of putting out small

Rear Admiral Muirhead-Gould with two Canberra survivors, c. 1942.

fires' and 'attempting to do what they could against the big ones' even as much as 'three hours after the action'. On different occasions McMahon was asked why he had ordered the evacuation of the engine rooms because the board believed this was done prematurely. McMahon emphasised again and again that because the boilers were destroyed and the engines subsequently dead, there was nothing more that could be done. Smoke and fumes rendered the engine rooms hazardous for personnel who he believed were better employed fighting fires and caring for the wounded. Board members remained unconvinced – they believed flooding turrets and spaces had been premature and probably caused the list. Engineer Commander McMahon argued that a large hole in the hull allowed sea water to enter, and additional, deliberate flooding probably prevented catastrophic explosions which would have killed many more.

McMahon became increasingly vocal about preparing *Canberra* for war duty. There had been too many shortcuts for *Canberra* to be completely operational; too little consideration in preparing the cruiser for war. Little advice had been taken in ensuring adequate countermeasures in case of battle damage and fire. The layers and layers of paint applied to and within *Canberra* during the 1930s had not been completely removed and this proved a major accelerant for fire.

In the catapult structure, which was one of the first places where intense fire broke out, I feel that varnishes or 'dope' used for painting aircraft structure may have been to blame. The flames there were so intense and blazed up so quickly that I feel that must be so. In the after control and that vicinity, fires were probably caused by a certain amount of woodwork ... I was always under the impression they were fireproof ... The spare aircraft wings stowed under the deck head of the Torpedo Space. Canvas sails for cutters stowed above the port torpedo tubes. Falls for Boats. Gear stowed in the 4" gun supports. Cinema film stowage ... supports. Canvas stowed just inside the starboard pom pom magazine. Lack of facilities to put them out they spread through woodwork, doors, furniture, fittings in cabins and enclosed messes and probably through the clothes in clothes lockers.[442]

Commander Otto Francis 'Mac' McMahon, OBE, RAN., c. 1940s.

McMahon reiterated his long-standing concern about personnel changes, how *Canberra* was constantly used as a training ship. Green recruits regularly replaced trained personnel, a constant interruption to cohesiveness and team development. Even as late as the last time the ship was in port 'there were drafts of between 10 and 20 second class stokers'.[443]

Otto Francis 'Mac' McMahon received an Order of the British Empire (OBE) for his actions on 9 August 1942 but was not promoted further than commander. He had said enough, perhaps too much; he had certainly seen too much and disillusionment had dispelled his RAN ambitions – he left the navy on 31 October 1946.

McMahon was not alone in expressing frustration concerning neglect and shortcomings. PO Russell Grantham Cope (17655) was the captain of 'X' turret. He testified that there were many deficiencies. 'The loss of the left cabin door', not replaced during the refit, caused injuries and gun damage – only the 'left cabinet bulkhead saved the gun house crew from being wiped out'. Cope complained of how too few 'torches' created problems, of how 'insufficient' his first aid box was when he was faced with severe shrapnel injuries to members of his crew. The lack of power completely affected not only the integrity of warship but also the ability to save the wounded. He was frustrated by the lack of compatibility between American hoses and Australian couplings that compounded the tragedy because fires could not be put out. He explained that too little fire-fighting equipment and too few 'Salvus' suits for sailors to enter and flood spaces was another problem. There was even a delay in flooding 'X' turret magazine and shell room because 'a suitable spanner' could not be found.[444] PO Cope had spent his life in the RAN, enlisting as a Boy Seaman in 1926. He had served throughout the fleet with distinction, and would continue his war service in HMAS *Shropshire* and *Hobart*. Cope hoped his testimony would be valued, but he remained unconvinced. Cope was not promoted to Chief Petty Officer and was given a medical discharge, on grounds of 'anxiety', in 1945.

An acute shortage of fresh water had hampered medical staff and caused further distress for the wounded. Surgeon Lieutenant Morris struggled with this and the lack of innovative medical supplies within *Canberra*.

> Fortunately the Americans had everything that opened and shut
> in the way of equipment and were more than generous with it.
> We used sulphathiazole powder on all wounds and by mouth
> in bad cases. The results were staggering ... the majority of the
> wounds were as clean as surgical incisions ... The Americans
> had a magnificent supply of dried plasma in a very handy
> apparatus. We used unbelievable quantities of it. The amount of
> morphine used was terrific.[445]

Canberra was designed and built in keeping with the Washington Naval

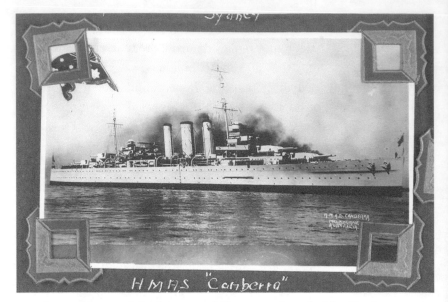

For those who served, Canberra *would be remembered with affection, c. 1930s.*

Agreement limit on British cruisers of displacement of 10,000 tons. This resulted in a poorly designed, poorly protected warship compounded by ACNB maintenance inaction. An example of one crucial oversight is the armour modification of *Canberra*.

In 1938 the decision was finally made to give both *Australia* and *Canberra* 4-inch side armour. For *Australia* the process took nearly 18 months to complete by which time *Canberra* could not be spared from the fleet. Some of this work was undertaken during the cruiser's 1942 refit but it was never completed. As such *Canberra* was poorly equipped for this new and brutal war. Inadequate fire-fighting equipment, generator space independent of the main propulsion spaces, casualty power systems, emergency fuel-oil service pumps and separate flammable stowage lockers with CO_2 systems, were just some of the dangerous shortcomings.

Canberra was the eighth Australian warship lost in this war, severely depleting the RAN. Questions needed to be asked not only about the readiness of warships for modern warfare but also of those who administered the RAN at the time. The problems were systemic and were allowed to persist from when Australia's navy was created in 1911. Instead blame and responsibility were deflected. Those within ACNB and their boards of enquiry attributed the loss of *Canberra* and 84 Australian officers and sailors to such minor details as 'if a really experienced [radar] operator had been available ...'[446]

Another board priority was to dismiss the possibility that *Canberra* had been hit by a torpedo fired by a United States warship, an allegation made by several crew. While survivor testimony was not conclusive on the issue, the preservation of Australian-American relations proved most influential and the Board dismissed the possibility. Yet as early as 1942 in Admiral Ernest Joseph King's covering letter accompanying a copy of the Hepburn report to the US Secretary for the Navy, USN Commander-in-Chief, King admitted that those in USS *Bagley* became disoriented, that the destroyer had continued to circle far to port during the 'significant delay' while torpedo primers were inserted, the starboard tubes brought to bear and four torpedoes fired. The Japanese fleet had departed north and *Bagley* was on the starboard side of *Canberra*.

For survivors on *Canberra*, particularly Midshipman (later Commodore) Bruce Loxton, RAN, it became a lifetime crusade to disprove the board's finding and have history record that *Canberra* was torpedoed by friendly fire from USS *Bagley*.[447]

Another significant fallacy concerned the complicity by the RAAF Hudson crew in the deaths of over 1,000 Allied navy personnel. Official US naval historian Rear Admiral Samuel Eliot Morison, USN, in his 15-volume *History of United States Naval Operations in World War II*, chronicled that the Australian pilot 'instead of breaking radio silence as he had orders to do' or returning to base, continued flying 'most of the afternoon before returning to Milne Bay, 'had his tea, and then reported the contact'.[448] Later American authors repeated this affront.[449]

A very determined and stubborn Australian named Eric Geddes refused to die before he cleared the reputation of his crew. Geddes was the Hudson radio operator and for 65 years, he besieged the US Department of the Navy with letters, even writing to US President Barack Obama. In October 2014, at the age of 96, Geddes received the long awaited apology in a letter from the US Department of the Navy agreeing that archival research now proved his Hudson crew had risked their lives in breaking radio silence, and on landing, as soon as they could, they reported the Japanese fleet steaming towards Savo Island[450] – the authorities to whom the Australian crew reported, had neglected to relay the intelligence immediately to the fleet.

Those who were killed and maimed were lost beneath official rhetoric, international misinformation and volumes of white paper covered in black type that lacked honest appraisal. The Battle of Savo Island veterans simply referred to the battle colloquially as 'The Battle of the Five Sitting Ducks'. *Canberra* survivors were left to support each other. In 1942 they had 'liberated' a gramophone from one of the US transports. It came with only one record so the song became the *Canberra* survivors' theme song and was played at every reunion: 'It's a lovely day tomorrow'.[451] Their emotions remained raw.

In his journal, Midshipman Bruce Loxton wrote a 'Requiem' to the cruiser.

> Thus was destroyed a ship which had never been able to win a
> name for herself and which will always be remembered as the
> ship that was sunk without firing a shot. It was not her fault, nor
> the fault of those who manned her. She was placed in a position
> where it was easy to surprise and attack her on a night when
> visibility was at a minimum. She was torpedoed exactly where it
> could do the most damage in such a short time after the alarm
> that the guns could not be brought to bear.[452]

Henry Hall had joined HMAS *Canberra* in February 1942 as a 19-year-old Able Seaman. He would forever remember the last words he exchanged with his mate Able Seaman Wallace Montrose Ross (22982); how they promised each other that they would contact with reverence next-of-kin should the worst occur.[453] Henry sat down to write that difficult letter after Wallace died of wounds onboard USS *Fuller* and continued to speak fondly of Wallace in 2015.

A distinguished RAN career followed for Hall that spanned four decades before he retired as a Lieutenant Commander in 1981. He remained an inspiring figure, never missing an opportunity to represent shipmates lost and an Australian cruiser, *Canberra*, which was a casualty of circumstance.

AB Stephen St George's memory was imprinted with the final words of PO James Haining: 'Don't forget to tell my wife and child, and go and see her'. So he did. Haining left behind a wife, a toddler and a baby he never met and who was named 'James' in honour of his father. The young family, like so many others, struggled on the small war pension just as others had after the 'war to end all wars'. Around the nation more names were

Lieutenant Commander Henry Hall, OAM, RAN (rtd), c. 2014.

carved on memorials. There are no graves for men lost at sea at which families can mourn. They were left to reflect on what could have been, what value their men could have added to families, communities and to the nation.

Supply Assistant Russell Keats with the intellect and musical talent which would have brightened a world, was killed instantly by a shell to the bridge and plot office. His father Horace had written to Russell for his twenty-first birthday. The letter was never delivered and was returned unopened. Horace was distraught and the letter remained unopened well after his death on 21 August 1945; the day before what would have been his son's twenty-fourth birthday. In the letter he had expressed his pride in Russell's achievements and how he hoped his son would be 'spared to see many more and happier birthdays'.[454] Horace Keats, the well-known composer, was unable to arrange more music but for one exception, a piece dedicated to Russell based on the poem 'Over the Quiet Waters'.

Over the quiet waters,
I hear your voice again
And it brings the old time gladness
And the old time tears and pain
Into the heart that loves you
Creeps a new ecstasy
Ever your dear song whispers,
Some day you'll come to me.[455]

On the morning of the 9 August 1942 the heavy cruiser HMAS Canberra was sunk after being severely damaged during the Battle of Savo Island in the Solomon Islands group.

In 1942 Australian politics clashed with English conservative convention. A Royal Australian Navy, controlled by the British Admiralty, struggled with its own identity and autonomy. A British Empire naval strategy based on outdated tradition, racist dogma and arrogance was now subordinate to that of the United States Navy. This destabilised the US and Australian joint operations in the war in the Pacific.

LEFT: Canberra *survivor, Stoker Roy Stephens shakes hands with fellow survivor, Alan Keys (left). Keys was an Ordinary Seaman II when* Canberra *was attacked and turned 18 the day after the cruiser sank.* RIGHT: *Stephens and Keys with other survivors of HMA ships* Canberra *and* Shropshire *at the commissioning of Amphibious Assault Ship (LHD) HMAS* Canberra III *in Sydney on 28 November 2014 (Courtesy of Gary Stephens).*

The consequence for the ships and crews of the screening fleet off Guadalcanal were dire. Eighty-four men – officers and sailors – onboard HMAS Canberra died. They and the families they left behind were casualties of circumstances beyond their control.

ENDNOTES

1 Gregory, MacKenzie, J. 'Ahoy – Mac's Web Log – Naval, Maritime, Australian History and more', http://ahoy.tk-jk.net (accessed 3 March 2016).

2 Gill, G. Hermon, *Australia in the War of 1939–1945, Royal Australian Navy 1942–1945*, Australian War Memorial, 1968, p. 140.

3 Gregory, http://ahoy.tk-jk.net.

4 Payne, A. *HMAS Canberra,* The Naval Historical Society of Australia, 1973, p.3.

5 Cunningham, I.J. *Work Hard, Play Hard: The Royal Australian Naval College 1913–1988*, AGPS, Canberra, 1988, p. 22.

6 The college was returned to Jervis Bay in January 1958 and commissioned as HMAS *Creswell*, after VADM Sir William Creswell, KCMG, KBE, the First Naval Member of the Naval Board (Chief of Navy) from 1911 to 1919.

7 Cunningham, I.J. *Work Hard, Play Hard: The Royal Australian Naval College 1913–1988*, AGPS, Canberra, 1988, p. 25.

8 ibid

9 Gregory, http://ahoy.tk-jk.net.

10 ibid.

11 ibid.

12 ibid.

13 ibid.

14 ibid.

15 ibid.

16 ibid.

17 King, N., 'Memoirs of a Reluctant Warrior 1936–1955', MS 1502, Australian War Memorial, Canberra.

18 ibid.

19 ibid.

20 ibid.

21 ibid.

22 ibid.

23 ibid.

24 HMAS *Australia II*.

25 National Archives Australia, 'HMAS *Canberra* commissioning', MS138/1, 603/255/1, Melbourne.

26 ibid.

27 Payne, A. *HMAS Canberra*, Naval Historical Society of Australia, 1973, p. 2.

28 ibid.

29 ibid.

30 ibid., p. 3.

31 ibid.

32 ibid.

33 Born in Liverpool, England, 3 November 1879. Appointed Captain, PNF on loan from Royal Navy which was terminated on reverting to the RN on 12 May 1930. Died 3 November 1937.

34 Payne, 1973, p. 4.

35 ibid.

36 ibid.; also National Archives of Australia, 'HMAS *Canberra* – Report of trials', MP138/1, 603/255/1504, Melbourne.

37 Choules, C., *The Last of the Last the Final Survivor of the First World War*, Mainstream, UK, 2011, p. 125.

38 ibid., p. 129.

39 King, N. 'Memoirs of a reluctant warrior 1936-1955', MSS 1502, Australian War Memorial, Canberra.

40 Choules, C. *The Last of the Last the Final Survivor of the First World War*, Mainstream, UK, 2011, p. 143.

41 Flags and pennants of the signal codes, disposed in as variegated and symmetrical a manner as possible. Except for the masthead ensigns, national flags and ensigns are not included, because the order in which they are flown could give offence. The flag of the senior officer on board, the Rear Admiral Commanding the Australia Squadron is flown at the head of the top mast.

42 Peek, R.I. PR85/419, Australian War Memorial, Canberra.

43 ibid.

44 Payne, 1973, p. 10.

45 Peek, R.I. PR85/419, Australian War Memorial, Canberra.

46 Choules, C. *The Last of the Last the Final Survivor of the First World War*, Mainstream, UK, 2011, p. 128.

47 Peek, R.I. PR85/419, Australian War Memorial, Canberra.

48 ibid.

49 ibid.

50 The life of Farquhar-Smith, Charles (1888–1968), RADM; b. 29 January 1888 Taree, NSW; education Sydney Boys High School; trained RN Coll. Portsmouth, Eng.; 1914–18 War (incl. at Heligoland, served in Sydney 1916–19); Asst. Chief of Naval Staff 1927; Chief Exec. Officer *Australia*; promoted Capt. 1930; Flag Capt. in *Canberra* 1931–33; Second Naval Member ANB 1933–35; with RN 1935–38; Dir. Naval Reserves 1938–39; District Naval Officer WA 1939–42; Naval Staff Officer *Hobart* 1942 (retd.); d. 17 June 1968.

51 Peek, R.I. PR85/419, Australian War Memorial, Canberra.

52 In 1941 Peek returned to Australia to join the light cruiser *Hobart* as Gunnery Officer, and saw action in the Mediterranean and the Far East. At the Battle of Leyte Gulf, he was on the bridge of *Australia*, standing near Captain Emile Dechaineux RAN, when a kamikaze aircraft struck the ship. Dechaineux and 30 men were killed and 56 wounded, including Peek, who suffered burns. For his skill and courage in helping to save the ship, he was appointed OBE. He was awarded the DSC for skill and devotion to duty during an earlier amphibious assault at Lingayen Gulf. Peek led the RAN contingent in the victory celebrations in London in 1945 and remained in England to complete a staff course, before becoming Commander, 1st Frigate Squadron in the River class frigate *Shoalhaven* in 1951. During the Korean War, while in command of the destroyer HMAS *Tobruk* he was awarded the US Legion of Merit. He was Deputy Chief of Naval Personnel in 1954 and again given command of *Tobruk* from 1956 to 1958 as Captain, 10th Destroyer Squadron. Four years later he commanded the aircraft carrier *Sydney*, and subsequently the Australian flagship, *Melbourne*. In 1964 he was promoted to Rear Admiral and was appointed 4th Naval Member and Chief of Supply of the ACNB. From 1965–67 he was Deputy Chief of Naval Staff. In 1967 Peek became Flag Officer Commanding Australian Fleet, before becoming Chief of Naval Personnel in 1968. In November 1970 he was promoted to Vice Admiral and became Chief of Naval Staff. A CB was granted in 1971, and a knighthood in 1972. A tireless advocate for naval veterans of all campaigns Vice Admiral Sir Richard Peek died 28 August 2010 [where is this information from: please reference this. Also, spell out what CB means in second last line.]

53 Payne, 1973, p. 10.

54 ibid, p. 11.

55 Ingleton, G.C. and Boyd, H.L. *Sea Noises*, HMAS *Canberra*, 1933.

56 ibid.

57 Officers were expected to pay for their alcohol consumption in the wardroom. For official receptions, some allowance was provided but often officers needed to contribute significant contributions for guests.

58 Ingleton, G.C. and Boyd, H.L. *Sea Noises*, HMAS *Canberra*, 1933.

59 *Australian Women's Weekly,* 21 April 1934.

60 ibid., 4 February 1939.

61 http://www.australiansatwarfilmarchive.gov.au/aawfa/interviews/76.aspx.

62 King, N., 'Memoirs of a Reluctant Warrior 1936–1955'.

63 ibid.

64 ibid.

65 *Australian Women's Weekly,* 6 October 1934.

66   *Sydney Morning Herald*, 20 October 1937.

67   ibid.

68   *The Argus*, 2 June 1927.

69   *Sydney Morning Herald*, 20 October 1937.

70   King, N., 'Memoirs of a Reluctant Warrior 1936–1955', MSS 1502, Australian War Memorial, Canberra.

71   ibid.

72   ibid.

73   ibid.

74   Burrell, H.M. *Mermaids Do Exist*, MacMillan, Melbourne, 1986, p. 14.

75   National Archives of Australia: Naval Board Minutes; A2585, 452/201/499, No. 165, 26 November 1932, No. 154, 12 October 1932.

76   ibid.

77   *The Age*, 9 November 1932.

78   ibid., 11 November 1932.

79   ibid.

80   National Archives of Australia: Canberra; A471/1, 22478, Court Martial, PO Edward Walter James Dickerson (10615).

81   ibid.

82   ibid.

83   *The Argus*, 11 October 1932.

84   A2585, 452/201/499, No. 232, 6 November 1936, National Archives, Canberra.

85   National Archives of Australia: Naval Board Minutes; No. 14, 16 January 1932.

86   *The Argus*, 11 November 1932.

87   ibid, 23 November 1932.

88   National Archives of Australia: Canberra; A5954/1, 1003/13, 'The Shedden Collection'.

89   Reville, F.W. 'Letters to Miss J Fraser', PR85/326, Australian War Memorial, Canberra.

90   National Archives of Australia: Melbourne; MP981/1, 564/201/161, Navy Office, general correspondence files, 1923–1950.

91   Payne, 1973, p. 13.

92   National Archives of Australia: Canberra; A5954/1, 1003/13,'The Shedden Collection'.

93   National Archives of Australia: Melbourne; MP981, 463/201/826, 'HMAS *Australia* and *Canberra*'.

94   ibid.

95   National Archives of Australia: Canberra; A5954/1, 1003/13, 'The Shedden Collection'.

96   Feakes, H. J. *White ensign, Southern Cross: a Story of the King's Ships of Australia's Navy*, Ure Smith, 1951, p. 268.

97   National Archives of Australia: Melbourne; MP525/1/0, 12/5/38.

98   National Archives of Australia: Melbourne; MP472/1/0, 5/20/1775.

99   National Archives of Australia: Melbourne; MP1049/1/0, 1917/0129.

100 ibid.

101 *Parliamentary Debates,* Vol. 14, 10 August 1926, pp. 3, 931.

102 ibid, Vol. 2, estimates 1926–1927.

103 Spurling, K. 'Life in the Lower Deck of the Royal Australian Navy 1911–1952', PhD thesis, UNSW@ADFA, 1999.

104 Carew, A. *The Lower Deck of the Royal Navy 1900–39*, Manchester University Press, 1981, pp. 177, 189.

105 ibid.

106 *Smith's Weekly*, 3 October 1931.

107 Spurling, K. 'Life in the Lower Deck of the Royal Australian Navy 1911–1952', PhD thesis, UNSW@ADFA, 1999.

108 Naval Board Minutes, No. 66, 13 May 1931, National Archives of Australia, Canberra.

109 Jay, P. 'Musings of Matelot Phillip Jay', MSS 1083, Australian War Memorial, Canberra.

110 National Archives of Australia: Canberra;.A461/7, N337/1/5.

111 Lloyd, C. and Rees, J., *The Last Shilling: A History of Repatriation in Australia*, Melbourne University Press, 1994, p. 227.

112 National Archives of Australia: Canberra;.Naval Board Minutes; No. 156, 10 November 1931,

113 ibid,, No. 82, 17 June 1931.

114 ibid,, No.125, 10 August 1932.

115 ibid,, No.73, 10 April 1935.

116 National Archives of Australia: Melbourne; 'Figures derived from *Commonwealth Year Book,* Volumes 1927–1937', MP98/1, 564/201/161.

117 National Archives of Australia: Canberra;.'Punishment Returns HMAS *Canberra*', A7111/1.

118 ibid., April 1933.

119 ibid., March 1933.

120 ibid., August 1933.

121 Sears, J. "'Though justice be thy Plea": Discipline in the Royal Navy 1913–1946', BA (Hons) thesis, UNSW@ADFA,1989, graph 4.1, p. 69, tables pp. 148–167.

122 National Archives of Australia: Canberra; A5954/1, 1003/13.

123 Burrell, H.M. *Mermaids Do Exist*, MacMillan, Melbourne, 1986, p. 14.

124 ibid., p. 65.

125 Jay, P. 'Musings of Matelot Phillip Jay', MSS 1083, Australian War Memorial, Canberra.

126 Radley, J. Diary, PR88/116, Australian War Memorial, Canberra.

127 Jay, P. 'Musings of Matelot Phillip Jay', MSS 1083, Australian War Memorial, Canberra.

128 Andrews, E. *The ANZAC Illusion: Anglo-Australian Relations during World War I*, Cambridge, 1994, p. 153.

129 Brock, G.M. (ed) HMAS *Quickmatch Book*, Bliss, 1943, p. 50.

130 ibid.

131 ibid.

132 National Archives of Australia: Canberra; 'The Shedden Collection', A5954/1, 1003/13.

133 Goldrick, J.V.P. 'The Australia Court-Martial of 1942', M.Litt. thesis, University of New England, 1983, p. 2.

134 ibid.

135 Roskill, S. *Admiral of the Fleet Earl Beatty The Last Naval Hero: An Intimate Biography*, Athenaeum, New York, 1981, p. 71.

136 National Archives of Australia: Canberra; 'The Shedden Collection', A5954/1, 1003/13.

137 Sears, J. 'Something Peculiar to Themselves? A Social History of the Executive Branch Officers of the Royal Australian Navy, 1913–1950', PhD thesis, UNSW@ADFA, 1997, p. 130.

138 This is the command that is piped to the ship's company for them to assemble to be given specific duties.

139 Jay, P. 'Musings of Matelot Phillip Jay', MSS 1083, Australian War Memorial, Canberra.

140 ibid.

141 ibid.

142 Reville, 'Letters to Miss J Fraser', PR85/326, Australian War Memorial, Canberra.

143 Radley, John, 'Diary', PR88/116, Australian War Memorial, Canberra.

144 *Daily Telegraph*, 16 February 1937.

145 ibid.

146 *Smith's Weekly* article included in MP981/1, 564/201/161, National Archives of Australia, Melbourne.

147 Commonwealth Year Book, Vols. 22, 24 and 25.

148 National Archives of Australia: Melbourne; MP981, 463/201/826.

149 ibid.

150 Gill, 1968, p. 30.

151 With the commencement of World War II, Mort re-enlisted and was accepted in the Royal Auxiliary Fleet Reserve (RAFR). He reclaimed his Chief Yeoman Signals crown in July 1943 and was demobilised from the navy in 1947. During his second RAN enlistment, he did not receive a 'moderate' notation on his service card.

152 National Archives of Australia: Canberra; 'Naval Board Minutes', No. 212, 7 October 1927.

153 ibid.

154 National Archives of Australia: Canberra; 'Prime Minister's Department, correspondence files, Hughes Ministry', A461/9, N337/1 1/5 ATT.

155 National Archives of Australia: Melbourne; 'Commonwealth Investigation Branch', B741/3, V6196.

156 *Commonwealth Year Book*, No. 26 (1933), p. 328 and No. 29 (1936), p. 347. In 1936, there were 370 officers, 44 midshipmen and 3,361 sailors.

157 *Smith's Weekly*, [no date other than year], 1936, in MP981/1, 564/201/161, National Archives of Australia, Melbourne.

158 *Daily Telegraph*, 16 February 1937.

159 ibid.

160 *The Sun*, 16 February 1937.

161 *Parliamentary Debates*, Vol. 120, 14 March 1929, p. 1227. Watkins was the Member for Newcastle.

162 ibid.

163 ibid., Vol. 122, 10 December 1929, pp. 966–967.

164 Robertson, J., 'The Distant War: Australia and Imperial Defence, 1919–41', p. 238 in McKernan, M and Browne, M. (eds) *Australia Two Centuries of War & Peace*, Allen and Unwin, 1988.

165 Roskill, S., *Naval Policy Between the Wars,* Collins, 1976, p. 348.

166 Hyslop, R., *Aye, Aye, Minister: Australian Naval Administration 1939–1959*, AGPS, 1990, p. 8.

167 Hyslop, R., Australian Dictionary of Biography website, http://adb.anu.edu.au/biography/hyde-sir-george-francis-6782.

168 Hopper, K.J. 'Midshipman Journal', PR91/006, Australian War Memorial, Canberra.

169 The Australian Naval Aviation Museum, *Flying Stations: A Story of Australian Naval Aviation*, Allen & Unwin, 1998, p. 17.

170 ibid.

171 ibid., p. 350.

172 ibid., p. 20.

173 Payne, 1973, p. 11.

174 National Archives of Australia: Canberra; A9376, 79, 'Report of 101 flight detachment in HMAS *Canberra* 12th July to 19th November 1935'.

175 The term 'Pussar' or 'Pusser' is derived from 'purser' a ship's supply, secretariat officer.

176 Australian Naval Aviation Museum, *Flying Stations: A Story of Australian Naval Aviation*, Allen & Unwin, 1998, p. 22.

177 John Bell's parents, John and Eva, faced years of uncertainty and further grief when John's brother, Corporal Alfred Napier Bell, AIF (SX1760 2/10 Bn), was killed in action in New Guinea on 20 January 1944, www.ww2roll.gov.au (accessed 3 March 2016)

178 Roskill, *Admiral of the Fleet Earl Beatty the Last Naval Hero: An Intimate Biography*, Athenaeum, New York, 1981, p. 161.

179 Neidpath, J. *The Singapore Naval Base and the Defence of Britain's Eastern Empire, 1913–1941*, Oxford, p. 138. See also Tracey, N. (ed) *The Collective Naval Defence of the Empire, 1900–1940*, Cambridge, 1997, p. 1.

180 McKernan, M. and Browne, M. (eds) *Australia Two Centuries of War and Peace*, AWM in concert with Allen & Unwin, 1988, p. 225.

181 McCarthy, J. *Australia and Imperial Defence 1919–39, A Study in Air and Sea Power*, University of Qld, 1976, p. 131.

182 Hall, H.A.L., 'Interview', 7 June 2015.

183 ibid.

184 ibid.

185 ibid.

186 Naval Historical Society of Australia, 'HMAS Canberra's 1935 cruise', first printed in the Sun & Guardian, 8 December, 1935, https://www.navyhistory.org.au/hmas-canberras-1935-cruise/ (accessed 3 March 2016)

187 Goldrick, J.V.P. 'The Australia Court-Martial of 1942', MLitt. Thesis, University of New England, 1983, p. 1.

188 Hopper, K.J., 'Midshipman Journal', PR91/006, Australian War Memorial, Canberra.

189 ibid.

190 ibid.

191 ibid.

192 ibid.

193 National Archives of Australia: Canberra; Storer, H.J., A6770.

194 *Sydney Morning Herald*, 22 February 1939

195 ibid., 10 May 1939

196 Australian War Memorial, Howell, H.L., PR86/145.

197 Australian War Memorial, 'Prime Minister Robert G. Menzies: wartime broadcast', www.awm.gov.au/encyclopedia/prime_ministers/menzies/ (accessed 3 March 2016).

198 Gregory, http://ahoy.tk-jk.net.

199 Farquhar, A.H., Papers, PR03381, Australian War Memorial, Canberra.

200 Naval Historical Society of Australia, 'HMAS *Canberra*'s 1935 cruise', 1983, p. 5.

201 Gilbert, M.F., *Winston S Churchill: Vol. VI, Finest Hour 1939–1941*, Heinemann, London, 1983, p. 410.

202 ibid.

203 Ross, J., *The Myth of the Digger: the Australian Soldier in Two World Wars*, Hale & Iremonger, 1985, pp. 120–121.

204 Goldrick J.V.P., 'The Australia Court-Martial of 1942', MLitt. Thesis, University of New England, 1983, p. 3.

205 *The Argus*, 3 December 1938.

206 National Archives of Australia: Canberra; A5854/1, 1924/8.

207 Australian War Memorial, Canberra, Howell H.L., PR86/145.

208 *Commonwealth Year Book*, Vol. 32, 1939, p. 239.

209 Australian War Memorial, Canberra, *HMAS*, 1942, p. 104.

210 In 1943, a special branch of the RANVR was created and all officers appointed since the outbreak of hostilities and engaged in specialised technical and operational duties were transferred – there were 592 officers serving by 1945.

211 Gill, G. Hermon. *Royal Australian Navy 1942–1945*, Collins/AWM, 1985, p. xiv. There were an additional 2,617 Women's Royal Australian Naval Service (WRANS) officers and ratings and 57 Royal Australian Naval Nursing Service (RANNS) sisters.

212 National Archives of Australia: Melbourne; MP981/1 429/206/94, HMAS *Canberra*, notification of casualties.

213 Rahmani, Z., 'Combining Two Professions: The Military Engineer', PhD Thesis, UNSW@ADFA, 1991.

214 Branch Colour: Accountant, White; Dental, Orange; Electrical, Dark Green; Engineer, Purple; Instructor, Blue; Medical, Scarlet; Ordnance, Dark Blue; R.N.V.R, Light Green; Schoolmaster, Light Blue; Shipwright, Silver–Grey; Wardmaster, Maroon. The practice of coloured stripes was discontinued in the mid 1950s.

215 National Archives of Australia: Melbourne; MP151/1/0 508/201/424.

216 National Archives of Australia: Melbourne; MP151/1/0 612/260/53.

217 ibid.

218 National Archives of Australia: Melbourne; MP138/1 603/255/1357–1365.

219 ibid.

220 Payne, 1973, p. 25.

221 ibid.

222 Australian War Memorial, Canberra, 'Memoirs of a reluctant warrior 1936–1955', MS1502.

223 Cowdroy was in the 2nd Anti Tank Atttack Regiment and served in the Pacific then promoted to the rank of sergeant (Sgt) in August 1943. Sgt Cowdroy returned to Australia in November 1945.

224 Farquhar, A.H., Papers, PR03381, Australian War Memorial, Canberra.

225 ibid.

226 ibid.

227 ibid.

228 ibid.

229 ibid.

230 ibid.

231 ibid.

232 Payne, 1973, p. 38.

233 Farquhar, A.H., Papers, PR03381, Australian War Memorial, Canberra.

234 ibid.

235 ibid.

236 ibid.

237 Payne, 1973, p. 41.

238 *Sydney Morning Herald*, 9 July 1940.

239 Keats, B., *Quiet Waters*, Wirripang, 2008, p. 43.

240 ibid., p. 44.

241 ibid., p. 25.

242 *The Herald*, 22 November 1940.

243 Keats, B., *Quiet waters: an account of HMAS Canberra and one of her sailors and three USS cruisers and their men, who rest in the deep quiet waters of Iron Bottom Sound*, Wirripang, 2008, p. 49.

244 Payne, 1973, p. 46.

245 Keats, 2008, p. 56.

246 ibid.

247 Payne, 1973, p. 48.

248 Gill, G. Hermon. *Australia in the War of 1939–1945: Series Two Navy. Volume 1, Royal Australian Navy, 1939–1942*, Australian War Memorial, Canberra, 1957, p. 370.

249 Keats, B. *Quiet waters: an account of HMAS Canberra and one of her sailors and three USS cruisers and their men, who rest in the deep quiet waters of Iron Bottom Sound*, Wirripang, 2008, p. 56.

250 Gill, G. Hermon *Royal Australian Navy 1942–1945: Australia in the War of 1939–1945*. AWM/Collins, 1985, p. 370. *Pinguin* was finally destroyed in May 1941 in a stunning battle with HMS *Cornwall*.

251 Payne, 1973, p. 48.

252 Gill, 1957, p. 458

253 National Archives of Australia: Canberra; SP109/3 309/27.

254 Keats, 2008, p. 56.

255 ibid.

256 Farquhar, A.H., Papers, PR03381, Australian War Memorial, Canberra.

257 The Partingtons formed their own band which had 'delighted dance audiences with their talent and melodies'. War came and the family wondered when next their band would play as three of the boys became RAN bandsmen. (Percival Kenneth (21938) was an accomplished trombonist and drafted to the light cruiser Perth. Sister light cruiser *Sydney* was home to Leslie Warburton (22696) another trombonist. See Spurling, K. *Cruel Conflict: the Triumph and Tragedy of HMAS Perth*, New Holland, 2008.

258 Payne, 1973, p. 53.

259 ibid., p. 57.

260 Maughan, B. *Tobruk and El Alamein, Australia in the War of 1939–1945,* Vol. 3, Australian War Memorial, 1966, p. 401.

261 National Archives of Australia: Melbourne; MP150/1/0 449/201/878.

262 ibid.

263 'Karl' appears to have been a nickname. This could have possibly been 17-year-old Assistant Cook Lionel Max Klein (S/5455).

264 Reville, 'Letters to Miss J. Fraser', PR85/326, Australian War Memorial, Canberra.

265 Martin, A.W. and Hardy, P. (eds) *Dark and Hurrying Days: Menzies' 1941 Diary*, National Library of Australia, 1993, p. 117.

266 Goldrick, J. 'Australian Naval Policy 1939–45' in Stevens, D. (ed) *The Royal Australian Navy in WWII*, 2005, p. 8.

267 Gill, 1957, p. 418.

268 ibid.

269 Both Colvin and Royle died in 1954.

270 Gill, 1957, p. 414.

271 ibid.

272 ibid., p. 415.

273 Keats, 2008, p. 63.

274 ibid., p. 67.

275 Gill, 1957, p. 412.

276 ibid.; Paravane is a device towed at the bow of a ship for cutting the moorings of underwater mines, so they will rise to the surface and be destroyed. Degaussing means removing a magnetic field in something such as electrical equipment or a ship's hull.

277 National Archives of Australia: Melbourne; MP138/1/0 603/248/2929; MP138/1 603/255/1348.

278 ibid.

279 ibid.

280 National Archives of Australia: Melbourne; MP981/1 201/004/930.

281 The county class ship, *Berwick*, had been decked in Douglas Fir but within six months it was 'condemned' and the timber was replaced by teak. It was realised Douglas Fir was unsuitable for tropical climates.

282 National Archives of Australia: Melbourne; MP981/1 201/004/930.

283 ibid.

284 National Archives of Australia: Melbourne; MP981/1/0 603/255/749.

285 MacMahon J., Letter, 7 August 2015.

286 National Archives of Australia: Canberra; MP1049/5 2026/3/501.

287 Gill, 1957, p. 425.

288 McIntyre, W.D. *The Rise and Fall of the Singapore Naval Base, 1939–1942*, MacMillan, 1979, p. 161.

289 Spurling, K. 'The Lower Deck of the RAN', PhD thesis, UNSW @ ADFA, 1999, pp. 306–307.

290 Gilbert, M. *Road to Victory: Winston S Churchill 1941–1945*, Heinemann, 1986, pp. 49–50.

291 Dower, J. *War Without Mercy: Race and Power in the Pacific War,* Faber & Faber, 1986, p. 99.

292 Attiwill, K. *The Rising Sunset*, Hale, 1957, p. 15.

293 King, N. 'Memoirs of a reluctant warrior 1936–1955', MS1502, Australian War Memorial, Canberra.

294 Gill, 1957, p. 446.

295 ibid., p. 482.

296 Keats, 2008, pp. 66–67.

297 Gill, 1957, p. 413.

298 ibid.

299 ibid., p. 414.

300 Stephens, G. email, 27 March 2015.

301 From author

302 Payne, 1973, p. 61.

303 ibid.

304 ibid.

305 Churchill, W., *The Hinge of Fate*, Houghton Mifflin, 1950, p. 164.

306 Spurling, K., *Cruel Conflict: The Triumph and Tragedy of HMAS Perth*, p. 127.

307 Gregory, MacKenzie, J., Ahoy – Mac's Web Log, 'Naval, Maritime, Australian History and more', http://ahoy.tk-jk.net (accessed October, 2015).

308 *Melbourne Herald*, 27 December 1941.

309 Day, D., *John Curtin: a Life*, Harper Collins, 1999, p. 448.

310 ibid.

311 ibid., p. 455.

312 ibid., p. 432.

313 *Sydney Morning Herald*, 19 February 1942.

314 ibid., 9 May 1942.

315 Goldrick, J., '1941–45: World War II: The War Against Japan' in Stevens, D. (ed), *Royal Australian Navy*, pp. 132–133.

316 National Archives of Australia: Melbourne; MP1049/5, 2026/3/501.

317 ibid.

318 *Sydney Morning Herald*, 9 May 1942.

319 Gill, 1968, p. 69.

320 Keats, 2008, p. 76.

321 National Archives of Australia: Melbourne; MP1049/5, 2026/3/501.

322 Payne, 1973, p. 64.

323 ibid.

324 National Archives of Australia: Canberra: Getting, F.E, A3978.

325 Gregory, MacKenzie, J., Ahoy – Mac's Web Log.

326 Keats, 2008, p. 88.

327 ibid., p. 89.

328 ibid., p. 90.

329 National Archives of Australia: Melbourne; MP1049/5, 2026/3/501.

330 Gregory, MacKenzie, J., Ahoy – Mac's Web Log.

331 Payne, 1973, p. 72.

332 ibid., p. 73.

333 Gregory, MacKenzie, J., Ahoy – Mac's Web Log.

334 8-inch cruisers: *Australia* and *Canberra* and USN cruisers *Chicago, Quincy, Astoria, Vincennes, Minneapolis, New Orleans, San Francisco, Salt Lake City* and *Portland*.

335 Gill, 1985, p.123.

336 Military uniforms and ranks were given to Coastwatchers in an effort to have them treated in accordance with the Geneva convention, but the Japanese forces failed to accord either. 337 Gill, J. C. H., 'Feldt, Eric Augustas (1899–1968)', Australian Dictionary of Biography, Vol. 14, Melbourne University Press, 1996, http://adb. anu.edu.au/biography/feldt-eric-augustas-10163 (accessed 22 March, 2016).

338 Feldt, E.A. *The Coast Watchers*, Oxford, 1979, p. 55.

339 Gill, 1985, p. 266.

340 ibid., p. 139.

341 Feldt, 1979, p. 83.

342 ibid.

343 Payne, 1973, p. 78.

344 Pickup, F. http://www.australiansatwar. gov.au

345 Australian War Memorial, Canberra, Morris, K. N., PR82/086.

346 Hoyt, E.P. *Guadalcanal*, Stein and Day, 1982, p.68.

347 Payne, 1973, p. 78.

348 ibid., p. 79.

349 ibid.

350 ibid.

351 ibid.

352 Hall, H.A.L, Interview, 6 June 2015.

353 National Archives of Australia: Melbourne; 'Lessons learnt from loss of HMAS *Canberra*' (including deck log book and related note book), MP1049/5 2026/3/501. Unless otherwise identified, information in this chapter, including quotes, has been compiled from this 480-page file.

354 Gregory, Ahoy – Mac's Web Log.

355 Payne, 1973, p. 80.

356 Newcomb, R.F., *The Battle of Savo Island*, New York: Harold Holt and Company, 1961, pp. 101–102.

357 uboat.net, http://uboat.net/allies/ commanders/4343.html

358 Payne, 1973, p. 81.

359 Gregory, Ahoy – Mac's Web Log.

360 *ABC News*, 28 October 2014

361 Payne, 1973, p. 91.

362 National Archives of Australia: Melbourne; MP1049/5 2026/3/501.

363 Gill, *1985*, p. 143.

364 Gregory, Ahoy – Mac's Web Log.

365 Loxton, B. with Coulthard-Clark, C. *The shame of Savo: the sinking of HMAS* Canberra *Anatomy of a Naval disaster*, Allen & Unwin, 1997, p. xxv.

366 ibid.

367 National Archives of Australia: Melbourne; MP1049/5 2026/3/501.

368 Loxton and Coulthard-Clark, 1997, p.xxv.

369 Gill, *1985*, p. 145.

370 Australian War Memorial: Canberra, Morris, K.N., PR82/086.

371 National Archives of Australia: Melbourne; MP1049/5 2026/3/501.

372 Entered from Melbourne at age 20 in 1926 and was a member of the commissioning crew of *Canberra*. When the retrenchments came he accepted a free discharge in 1929. Gorham realised his mistake and re-entered the RAN two years later. He took every advantage of additional training and promotion. Enthusiasm and hard work reaped benefits and he was promoted in Stoker PO in 1936 before accepting intensive mechanical training at *Cerberus* to qualify for the rating of 'Mechanician' and was promoted to Chief.

373 National Archives of Australia: Melbourne; MP1049/5 2026/3/501.

374 ibid.

375 ibid.

376 ibid.

377 ibid.

378 ibid.

379 ibid.

380 ibid.

381 Tommy Thurlow from Melbourne, survived the war.

382 National Archives of Australia: Melbourne; MP1049/5 2026/3/501.

383 ibid.

384 ibid.

385 ibid.

386 Jones, T. M. and Idries, Ion L., The silent service – action stories of the Anzac Navy, 2nd ed., Sydney: Angus & Robertson, 1952, p. 322.

387 ibid., p. 323.

388 ibid.

389 ibid., p. 322.

390 Gill, 1985, p. 123.

391 Australian War Memorial: Canberra, Morris, K.N., PR82/086.

392 National Archives of Australia: Melbourne; MP1049/5 2026/3/501.

393 ibid.

394 Pickup, F. www.australiansatwar.gov.au

395 Stephens, G., email, 27 March 2015.

396 ibid.

397 ibid.

398 ibid.

399 Gregory, MacKenzie, J., Ahoy – Mac's Web Log; Bruce Loxton survived his WWII RAN career and went on to write Loxton, B. with Coulthard-Clark, C. The shame of Savo: the sinking of HMAS Canberra Anatomy of a Naval disaster, Allen & Unwin, 1997, spending his life attempting to expunge the Canberra crew of blame.

400 Payne, 1973, p. 97.

401 Jones and Idriess, 1952, pp. 326–327.

402 ibid.

403 Courtesy of Henry Hall.

404 Hall, H.A.L. Interview, 7 June 2015.

405 ibid.

406 ibid.

407 Jones and Idriess, 1952, p. 328.

408 Hall, Interview, 7 June 2015.

409 ibid.

410 National Archives of Australia: Melbourne; MP1049/5 2026/3/501, 'Lessons learnt from loss of HMAS Canberra'.

411 Bates, R., 'The Battle of Savo Island', Strategical and Tactical Analysis Part 1, Naval War College, 1950, pp. 290–291.

412 Gregory, MacKenzie, J. Ahoy – Mac's Web Log.

413 Figures vary depending on sources, this is partly due to several ships, including Canberra, had non-RAN personnel, exchange personnel. One report had the Allied deaths as 12,700. Canberra had USN and RN personnel as well as three civilian canteen staff onboard. What was the report that had Allied deaths as 12,700? Please state.

414 National Archives of Australia: Melbourne; MP151/1 429/206/67; MP981/1 201/004/930.

415 Born on 4 December 1918 in Memphis, Tenn. Enlisted in the Naval Reserve on 26 July 1940 as an apprentice seaman. After serving at sea in Arkansas (BB-33) during the late summer and early fall, he was appointed Midshipman on 22 November and commissioned Ensign on 28 February 1941, and joined Parrott (DD-218) in the Philippine Islands on 16 April. Parrott and her sister ships joined the American-British-Dutch-Australian (ABDA). For his gallantry during the Battle of Makassar Strait and the Battle of Badoeng Strait, Ens. Vance was awarded the Bronze Star. Promoted to Lieutenant (junior grade) on 15 June 1942. Vance was then attached to Canberra. He was killed when a shell hit the Cypher Officer.

416 National Archives of Australia: Melbourne; MP151/1 429/206/67; MP981/1 201/004/930.

417 The Argus, 21 August 1942.

418 The Examiner, 21 August 1942.

419 Daily Advertiser (Wagga Wagga), 21 August 1942.

420 Advocate, 22 August 1942.

421 Northern Star, 16 September 1942.

422 The Argus, 21 August 1942.

423 ibid.

424 Western Mail, 17 September 1942.

425 *The Argus*, 17 September 1942.

426 *Advocate*, 22 August 1942

427 *Newcastle Morning Herald & Miners Advocate*, 5 September 1942.

428 *Advocate*, 22 August 1942.

429 National Archives of Australia: Melbourne; MP151/1/0, 429/206/67.

430 National Archives of Australia: Melbourne; MP1049/5 2026/3/501.

431 ibid.

432 In early 1943 President Franklin Delano Roosevelt ordered that a new heavy cruiser be named USS *Canberra* as a special tribute, the first ever named after a foreign naval vessel or foreign capital. Since then, there have been two ships commissioned, HMAS *Canberra* II, HMAS Canberra III.

433 National Archives of Australia: Melbourne; MP1049/5 2026/3/501.

434 ibid.

435 National Archvies of Australia: Canberra; A5954 654/29, 'Loss of HMAS Canberra in Operations in Solomon Islands – August 1942. Summary of Report by Admiral Hepburn. 22/12/43'.

436 National Archives of Australia: Melbourne; MP1049/5 2026/3/501.

437 Frank, R. B., *Guadalcanal: The Definitive Account of the Landmark Battle*, Penguin, 1990, p. 123.

438 Loxton and Coulthard-Clark, 1997, p. xxvi.

439 National Archives of Australia: Melbourne; MP1049/5 2026/3/501.

440 ibid.

441 ibid.

442 ibid.

443 ibid.

444 ibid.

445 Morris, K.N. PR82/086, Australian War Memorial, Canberra.

446 National Archives of Australia: Melbourne; MP1049/5 2026/3/501.

447 In a letter dated 10 November 1942, the highly experienced and respected Captain (later Vice Admiral Sir) John Augustine Collins, RAN, ex-Captain of HMAS *Sydney*, wrote to the ACNB that after examining the reports in detail 'I consider it likely that *Canberra* was hit by a torpedo in the starboard side abreast the boiler rooms'.

448 Morison, S.E. *Struggle for Guadalcanal*, Vol. 5 first published in 1949, p. 25, of 15 volume *History of United States Naval Operations in World War II*, Little Brown, 1947–1962.

449 Further reports about this incident include: Richard F. Newcomb in his 1961 book *The Battle of Savo Island* wrote that the RAAF pilot 'was to report immediately. He did not' and that the Australian 'finally landed in late afternoon, had his tea, then reported his sighting'. So too Edwin P. Hoyt in his 1982 book *Guadalcanal*, with reprints as late as 1999, and Eric Larrabee in 1988 in *Commander in Chief*.

450 *ABC News*, 28 October 2014.

451 McMahon, J. Letter, 7 August 2015.

452 Payne, 1973, p. 108.

453 Hall, H.A.L., Interview, 7 June 2015.

454 Keats, 2008, p. 112.

455 ibid.

PHOTO CREDITS

All images have been sourced from the public domain apart from those listed below.

Freestone family: 152

Gary Stephens: 144, 174, 222

Henry Hall: 92, 202

Kathryn Spurling: 255

Keva North, www.ahoy.tk-jk.net: 107, 216

Margaret Hadfield: 221

ACKNOWLEDGEMENTS

I was able to write this book because of the easy access to the National Archives of Australia records in Canberra and Melbourne. There are official moves to restrict access to Australian Defence Force files, particularly personnel records. This would severely handicap historians from revealing the human side of the service and the sacrifice of so many Australians in conflict.

Lieutenant Commander Henry Hall, MBE, OAM, RAN (rtd) was a strong motivating force behind the writing of the book. At 93, this survivor of HMAS *Canberra 1* is an inspiration – an example to us all of how we should never take life for granted and should live it to the fullest. Thank you, Henry.

I am honoured that the Chief Minister of the ACT, the Hon. Andrew Barr, MLA, has seen the book as worthy of his foreword.

I would like to thank Elizabeth Van Der Hor, friend and words guru, for her continued support. Her review skills allow me to say what I really intended to. Thanks also to my children and grandchildren for their ongoing support.

ABOUT THE AUTHOR

Kathryn Spurling served with the Women's Royal Australian Naval Service (WRANS). She completed an honours degree in history at the Australian National University (ANU); a Master of History Degree (hons) and a PhD in military history at University of New South Wales (UNSW).

Between 1996 and 2011 Kathryn was attached to the School of History, and then the School of Humanities and Social Sciences, UNSW, Australian Defence Force Academy, Canberra, where she tutored history and strategic studies. In 1999 she initiated the *Women in Uniform: Perceptions and Pathways* Conference and co-edited the book of the same name. Dr Spurling has lectured and published extensively within Australia and internationally on military history, peacekeepers and women in the military. She was the first Australian invited to speak at NATO in Brussels on women in the military and was the first Australian appointed as a Summer History Fellow, at the United States Military Academy (West point).

As part of the RAN submarine centenary commemorations on ANZAC Day 2014, Dr Spurling gave the commemorative address in Rabaul, New Britain, in August 2014.

Dr Spurling was appointed to the ACT Veterans Council by the ACT Chief Minister, the Hon. Katy Gallagher, MLA, in 2011, and continues to serve on this committee for the ACT Chief Minister the Hon. Andrew Barr, MLA.

During 2012 and 2013 Dr Spurling was Visiting Scholar, School of History, Australian National University. In 2014 she was appointed Adjunct Research Associate, School of Education and Humanities, Flinders University.

Other books by the author published by New Holland Publishers:
Cruel Conflict: The Triumph and Tragedy of HMAS Perth I, 2008.
A Grave Too Far Away: A Tribute to Australians in Bomber Command Europe, 2012.
Abandoned and Sacrificed: The Tragedy of Montevideo Maru, 2017.